1- and 2- Family Study Guide

Electrical Inspector Certification Program

Electrical General Study Guide

ELECTRICAL INSPECTOR CERTIFICATION PROGRAM

Updated to the
2014 *NEC*

International Association of Electrical Inspectors
Richardson, Texas

Copyright © 1981, 1984, 1987, 1990, 1993, 1996, 1999, 2004, 2006, 2008, 2012, 2013 by
International Association of Electrical Inspectors
901 Waterfall Way, Suite 602
Richardson, TX 75080-7702

All rights reserved. First edition published 1981
Printed in the United States of America
17 16 15 14 13   5 4 3 2 1

ISBN-10:1-890659-67-3
ISBN-13:978-1-890659-67-7

Notice to the Reader

This book has not been processed in accordance with NFPA Regulations Governing Committee Projects. Therefore, the text and commentary in it shall not be considered the official position of the NFPA or any of its committees and shall not be considered to be, nor relied upon as a formal interpretation of the meaning or intent of any specific provision or provisions of the 2014 edition of NFPA 70, *National Electrical Code.*[®1]

Publishers do not warrant or guarantee any of the products described herein or perform any independent analysis in connection with any of the product information contained herein. Publisher does not assume, and expressly disclaims, any obligation to obtain and include information referenced in this work.

The reader is expressly warned to consider carefully and adopt all safety precautions that might be indicated by the activities described herein and to avoid all potential hazards. By following the instructions contained herein, the reader willingly assumes all risks in connection with such instructions.

THE PUBLISHERS MAKE NO REPRESENTATIONS OR WARRANTIES OF ANY KIND, INCLUDING, BUT NOT LIMITED TO, THE IMPLIED WARRANTIES OF FITNESS FOR PARTICULAR PURPOSE, MERCHANTABILITY OR NON-INFRINGEMENT, NOR ARE ANY SUCH REPRESENTATIONS IMPLIED WITH RESPECT TO SUCH MATERIAL. THE PUBLISHERS SHALL NOT BE LIABLE FOR ANY SPECIAL, INCIDENTAL, CONSEQUENTIAL OR EXEMPLARY DAMAGES RESULTING, IN WHOLE OR IN PART, FROM THE READER'S USES OF OR RELIANCE UPON THIS MATERIAL.

Table of Contents

Chapter 1	Techniques for Testing	6
Chapter 2	How to Use the *NEC*	9
Chapter 3	Raceways	14
Chapter 4	Cables	28
Chapter 5	Conductors	43
Chapter 6	Service Equipment	60
Chapter 7	Control Devices	77
Chapter 8	Utilization Equipment	91
Chapter 9	Cabinets	108
Chapter 10	Calculations	121
Chapter 11	Swimming Pools	139
Chapter 12	Charts, Formulas, and Useful Information	157
Chapter 13	Answers	183

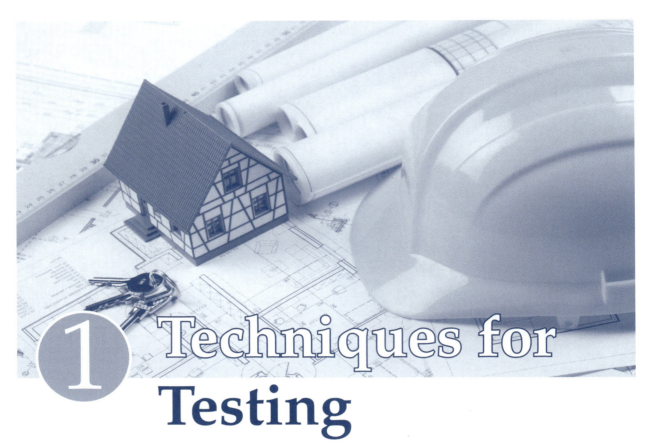

1 Techniques for Testing

People study for a variety of reasons. Some study to improve their understanding and grasp of their chosen field, but the vast majority study because they will be required to show their competence in a given subject. Competence is generally measured by test scores. Unfamiliarity with the specific subject is one of the main reasons for low scores. Another reason is, a person's performance is only a sample of his or her behavior at that point in time. In other words, test scores are not set in concrete and you can improve your score by preparing better, improving your attitude, and understanding the best methods to use in test taking.

The easiest way to improve your test performance is to reduce your anxiety level. The study guides sponsored by the International Association of Electrical Inspectors are designed to improve your understanding of how to find information in the *National Electrical Code*. The questions are designed to be similar to test formats you are likely to find in electrical inspector certification examinations. It should be understood that no effort is made to duplicate those questions exactly. To do so, would be nonproductive as questions are changed from time to time. Rather, the approach used in these study guides is to help you master locating information quickly and accurately. You can then master any test question. The refresher courses are available in three modules: *Electrical General Study Guide*, *One- and Two-Family Dwellings Study Guide*, and *Plan Review Study Guide*.

The goal of these courses is to ensure your best possible performance by understanding how to use the *National Electrical Code®* and thus reduce your anxiety level. The courses may be used for individual home study and are also ideally suited for an instructor/pupil classroom approach.

Examination for Certification
Methods to Improve Your Test Scores

1. *Prepare by studying.* The questions in this refresher course are designed to teach you how to find the rules quickly and efficiently. If you learn how to use the table of contents and index properly, you will find the material in a reasonably short period. This knowledge and confidence will help reduce your anxiety and raise your scores. Consistent study leads to a higher retention level than cramming just prior to the examination date. The ultimate

goal is to become familiar with the use of the *NEC* and testing format.

2. *Arrive on time.* Make sure you allow plenty of time to arrive promptly, but not too early. Since nervousness is contagious, don't associate too closely with the other examinees as you may pick up their anxiety level.

3. *Eliminate wrong answers.* If the test is multiple choice and you have four alternatives, the odds are 4 to 1 that you can guess the right answer. If you eliminate any two alternatives, your chances are increased to 50-50.

4. *Read directions carefully.* Many mistakes are made merely because the directions have been misunderstood. If, after reading carefully, you still are not sure, ask the proctor for clarification.

5. *Allow yourself enough time.* Based on the number of questions you have to answer, allot a specific amount of time for each question.

6. *Answer question first.* If the question has several alternatives, attempt to answer the question before you check the alternatives. In this way you can evaluate your answer against the alternatives.

7. *Skip difficult questions.* If you are unsure of the answer or know that you are familiar with the material but don't have a ready answer, skip the question and go on to other material. Complete known questions then return to those you don't know. Chances are, your mind will subconsciously work out the answer so that it will be easier when you return to it.

8. *First choice is usually best.* If you pick an answer to a multiple choice question and have later reservations about the right answer, remember that your first choice is usually best. If on later evaluation you know you have made a mistake, by all means change your answer.

9. *Read questions carefully.* Make sure you note key words that might change the meaning of the questions. Note negative disclaimers such as, "which of the following are not...". A handy way to increase understanding is to underline key words. This has a tendency to channel your thinking along the right path.

10. *Make sure you are comfortable.* If you have on too many clothes, remove some. Being too warm has a tendency to make you drowsy, which leads to a loss of concentration.

11. *Re-check your work.* The last thing you should do before handing in your paper is to recheck and make sure you have not made any clerical mistakes. Many times you will know the right answer, but lose points on your score because of a clerical error.

Study Plan

Familiarize yourself completely with the codebook. Until one is familiar with the *Code* to the extent that location of specific requirements is committed to memory, use of the index is the best way to find information. The index contains in alphabetical order a list of what is in the *Code*, telling where to find topics covered.

Even though you may know the answer to a question, follow this sequence to establish the answer:

1. Check the table of contents to find the proper code article.

2. Select key words from the question that will identify the code article and subject matter that will be used to find the requirements in the index.

Select key words from the question that will identify the code article and subject matter that will be used to find the requirements in the index.

For example, you have been asked to verify the size of a grounding electrode conductor for a 200 ampere AC service supplying a dwelling. The dwelling unit has a metal water pipe and the service-entrance conductors are 3/0, THWN, copper.

From the question, you can identify the subject of the question is a grounding electrode conductor. Specifically, you are being asked to determine the size. Additional key words or subject matter are the *size of the service-entrance conductors* and the fact the dwelling is supplied by a *metal water pipe*.

Looking in the index, you find "Grounding electrode conductors" under which you will find "Sizing 250.30(A)(6)(a), 250.66 and

250.166." Scanning 250.30(A)(6) you quickly realize this is related to separately derived systems; so the next choice was 250.66 from the index. Section 250.66 is titled "Size of Alternating-Current Grounding Electrode Conductors."

The opening paragraph of 250.66 states the grounding electrode conductor cannot be less than given in Table 250.66 except as permitted in (A)–(C). Scanning 250.66(A)–(C), you find they are not applicable to the question; so Table 250.66 must be used.

Table 250.66 is based on the size of the service-entrance conductors; so in our case, we determine a 4 AWG copper grounding electrode conductor is required for an AC service supplied by 3/0 copper conductors.

3. If, in the index, you do not readily find the location of the requirements related to the question, scan the bold face titles of the appropriate sections in the body of the code to locate quickly the subject material.

The Table of Contents lists in numerical sequence the subjects covered by each chapter and each article. So it provides the article number, part number if applicable, and a page number that can be used to find a location to start scanning section and subsection titles. Experienced users of the *NEC* are generally familiar with the content of *NEC* articles and, therefore, often use the Table of Contents of to find a page number as a starting point.

Using the above question, an experienced user of the *NEC* would know that grounding and bonding requirements are found in Article 250. Scanning the information in the Table of Contents, we find the requirements for the "Grounding Electrode System and Grounding Electrode Conductor" are in Part III of Article 250 and they start on Page 117. Scanning the boldfaced section and subsection titles starting on page 119, we find 250.66 "Size of Alternating-Current Grounding Electrode Conductors on page 121."

This study guide is divided into subject categories and each category has several questions. Each question is followed by the procedure for finding the correct answer. Follow the procedures step by step to learn good work habits. The answers are listed in the back of the book. Do not look up the answers until you have completed work in the entire category.

Remember, you are only shortchanging yourself by not following the step-by-step method of problem solving. The goal is to learn how to find code information in the most efficient manner.

This study guide is based on the *National Electrical Code*, 2014 edition.

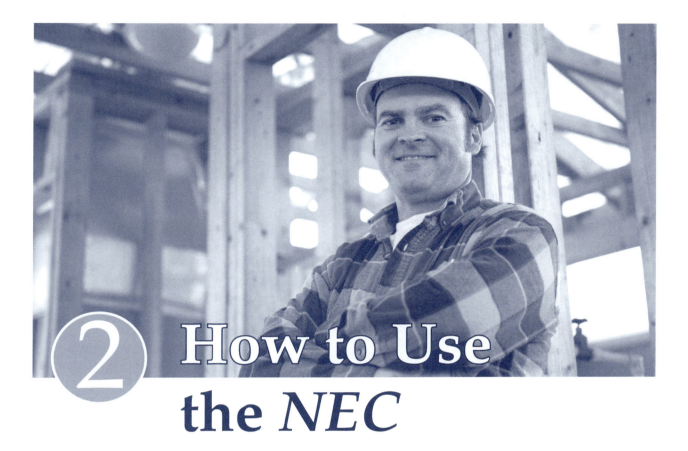

2 How to Use the NEC

The *National Electrical Code*, sponsored by the National Fire Protection Association, is the most widely adopted code in the world. It is also, in all probability, the most widely misinterpreted code in the world. The *NEC* is adopted by federal, state and local governments as well as by private industry. As far as NFPA is concerned, the *NEC* is purely advisory. It becomes enforceable as law only upon adoption by an agency having authority to enforce its rules. Requirements for electrical inspection of installations, licensing of electrical contractors and electricians, as well as qualifications of electrical inspectors usually are contained in laws or ordinances that are associated with adoption and enforcement of electrical codes.

Scope of the *Code*

Article 90 serves as an introduction to the *NEC* and provides a scope to specify the electrical installations that are covered and those that are not covered. The *Code* covers installations of electric conductors and equipment within or on public and private buildings or other structures, including mobile homes, recreational vehicles, and floating buildings; and other premise wiring such as yards, carnival, parking, and other lots, and industrial substations. The *Code* also covers installations of conductors and equipment that connect to the supply of electricity, installations of other outside conductors and equipment on the premises, as well as installations of signaling and communications conductors and equipment and optical fiber cable.

In addition, the *Code* covers installations in buildings used by the electric utility, such as office buildings, warehouses, garages, machine shops and recreational buildings that are not an integral part of a generating plant, substation or control center.

The *Code* does *not* cover installations in ships, watercraft other than floating buildings, railway rolling stock, aircraft, or automotive vehicles other than mobile homes and recreational vehicles.

It also does not cover underground mines, railway conductors, or installations of communications equipment under the exclusive control of the communications utility. This latter requirement generally applies to overhead and underground communications conductors up to their termination in a locked room under the exclusive control of the communications utility. Installations, such as telephone distribution conductors, in hung ceilings or other accessible locations, are not normally under the exclusive control of the telephone company and are, therefore, covered by Article 800. Electric utility generation, transmission, transformation and distribution conductors including associated lighting are not normally covered by the *NEC*.

Enforcement
It is intended that the authority having jurisdiction interpret the rules in the *Code* and approve all devices, materials, equipment and conductors.

> **90.4 Enforcement.** This *Code* is intended to be suitable for mandatory application by governmental bodies that exercise legal jurisdiction over electrical installations, including signaling and communications systems, and for use by insurance inspectors. The authority having jurisdiction for enforcement of the *Code* has the responsibility for making interpretations of the rules, for deciding on the approval of equipment and materials, and for granting the special permission contemplated in a number of the rules.

While the code is primarily intended to apply to new construction, the second paragraph of 90.4 permits the authority having jurisdiction to use his or her judgment in applying the code to rewiring in old installations.

By special permission, the authority having jurisdiction may waive specific requirements in this code or permit alternative methods where it is assured that equivalent objectives can be achieved by establishing and maintaining effective safety.

In discharging the responsibilities granted in 90.4, authorities having jurisdiction should enforce the requirements of 110.3(B) to assure that equipment is used as intended by the manufacturer and electrical products testing laboratory.

All mandatory rules are characterized by the use of the word "shall." Where the word "may" is used it means that the authority having jurisdiction has the prerogative of granting permission.

This should not be confused with the permissive term "may," which has largely been replaced in current editions of the code by the term "shall be permitted."

90.5 Mandatory Rules, Permissive Rules, and Explanatory Material.
(A) Mandatory Rules. Mandatory rules of this *Code* are those that identify actions that are specifically required or prohibited and are characterized by the use of the terms *shall* or *shall not*.

(B) Permissive Rules. Permissive rules of this *Code* are those that identify actions that are allowed but not required, are normally used to describe options or alternative methods, and are characterized by the use of the terms *shall be permitted* or *shall not be required*.

(C) Explanatory Material. Explanatory material, such as references to other standards, references to related sections of this *Code*, or information related to a *Code* rule, is included in this *Code* in the form of informational notes. Informational notes are informational only and are not enforceable as requirements of this *Code*.

Brackets containing section references to another NFPA document are for informational purposes only and are provided as a guide to indicate the source of the extracted text. These bracketed references immediately follow the extracted text.

Informational Note: The format and language used in this *Code* follows guidelines established by NFPA and published in the *NEC Style Manual*. Copies of this manual may be obtained from NFPA.

(D) Informative Annexes. Nonmandatory information relative to the use of the *NEC* is provided in informative annexes. Informative annexes are not part of the *NEC*, but are included for informative purposes only.

Informational notes are sometimes mistakenly enforced as mandatory requirements. They are intended to provide information or explanatory material and are not intended to be enforced as a part of the requirements. Where more than one Informational Note follows a section, they are numbered consecutively such as Informational Note No. 1, Informational Note No. 2, etc.

Use the Table of Contents and Index

To save time, one should use the table of contents to his or her best advantage. The table of contents lists in numerical sequence the subjects covered by each chapter and each article. Review of the table of contents gives an excellent overview of where the *Code* covers specific subjects or equipment.

Until one is familiar with the *Code* to the extent that location of specific requirements is committed to memory, use of the index is the best way to find information. The index contains in alphabetical order a list of what is in the *Code*, telling where to find topics covered. In some cases, the location of topics can be found in more than one way. For instance, the ampacities for conductors can be found under the heading "Ampacities" and also under the heading "Conductors."

Seemingly vague requirements can often become crystal clear by making use of the definitions in Article 100. For instance, the definition of *overload* says that a fault, such as a short circuit or ground fault, is not an overload.

Code Arrangement

The arrangement of the *Code* is explained in 90.3. One should become thoroughly familiar with this concept for proper application of code rules. General rules in early chapters are sometimes supplemented or modified by later chapters.

> **90.3 Code Arrangement.** The *Code* is divided into the introduction and nine chapters, as shown in Figure 90.3. Chapters 1, 2, 3, and 4 apply generally; Chapters 5, 6, and 7 apply to special occupancies, special equipment, or other special conditions. These latter chapters supplement or modify the general rules. Chapters 1 through 4 apply except as amended by Chapters 5, 6, and 7 for the particular conditions.
>
> Chapter 8 covers communications systems and is not subject to the requirements of Chapters 1 through 7 except where the requirements are specifically referenced in Chapter 8.
>
> Chapter 9 consists of tables.
>
> Annexes are not part of the requirements of the *Code* but are included for informational purposes only.

Chapter Arrangement

Many articles have a scope that explains what is covered by that article. Mistakes in understanding and application of *Code* requirements are often avoided by reviewing the article scope before assuming general coverage of a requirement. Let's look at the scope of Article 555.

> **555.1 Scope.** This article covers the installation of wiring and equipment in the areas comprising fixed or floating piers, wharves, docks, and other areas in marinas, boatyards, boat basins, boathouses, yacht clubs, boat condominiums, docking facilities associated with residential condominiums, any multiple docking facility, or similar occupancies, and facilities that are used, or intended for use, for the purpose of repair, berthing, launching, storage, or fueling of small craft and the moorage of floating buildings. Private, noncommercial docking facilities constructed or occupied for the use of the owner or residents of the associated single-family dwelling are not covered by this article.

Chapter 8 covers communication systems and is not subject to the requirements of Chapters 1 through 7, except where the requirements are specifically referenced therein. For example, refer to 800.44(A)(3), Climbing Space. "The climbing space through communications wires and cables shall comply with the requirements of 225.14(D)." Without a reference like this, there would not be any requirements for climbing space relative to communications conductors unless specifically included in Article 800.

Numbering System

Essential to the understanding of any standard is familiarizing oneself with the arrangement and numbering system employed. The numbering system utilized for the *NEC* consists of the introduction Article 90, along with chapters numbered from 1 through 9.

Chapters are further divided into several articles consisting of numbers in hundreds such as Article 100, Article 200, Article 300, etc. All articles in Chapter 1 begin with 100, Chapter 2 with 200, etc.

Some articles have several parts which are in roman numerical sequence such as I, II, III, IV, etc. Common requirements are grouped in parts of articles. Part I, General, usually contains provisions that apply to all the other parts of the article. Other parts contain provisions that are independent of all other parts; except Part I General. For instance, Part II of Article 680 contains provisions for permanently installed pools, and Part III contains provisions for storable pools. Each part is separate and independent of the other, but all parts must comply with the applicable general requirements of Part I; unless specifically stated otherwise.

All articles are divided into sections such as 110.3, 110.5, 110.8, 110.26, etc. Subsections are further numbered with lower case alphabetical characters similar to 110.26(A), 110.26(B), 110.26(C). In some cases, paragraphs following subsections are numbered similar to 110.27(A)(1), 110.27(A)(2), 110.27(A)(3), etc.

Parallel Numbering
The *NEC*-2002 introduced a new parallel numbering system. Common types of rules or information are assigned the same numbered section in each article. As an example, article scopes are designed as ".1" and definitions for the specific article are assigned as ".2". Uses permitted are ".10" in all articles. This will help users of the *Code* locate this type of common material without having to search for it in different locations on each article.

General Requirements
Users often miss important requirements by failing to review the general requirements before deciding that the subject is not covered in the Code. Article 110 contains general requirements for electrical installations that are applied throughout all the other articles, unless modified by other articles. Article 300 provides the general requirements for wiring methods and materials. By its scope it can be modified by other articles within Chapter 3. Remember that per 90.3 the general requirements of chapters one through three can be modified by other articles in chapters five, six or seven. Only those sections in Article 300 that are referenced in Articles 725, 760, 770, 800, 810, 820, 830, and 840, apply in the latter articles. The sections of Article 300 that apply to those later articles can be found under "Other Articles" which is typically in ".3" of the respective article. This is due to the unique nature of the requirements in the latter articles.

Table Notes
Tables utilize a smaller font size for the footnotes, which are mandatory to the application of the table. For example, see the footnotes that follow Table 300.5 that read as follows:

Notes:
1. Cover is defined as the shortest distance in millimeters (inches) measured between a point on the top surface of any direct-buried conductor, cable, conduit, or other raceway and the top surface of finished grade, concrete, or similar cover.
2. Raceways approved for burial only where concrete encased shall require concrete envelope not less than 50 mm (2 in.) thick.
3. Lesser depths shall be permitted where cables and conductors rise for terminations or splices or where access is otherwise required.
4. Where one of the wiring method types listed in Columns 1–3 is used for one of the circuit types in Columns 4 and 5, the shallowest depth of burial shall be permitted.
5. Where solid rock prevents compliance with the cover depths specified in this table, the wiring shall be installed in metal or nonmetallic raceway permitted for direct burial. The raceways shall be covered by a minimum of 50 mm (2 in.) of concrete extending down to rock.

Note also, in the case of Table 300.5, the definition of *cover*, which is located as note 1.

Exceptions
Basic rules are stated in standard (Roman) type and are followed by all the exceptions to the basic rule. Exceptions are set in italics. It is important to clearly read and understand the requirements of the basic rule be-

fore applying the exception. Exceptions apply only to the section or subsection they follow, unless stated differently in the rule. See the following example.

Several sections use a type of exception that can be considered "except as provided in _____ through_____." Look at 240.21 for an example of this concept. The general rule for location of the overcurrent device applies "except as specified in 240.21(A) through (H)."

Installation and Use
"Listed or labeled equipment shall be installed and used in accordance with any instructions included in the listing or labeling" [110.3(B)].

Purpose
The *Code* is not intended as a design specification, and proper application dictates the use of nationally recognized product safety standards. Neither is the *Code* an instruction manual for untrained persons.

> **90.1(A) Purpose.** The purpose of this Code is the practical safeguarding of persons and property from hazards arising from the use of electricity. This *Code* is not intended as a design specification or an instruction manual for untrained persons.

Definitions
Article 100, Definitions, generally contains definitions of terms only where used in two or more articles as stated in the Scope. When an article requires a definition of a term not used in other parts of the *Code*, that definition will be found within the article in which it is used at ".2" in the parallel numbering system. In most other cases, *Webster's Dictionary* or the *Institute of Electrical and Electronics Engineers Dictionary* will suffice. The cultivation of an electrical technical vocabulary is a must to understand the more intricate requirements. The *IEEE Standard Dictionary of Electrical Terms* proves helpful even to the seasoned veteran.

Applying the subtle rules that are used in writing the *Code* will assist old hands as well as the beginner. Failure to follow the simple rules leads to controversy and non-uniformity.

3 Raceways

QUESTION 1. Under general conditions conductors installed in raceways shall be stranded if larger than what size?

A. 12 AWG
B. 10 AWG
C. 8 AWG
D. 6 AWG

ANSWER _____

PROCEDURE TO ESTABLISH ANSWER
The question is about stranded conductors installed in raceways.

▶ 1. In Index, find "Conductors."

▶ 2. Under "Conductors," find "Stranded, 310.106(C)."

▶ 3. Section 310.106(C) provides that when installed in raceways, conductors of size 8 AWG and larger shall be stranded, except as permitted or required elsewhere in this *Code*.

▶ 4. When answering a question such as this, one has to really think before selecting the answer. As noted in Step 3, the *NEC* section is noting that conductors of 8 AWG and larger have to be stranded but the question is essentially asking, what is the largest size solid conductor that can be installed in a raceway?

▶ 5. The correct answer is B.

QUESTION 2. Raceways for service conductors are considered outside a building or structure if the raceway is installed:

A. in the hollow spaces of the building or structure
B. within rigid metal conduit (Type RMC) or intermediate metal conduit (Type IMC) used to accommodate the clearance requirements in 230.24 and routed directly through an eave but not a wall of a building

14 | 1- and 2-Family Study Guide | Raceways

C. within insulation between studs in an outside wall
D. exposed in a crawlspace under a building

ANSWER _____

PROCEDURE TO ESTABLISH ANSWER
The question is about when service conductors are considered to be outside a building.

▶ 1. In Index, find "Service-entrance conductors" under which find "Considered outside of building, 230.6."

▶ 2. Section 230.6(5) indicates that statement B is the correct answer.

▶ 3. The correct answer is B.

QUESTION 3. Which one of the following statements applies to a short section of raceway used to protect exposed wiring from physical damage?

A. It may be filled to 53 percent only.
B. It may be filled to 31 percent only.
C. It may be filled to 40 percent only.
D. Fill requirements do not apply.

ANSWER _____

PROCEDURE TO ESTABLISH ANSWER
The question is about conduits used to protect conductors from physical damage.

▶ 1. In Index, find "Conduits" under which find "Conductors, number in, Chap. 9, Table 1, Annex C, Tables C1 through C12(A)."

▶ 2. In Chapter 9, Tables, find note 2 under the heading "Notes to Tables," which states short nipples or sections of conduit or tubing used to protect exposed wiring from physical damage are exempt from Table 1.

▶ 3. The correct answer is D.

QUESTION 4. The smallest size of electrical metallic tubing (EMT) that can be used for a residential service with two 2/0 AWG Type THW conductors and one 4 AWG bare conductor

A. Metric Designator 27 (trade size 1)
B. Metric Designator 35 (trade size 1¼)
C. Metric Designator 41 (trade size 1½)
D. Metric Designator 103 (trade size 4)

ANSWER _____

PROCEDURE TO ESTABLISH ANSWER
This question is related to various sizes of conductors in the same raceway so we are talking about number of conductors in a raceway or the "conductor fill." The fact that it is a residential service has no bearing on the answer.

▶ 1. There are at least two easily identifiable avenues in the Index to find this answer. In the Index find "Conduits" under which find "Conductors, number in, Chap. 9, Table 1, Annex C, Tables C1 through C12(A)." The reference to Table 1 is probably the more direct pathway of the two we are noting but may not be the most effective if the reader does not already know the number of conductors cannot exceed the percentage fill in Table 1.

Alternatively, you can find "Conductor fill" in the Index under which find "Electric Metallic Tubing, 358.22. Section 358.22 notes the number of conductors permitted shall not exceed the percentages allowed in Table 1, Chapter 9. As there are in most *NEC* tables, there are "Notes to Tables" in Table 1, Chapter 9. Notes to tables should always be considered as they are extremely important and will generally affect the use of the table.

▶ 2. Annex C was noted in the Index reference in Step 1 but Note 1 to Table 1, Chapter 9 states Annex C only applies to conduit and tubing fill for conductors and fixture wires of all the same size. Since the question states there are different conductor sizes, Annex C cannot be used.

▶ 3. Scanning the Notes to Tables, you will find that Note 6 applies to combinations of conductors of different sizes. It states that for combinations of conductors of different sizes, Table 5 and Table 5A can be used for conductor dimensions and Table 4, for the applicable conduit or tubing dimensions.

▶ 4. Under Table 5 of Chapter 9, find the column for "Approximate Area" and use "in.^{2}." Under the "Type" column find THW, and then under the "Size" column find 2/0 AWG. It shows an approximate area of .2624 in.^{2} x 2 conductors = .5248 in.^{2}

▶ 5. Note 8 states that where bare conductors are permitted, the dimensions for bare conductors listed in Chapter 9, Table 8 can be used. Look under the "Conductors" column and then find the "Overall" column, followed by the "Area, in.^{2}"
4 AWG overall = 0.042. Adding the 0.042 to the .5248 for the 2/0 conductors there is a total sq. in. area of .5668 in.^{2}

▶ 6. To find tubing size for this fill, go to Chapter 9, Table 4, "Article 358—Electrical Metallic Tubing," "Over 2 Wires 40% column," and then "in.^{2}" A metric designator 27 (1 in.) tubing is permitted to have a conductor fill of only 0.346 square inches, which is not large enough. A metric designator 35 (1¼ in.) tubing is permitted to have conductor fill of 0.598 square inches at 40% fill.

▶ 7. To meet the minimum overall conductor fill of 0.5668 in.^{2}, a metric designator 35 (1¼ in.) EMT conduit would be required.

▶ 8. The correct answer is B.

QUESTION 5.
Generally, electrical nonmetallic tubing shall be secured within a minimum of how many inches from each outlet box?

A. 300 mm (12 in.)
B. 450 mm (18 in.)
C. 600 mm (24 in.)
D. 900 mm (36 in.)

ANSWER _____

PROCEDURE TO ESTABLISH ANSWER
The question is about securing electrical nonmetallic tubing.

▶ 1. In Index, find "Electrical nonmetallic tubing" under which find "Securing and supporting, 362.30."

▶ 2. Section 362.30(A) requires ENT to be securely fastened within 900 mm (3 ft) of each outlet box.

▶ 3. The correct answer is D.

QUESTION 6.
What is the minimum size Schedule 40 rigid polyvinyl chloride conduit (PVC) permitted for three 4 AWG Type THW copper conductors used for a 100-ampere dwelling service?

A. Metric Designator 21 (trade size ¾)
B. Metric Designator 27 (trade size 1)
C. Metric Designator 35 (trade size 1¼)
D. Metric Designator 41 (trade size 1½)

ANSWER _____

PROCEDURE TO ESTABLISH ANSWER
The question is about conductor fill. The fact that it is a dwelling unit service had no bearing on the question.

▶ 1. In Index, find "Conductor fill" under which find "Rigid polyvinyl chloride conduit, 352.22."

▶ 2. Section 352.22 refers to Table 1, Chapter 9, which permits 40 percent fill for over two conductors.

▶ 3. Note 1 to table permits the use of Annex C for conductors of same size.

▶ 4. Table C10 applies to the maximum number of conductors permitted in polyvinyl chloride conduit (PVC), Schedule 40.

▶ 5. For Type THW conductors, size 4 AWG, a metric designator 27 (1 in.) conduit may contain three conductors. A metric designator 21 (¾ in.) conduit will accept only one conductor, so the 1 in. conduit is required.

▶ 6. The correct answer is B.

QUESTION 7. The maximum permitted spacing between supports for flexible metal conduit run exposed along the outside of a wall between two outlet boxes is:

A. 450 mm (1½ ft)
B. 1.4 m (4½ ft)
C. 1.8 m (6 ft)
D. 3.0 m (10 ft)

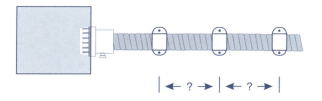

ANSWER _____

PROCEDURE TO ESTABLISH ANSWER
The question is about supports for flexible metal conduit.

▶ 1. In Index, find "Flexible metal conduit" under which find "Securing and supporting, 348.30."

▶ 2. Section 348.30(A) requires flexible metal conduit to be supported at intervals not exceeding 1.4 m (4½ ft).

▶ 3. Since none of the four exceptions applies in this question, assume that the general conditions apply.

▶ 4. The correct answer is B.

QUESTION 8. Generally, flexible metal conduit shall be securely fastened within how many inches from an outlet box?

A. 150 mm (6 in.)
B. 200 mm (8 in.)
C. 300 mm (12 in.)
D. 450 mm (18 in.)

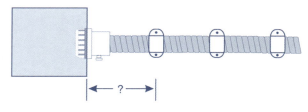

ANSWER _____

PROCEDURE TO ESTABLISH ANSWER
The question is about securing flexible metal conduit.

▶ 1. In Index, find "Flexible metal conduit" under which find "Securing and supporting, 348.30."

▶ 2. Section 348.30(A) requires flexible metal conduit to be securely fastened within 300 mm (12 in.) on each side of every outlet box or fitting.

▶ 3. Since none of the four exceptions is stated in the question, assume that the general conditions apply.

▶ 4. The correct answer is C.

QUESTION 9. Rigid polyvinyl chloride conduit is installed underground as a raceway between a dwelling and an outdoor post light. Two 12 AWG Type THW insulated conductors and a bare 12 AWG equipment grounding conductor are pulled into the raceway. The circuit is protected by a 20-ampere GFCI circuit breaker. What is the minimum burial depth permitted for the raceway?

A. 150 mm (6 in.)
B. 300 mm (12 in.)
C. 450 mm (18 in.)
D. 600 mm (24 in.)

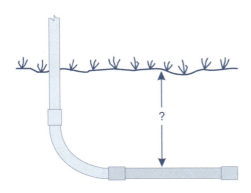

ANSWER _____

PROCEDURE TO ESTABLISH ANSWER
The question is about burial depth of rigid nonmetallic conduit for a branch circuit.

▶ 1. In Index, find "Direct burial" under which find "Rigid polyvinyl chloride conduit, 300.50, 352.10(G)."

▶ 2. Section 352.10(G) refers to 300.5, and 300.5(A) refers to Table 300.5 for minimum cover requirements.

▶ 3. Table 300.5, Column 4, allows 300 mm (12 in.) of cover for a residential branch circuit rated 120 volts or less with GFCI protection and a maximum overcurrent protection of 20 amperes.

▶ 4. The correct answer is B.

QUESTION 10.
A 40-ampere, 240-volt feeder between a dwelling and garage in Schedule 80 rigid polyvinyl chloride conduit (PVC), buried in earth, shall be installed at a minimum depth of:

A. 150 mm (6 in.)
B. 300 mm (12 in.)
C. 450 mm (18 in.)
D. 600 mm (24 in.)

ANSWER _____

PROCEDURE TO ESTABLISH ANSWER
The question is about burial depth of rigid nonmetallic conduit.

▶ 1. In Index, find "Direct burial" under which find "Rigid polyvinyl chloride conduit, 300.50, 352.10(G)."

▶ 2. Section 352.10(G) refers to 300.5, and 300.5(A) refers to Table 300.5 for minimum cover requirements.

▶ 3. Column 3 of Table 300.5 requires 450 mm (18 inches) of cover for all locations not specified below listed conditions.

▶ 4. Scan all conditions under "Location of Wiring Method or Circuit" as well as the notes below the table. The basic requirement of 450 mm (18 in.) applies.

▶ 5. The correct answer is C.

QUESTION 11.
Raceways may be used as a means of support for which one of the following?

A. A raceway containing power supply conductors supplying power to a piece of electrical equipment is permitted to provide support for the Class 2 control circuit conductors for that same piece of equipment
B. Other raceways
C. Telephone cables
D. Nonelectric equipment

ANSWER _____

PROCEDURE TO ESTABLISH ANSWER
The question is about raceways used as a means of support.

▶ 1. In Index, find "Raceways" under which find "Support for nonelectrical equpment, 300.11(B)."

▶ 2. Section 300.11(B) prohibits raceways from being used as a means of support for other raceways, cables, or nonelectrical equipment.

▶ 3. Section 300.11(B)(2), however, permits raceways containing power conductors to support

Class 2 circuit conductors for the specified purpose.

▶ 4. The correct answer is A.

Note: An example would be the 24-volt, Class 2 thermostat circuit conductors for a furnace, which may be supported by the furnace conduit.

QUESTION 12.
All of the following wiring methods are acceptable for use as service-entrance conductors within a dwelling occupancy EXCEPT:

A. surface metal raceway
B. liquidtight flexible nonmetallic conduit
C. flexible metal conduit
D. electrical nonmetallic tubing

ANSWER _____

PROCEDURE TO ESTABLISH ANSWER
The question is about permitted wiring methods for service-entrance conductors to a dwelling.

▶ 1. In Index, find "Service-entrance conductors" under which find "Wiring methods, 230.43."

▶ 2. Section 230.43 lists nineteen types of wiring methods approved for service-entrance conductors.

▶ 3. Surface metal raceway is not listed as one of the approved wiring methods.

▶ 4. The correct answer is A.

QUESTION 13.
All of the following statements regarding metal enclosures and raceways enclosing grounding electrode conductors are true EXCEPT:

A. They shall be a minimum of a metric designator 21 (¾ in.) raceway.
B. They shall be electrically continuous from the service equipment to the electrode, and shall be securely fastened to the ground clamp or fitting.
C. Bonding shall apply at each end of a ferrous raceway, including all boxes and enclosures between the service equipment and the grounding electrode.
D. Electrical metallic tubing may be used to protect 6 AWG grounding electrode conductors subject to physical damage.

ANSWER _____

PROCEDURE TO ESTABLISH ANSWER
The question is about enclosures for grounding electrode conductors.

▶ 1. In Index, find "Grounding electrode conductors" under which find "Installation, 250.64." Section 250.64(B) permits electrical metallic tubing to protect conductors.

▶ 2. Scan through 250.64, and find that 250.64(E) requires metal enclosures to be electrically continuous and be securely fastened to the ground clamp or fitting.

▶ 3. No minimum size of conduit is given.

▶ 4. The correct answer is A.

QUESTION 14.
Generally, electrical metallic tubing shall be securely fastened in place within how many feet of each outlet or junction box?

A. 300 mm   (1 ft)
B. 900 mm   (3 ft)
C. 1.4 m   (4½ ft)
D. 1.8 m   (6 ft)

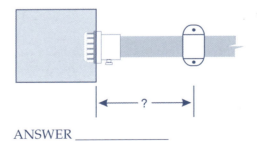

ANSWER _____

Raceways | 1- and 2-Family Study Guide | 19

PROCEDURE TO ESTABLISH ANSWER

The question is about securing electrical metallic tubing.

▶ 1. In Index, find "Electrical metallic tubing" under which find "Securing and supporting, 358.30."

▶ 2. Section 358.30(A) requires that EMT be supported within 900 mm (3 ft) of each outlet box, etc.

▶ 3. The correct answer is B.

QUESTION 15. A large residence requires a service of three 4/0 AWG Type THW copper conductors. Which of the following code references would you use to determine the proper rigid metal conduit size for these conductors?

A. Annex C
B. Table 1, Chapter 9
C. Section 344.22
D. All the above

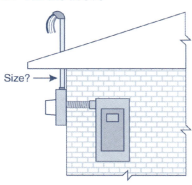

ANSWER _____

PROCEDURE TO ESTABLISH ANSWER

The question is about the size or number of conductors permitted in rigid metal conduit.

▶ 1. In Index, find "Rigid metal conduit" under which find "Number of conductors, 344.22, Chapter 9, Table 1."

▶ 2. Section 344.22 refers to Table 1, Chapter 9 for number of conductors permitted.

▶ 3. As with any *NEC* table, the notes must be reviewed as they will affect the use of the table or provide information on how the table is to be used. In this case, Note 1 to Table 1, Chapter 9 refers to Annex C when all conductors are the same size.

▶ 4. Scan Annex C and find that Table C.8 is applicable for rigid metal conduit.

▶ 5. The correct answer is D.

QUESTION 16. Which of the following is not true regarding a rigid metal conduit raceway used as a service mast to support a service-drop or overhead service conductors:

A. service-drop conductors cannot be attached to the mast between a weatherhead and a coupling, where the coupling is located above the last point of securement to the building
B. the top of the open mast or weatherhead must be at least 750 mm (30 in.) above the roof
C. the mast must be of adequate strength or braced or guyed
D. hubs intended for use with a conduit that serves as a service mast must be identified for use with service-entrance equipment

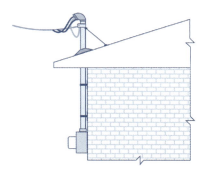

ANSWER _____

PROCEDURE TO ESTABLISH ANSWER

The question is about a raceway used as a service mast to support a service-drop or overhead service conductors.

▶ 1. In Index, find "Service drops" under which there is no longer any direct reference to a point of attachment. However, in the Index find "Overhead service conductors" under which find "Point of attachment, 230.26, 230.28."

► 2. Section 230.28(A) requires that when a mast is used to support service-drop conductors, it shall be of adequate strength or be supported by braces or guys, etc., and that hubs intended for use with a service mast be identified for use with service-entrance equipment. Answers C and D are true.

► 3. Section 230.28(B) prohibits service-drop or overhead service conductors from being attached to the service mast above the building or other structure or where the coupling is located above the last point of securement to the building or other structure. Answer A is true.

► 4. There is no mention of a minimum height requirement to the top of an open service mast or the weatherhead. Answer B is not true.

► 5. The correct answer is B.

QUESTION 17. At the point of connection to the service-drop or overhead service conductors, service raceways shall be equipped with a service head that is:

A. listed for a wet location
B. rainproof
C. weatherproof
D. raintight

ANSWER _____

PROCEDURE TO ESTABLISH ANSWER
The question is about service head connections at service drops.

► 1. In Index, find "Service drops" under which find "Connections, service head, 230.54."

► 2. Section 230.54(A) requires service raceways to be equipped with a service head that is listed for use in wet locations.

► 3. The correct answer is A.

QUESTION 18. A 500-mm (20-inch) length of rigid metal conduit between a pull box and a panelboard contains 30 current-carrying conductors. These conductors would be subject to ampacity adjustment (derating) of:

A. 80 percent
B. 70 percent
C. 45 percent
D. no ampacity adjustment (derating) required

ANSWER _____

PROCEDURE TO ESTABLISH ANSWER
The question is about conductor ampacity adjustment due to the number of conductors in a raceway.

► 1. In Index, find "Ampacities" under which find "Conductors, 310.15, etc."

► 2. Section 310.15(A) states that ampacities of conductors shall be determined by tables as permitted in 310.15(B) or under engineering supervision as in 310.15(C). Since the question is not specific to using engineering supervision, we will use the tables as modified by 310.15(B).

► 3. Section 310.15(B) states the allowable ampacity for conductors shall be as specified in the Allowable Ampacity Tables 310.15(B)(16) through 310.15(B)(19), as modified by 310.15(B)(1) through (B)(7).

► 4. Section 310.15(B)(3)(a) and Table 310.15(B)(3)(a) apply where there are more than three current-carrying conductors in a raceway or cable. Where there are 30 current-carrying conductors in a raceway, Table 310.15(B)(3) would require their ampacity to be adjusted to 45 percent of the value from the Allowable Ampacity Tables.

► 5. However, in our question, the raceway installed between the pull box and the panelboard is only 20" in length. Section 310.15(B)(3)(a)(2) notes the adjustment factors do not apply to conductors in raceways not exceeding 600 mm (24 in.) in length.

► 6. The correct answer is D.

QUESTION 19. When a 500-mm (20-inch) long section of electrical metallic tubing is installed between two outlet boxes, the tubing shall be permitted to be filled to a maximum of:

A. 31 percent
B. 40 percent
C. 60 percent
D. no limit, as many conductors as the conduit will physically hold

ANSWER _____

PROCEDURE TO ESTABLISH ANSWER
The question is about number of conductors in electrical metallic tubing.

▶ 1. In Index, find "Electrical metallic tubing" under which find "Number of conductors in, 358.22."

▶ 2. Section 358.22 refers to Table 1, Chapter 9.

▶ 3. The general requirements in Chapter 9, Table 1, specify not more than 53% fill for a single conductor, 31% fill for two conductors and 40% fill of more than two conductors. However, Note 4 provides that where tubing has a maximum length not exceeding 600 mm (24 in.) and is installed between boxes, it shall be permitted to be filled to 60 percent.

▶ 4. The correct answer is C.

QUESTION 20. Which one of the following methods is NOT acceptable for bonding a metal service raceway to a service panelboard enclosure?

A. Threaded hub on top of enclosure
B. Sealing-type locknut outside and bonding-type locknut inside enclosure
C. Sealing-type locknut outside, standard locknut and bonding bushing with bonding jumper inside enclosure
D. Standard locknuts both inside and outside of enclosure

ANSWER _____

PROCEDURE TO ESTABLISH ANSWER
The question is about bonding of service equipment.

▶ 1. In Index, find "Bonding" under which find "Service equipment, 250.92, 250.94."

▶ 2. Section 250.92(B) covers the methods of bonding at the service and 250.92(B)(1), (B)(2), (B)(3), and (B)(4) recognize threaded hubs, bonding jumpers and bonding locknuts.

▶ 3. The second sentence of 250.92(B) provides that standard locknuts or bushings can be used to provide the mechanical connection of the raceway to the enclosure but they shall not be the only means for the required bonding.

▶ 4. The correct answer is D.

QUESTION 21. Surface metal raceway shall be permitted to be installed in which one of the following locations?

A. Dry locations
B. Damp locations
C. Where subject to physical damage
D. More than one surface metal raceway section joined together and concealed behind drywall

ANSWER _____

PROCEDURE TO ESTABLISH ANSWER
The question is about the use of surface metal raceway.

▶ 1. In Index, find "Surface metal raceways" under which find "Uses permitted, 386.10."

▶ 2. Of our choices, Section 386.10 limits the use to dry locations, which eliminates damp locations.

▶ 3. The uses not permitted in 386.12 include: (1) where subject to physical damage, and (5) where concealed except when in compliance with 386.10. Section 386.10(4) would only permit the surface metal raceway to be installed concealed in a wall if it was passing transversely through the wall and the length is unbroken. As noted in the question, two raceways were joined within the wall and as indicated in 386.10(4), the surface metal raceway can only pass transversely through the wall.

▶ 4.   The correct answer is A.

QUESTION 22. A metric designator 35 (1¼ in.) rigid polyvinyl chloride conduit (PVC) must be securely fastened in place at least every _____ feet and within _____ feet of each outlet box, cabinet or fitting.

A. 900 mm (3 ft) and 900 mm (3 ft)
B. 1.5 m (5 ft) and 900 mm (3 ft)
C. 1.5 m (5 ft) and 1.5 m (5 ft)
D. 3.0 m (10 ft) and 1.5 m (5 ft)

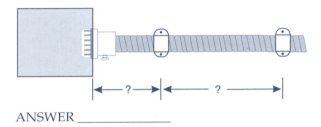

ANSWER _____

PROCEDURE TO ESTABLISH ANSWER
The question is about securing rigid polyvinyl chloride conduit (PVC) conduit.

▶ 1.   In Index, find "Rigid polyvinyl chloride conduit" under which find "Supporting and securing, Table 352.30(B)."

▶ 2.   Section 352.30(A) requires support within 900 mm (3 ft) of each outlet box, etc.

▶ 3.   Section 352.30(B) refers to Table 352.30(B), which requires the conduit to be supported every 1.5 m (5 ft).

▶ 4.   The correct answer is B.

QUESTION 23. The largest size electrical metallic tubing recognized in the *Code* is:

A. metric designator 53 (trade size 2)
B. metric designator 78 (trade size 3)
C. metric designator 103 (trade size 4)
D. metric designator 155 (trade size 6)

ANSWER _____

PROCEDURE TO ESTABLISH ANSWER
The question is about the size of electrical metallic tubing.

▶ 1.   In Index, find "Electrical metallic tubing" under which find "Size, 358.20."

▶ 2.   Section 358.20(B) limits the maximum size to metric designator 103 (trade size 4).

▶ 3.   The correct answer is C.

QUESTION 24. Which one of the following statements about intermediate metal conduit is true?

A. Conduit smaller than metric designator 16 (trade size ½) may be used.
B. Conduit larger than metric designator 103 (trade size 4) may be used.
C. Conduit shall be supported at least every 3 m (10 ft).
D. Generally, conduit shall be securely fastened within 1.8 m (6 ft) of each outlet box.

ANSWER _____

PROCEDURE TO ESTABLISH ANSWER
The question is about intermediate metal conduit.

▶ 1.   In Index, find "Intermediate metal conduit" under which find "Size, 342.20" and "Supports and securing, 342.30."

▶ 2.   Section 342.20(A) restricts the minimum size to metric designator 16 (trade size ½).

Raceways | 1- and 2-Family Study Guide | 23

► 3. Section 342.20(B) does not permit use of IMC larger than metric designator 103 (trade size 4).

► 4. Section 342.30(B)(1) requires the conduit to be supported at least every 3 m (10 ft).

► 5. Section 342.30(A) requires IMC to be securely fastened within 900 mm (3 ft) of each outlet box, etc., with rules allowing securing at various distances from outlet box, but not at 1.8 m (6 ft). Answers A, B, and D are not true.

► 6. The correct answer is C.

QUESTION 25.
Bends in electrical metallic tubing between any two pull points shall not exceed the equivalent of _____ quarter-bends.

A. two
B. four
C. six
D. eight

ANSWER _____

PROCEDURE TO ESTABLISH ANSWER
The question is about bends in electrical metallic tubing.

► 1. In Index, find "Electrical metallic tubing," under which find "Bends, 358.24, 358.26."

► 2. Section 358.26 states that there shall not be more than the equivalent of four quarter bends (360 degrees total) between pull points.

► 3. The correct answer is B.

QUESTION 26.
Which one of the following statements about flexible metal conduit is NOT true?

A. Flexible metal conduit is permitted to be installed in a concealed location.
B. Flexible metal conduit containing Type THW conductors may be installed in wet locations.
C. Flexible metal conduit can be used to enclose service-entrance conductors only under specific conditions.
D. Flexible metal conduit is not permitted to be used underground.

ANSWER _____

PROCEDURE TO ESTABLISH ANSWER
The question is about the use of flexible metal conduit.

► 1. In Index, find "Flexible metal conduit" under which find "Uses not permitted, 348.12" and "Uses permitted, 348.10."

► 2. Section 348.10 allows FMC in both exposed and concealed locations. Answer A is true.

► 3. Section 348.12(1) prohibits the use of flexible metal conduit in wet locations regardless of the type of conductors utilized. Answer B is not true.

► 4. Section 348.12 does not list flexible metal conduit as a prohibited wiring method for service-entrance conductors. In Index, find "Service-entrance conductors" under which find "Wiring methods, 230.43." In 230.43, flexible metal conduit is permitted to enclose service-entrance conductors, when certain requirements are met. Answer C is true.

► 5. Section 348.12(6) prohibits the use of flexible metal conduit underground. Answer D is true.

► 6. The correct answer is B.

QUESTION 27.
The use of rigid polyvinyl chloride conduit (PVC) and fittings approved for the purpose shall be permitted under all of the following conditions EXCEPT:

A. for the support of luminaires (lighting fixtures) from a conduit body (cast aluminum or steel boxes with threaded hub or entries such as "Mulbury," "Red Dot" or "bell boxes" are listed as conduit bodies)
B. concealed in an insulated wall
C. in cinder fill
D. for underground installations

ANSWER _____

PROCEDURE TO ESTABLISH ANSWER
The question is about uses for rigid nonmetallic conduit.

▶ 1. In Index, find "Rigid polyvinyl chloride conduit" under which find "Uses permitted, 352.10" and "Uses not permitted, 352.12."

▶ 2. Section 352.10(A) permits PVC to be installed concealed in walls.

▶ 3. Section 352.10(C) permits PVC installations in cinder fill.

▶ 4. Section 352.10(G) permits PVC installations underground.

▶ 5. Section 352.12(H) prohibits PVC for support of luminaires (lighting fixtures).

▶ 6. The correct answer is A.

QUESTION 28. All of the following types of conductor insulation are suitable for installing in an underground raceway extending from a dwelling to a detached garage EXCEPT?

A. TW
B. THW
C. THWN
D. THHN

ANSWER _____

PROCEDURE TO ESTABLISH ANSWER
The question is about types of conductor insulation that are suitable for installation in underground raceways.

Note: Any underground installation has to be considered a wet location (see Article 100, Definitions, for *Location, Wet*).

▶ 1. In Index, find "Conductors" under which find "Wet location, 225.4, 310.10(C), Table 310.104(A)."

▶ 2. Section 310.10(C) permits conductors that are marked TW, THW or THWN to be used in wet locations.

▶ 3. Section 310.104(A) requires conductors to meet the provisions of Table 310.104(A). In Table 310.104(A) find the "Application Provisions" column and locate Types TW, THW and THWN insulation. Note that all three insulation types are suitable for dry and wet locations. Also find "THHN" insulation is only suitable for dry and damp locations.

Further, the designation "W" stands for "Moisture resistant" according to the UL *Wire and Cable Marking Guide*. Therefore, a conductor without a "W" in its type letters is not suitable for wet locations.

▶ 4. The correct answer is D.

QUESTION 29. Where a raceway containing insulated conductors enters a cabinet, the conductors shall be protected by an insulated fitting (bushing) that provides a smoothly rounded insulating surface, if the conductors are of what AWG size or larger?

A. 2 AWG
B. 4 AWG
C. 6 AWG
D. 8 AWG

ANSWER _____

PROCEDURE TO ESTABLISH ANSWER
The question is about insulation at bushings at a cabinet.

▶ 1. In Index, find "Cabinets, cutout boxes, and meter socket enclosures" under which find "Insulation at bushings, 300.4(G), 312.6(C)."

▶ 2. Section 312.6(C) refers to 300.4(G) which provides the requirements for protecting conductors in raceways entering a cabinet and requires protection for conductors 4 AWG and larger.

▶ 3. The correct answer is B.

QUESTION 30. Which of the following statements about the use of a raceway through which nonmetallic-sheathed cables enter a panelboard without being secured is true?

A. Flexible metal conduit is permitted.
B. The raceway is permitted to enter the top, sides or bottom of the panelboard.
C. The cables are required to be secured to the structure within 300 mm (12 in.) of the point where they enter the outer end of the raceway.
D. The raceway is required to be between 300 mm (12 in.) and 1.2 m (48 in.).

ANSWER _____

PROCEDURE TO ESTABLISH ANSWER
The question is about rules under which cables are not required to be secured to panelboard cabinets.

▶ 1. In Index, find "Cabinets, cutout boxes, and meter socket enclosures, Art. 312."

▶ 2. Since there is no direct reference to cables in raceways, turn to Article 312.

▶ 3. Scan Article 312 and find "312.5(C), Cables."

▶ 4. The main rule of this section is for the cable to be secured to the cabinet. The opening paragraph of the exception permits nonmetallic-sheathed cables to enter the top of an enclosure through a "nonflexible" raceway. Answer A is not true as it is a flexible raceway and Answer B in not true as the raceway must enter the top of the enclosure.

▶ 5. The opening paragraph of the exception requires the raceway to be between 450 mm (18 in.) and 3.0 m (10 ft) in length. Answer D is not true.

▶ 6. Section 312.5(C) Exception, part (a) requires the cables to be secured to the structure within 300 mm (12 in.) of the point where they enter the outer end of the raceway. Answer C is true.

▶ 7. The correct answer is C.

QUESTION 31. In the *NEC*, conduit bending radius tables for field bends of rigid metal conduit are found in:

A. Table 344.24
B. Section 344.26
C. Annex C
D. Chapter 9, Table 2

ANSWER _____

PROCEDURE TO ESTABLISH ANSWER
The question is about the location of conduit bending radius tables for field bends of rigid metal conduit.

▶ 1. In Index, find "Rigid Metal Conduit, Art. 344," under which find "Bends, 344.24, 344.26."

▶ 2. Section 344.24 states that the radius of a curve of any field-bend to the centerline of the conduit shall not be less than indicated in Table 2, Chapter 9.

▶ 3. The correct answer is D.

QUESTION 32. All of the following statements regarding support of flexible metal conduit are true EXCEPT?

A. In an accessible ceiling, flexible metal conduit is permitted to be securely fastened for connection within 6 feet of a luminaire or other equipment.
B. Generally, flexible metal conduit shall be securely fastened by an approved means within 300 mm (12 in.) of each box, cabinet, conduit body, or other conduit termination, and shall be supported and secured at intervals not to exceed 1.4 m (4½ ft).
C. Horizontal runs of flexible metal conduit supported by openings in framing members at intervals not greater than 1.4 m (4½ ft) and securely fastened within 300 mm (12 in.) of termination points are permitted.
D. Trade size ¾ inch flexible metal conduit, installed to a motor terminal box where flexibility is required, must be supported within 300 mm (12 in.) of the motor terminal box.

ANSWER _____

PROCEDURE TO ESTABLISH ANSWER
The question is about supporting and securing flexible metal conduit.

▶ 1. In Index, find "Flexible metal conduit (Type FMC), Art. 348" under which find "Securing and supporting, 348.30."

▶ 2. Scan 348.30, and find that Answers A, B, and C are all true.

▶ 3. Section 348.30(A) Exception No. 2, (1), permits metric designator 21 (trade size ¾) flexible metal conduit to be supported at lengths not exceeding 900 mm (3 ft.) at terminals where flexibility is required.

▶ 4. The correct answer is D.

4 Cables

QUESTION 1. What is the minimum cover requirement for 12 AWG Type UF cable used for an underground residential branch circuit rated 120 volts and connected to a GFCI circuit breaker?

A. 150 mm (6 in.)
B. 300 mm (12 in.)
C. 450 mm (18 in.)
D. 600 mm (24 in.)

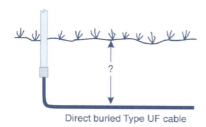

Direct buried Type UF cable

A. 150 mm (6 in.)
B. 300 mm (12 in.)
C. 450 mm (18 in.)
D. 600 mm (24 in.)

ANSWER _____

PROCEDURE TO ESTABLISH ANSWER
The question is about minimum cover requirements for underground cable.

▶ 1. In Index, find "Underground wiring" under which find "Minimum cover requirements, 300.5(A)."

▶ 2. Section 300.5(A) references Table 300.5, which in Column 4 allows a 20-ampere, 120-volt residential branch circuit with GFCI protection to be buried a minimum of 300 mm (12 in.).

▶ 3. The correct answer is B.

QUESTION 2. Nonmetallic-sheathed cable shall be which one of the following types?

A. AC
B. USE
C. NM
D. SJO

28 | 1- and 2-Family Study Guide | Cables

ANSWER _____

PROCEDURE TO ESTABLISH ANSWER
The question is about types of nonmetallic-sheathed cable.

▶ 1. In Index, find "Cables."

▶ 2. Under "Cables," find "Nonmetallic-sheathed (Types NM, NMC, and NMS)," which refers to "Nonmetallic-sheathed cable (Types NM, NMC, and NMS)."

▶ 3. In Index, find "Nonmetallic-sheathed cable (Types NM, NMC, and NMS), Art. 334."

▶ 4. Article 334 provides the requirements for the construction, installation, and use of Type NM cable.

▶ 5. The correct answer is C.

QUESTION 3. What is the minimum cover requirement for Type UF cable used as a residential 30-ampere feeder under a driveway for a two-family dwelling?

A. 150 mm (6 in.)
B. 300 mm (12 in.)
C. 450 mm (18 in.)
D. 600 mm (24 in.)

ANSWER _____

PROCEDURE TO ESTABLISH ANSWER
The question is about burial depth for Type UF cable.

▶ 1. In Index, find "Cables" under which, find "Underground feeder and branch-circuit Type UF" *see* Underground feeder and branch-circuit cable (Type UF)."

▶ 2. In Index, find "Underground feeder and branch-circuit cable (Type UF), Art. 340."

▶ 3. In 340.10, Uses Permitted, find subsection (1) which refers to 300.5 for underground requirements.

▶ 4. Section 300.5(A) references Table 300.5.

▶ 5. Column 1 of Table 300.5 would fit our described situation since we are dealing with a 30-ampere feeder installed under a one- and two-family dwelling driveway.

▶ 6. We would need a minimum burial depth of 450 mm (18 in.) in this situation.

▶ 7. The correct answer is C.

QUESTION 4. Which of the following applications is a permitted use for Type NM nonmetallic-sheathed cable?

A. Where embedded in attic insulation of a one- or two-family dwelling
B. In a location subject to excessive moisture or dampness
C. As service-entrance cable
D. Where embedded in poured concrete

ANSWER _____

PROCEDURE TO ESTABLISH ANSWER
The question is about the use of nonmetallic-sheathed cable.

▶ 1. In Index, find "Nonmetallic-sheathed cable" under which find "Uses not permitted, 334.12" and "Uses permitted, 334.10."

▶ 2. Section 334.10(1) permits Type NM cable in one- and two-family dwellings and their attached or detached garages and their storage buildings. Answer A is true.

▶ 3. Section 334.10(A)(1) permits Type NM cable in a dry location such as an attic.

▶ 4. Section 334.12(B)(4) prohibits Type NM cable in damp or wet locations. Answer B is not true.

▶ 5. Section 334.12(A)(3) does not permit Type NM Cable to be used as service-entrance cable. Answer C is not true.

▶ 6. Section 334.12(A)(9) prohibits Type NM cable from being embedded in poured concrete. Answer D is not true.

▶ 7. The correct answer is A.

QUESTION 5.
Where ampacity adjustment or correction (derating) of conductors is not required, the ampacity of 6 AWG copper Type NM cable shall be:

A. 50 amperes
B. 55 amperes
C. 60 amperes
D. 65 amperes

ANSWER _____

PROCEDURE TO ESTABLISH ANSWER
The question is about the ampacity of the conductors in Type NM cable.

▶ 1. In Index, find "Nonmetallic-sheathed cable" under which find "Ampacity, 334.80."

▶ 2. Section 334.80 requires the ampacity of Type NM cable to be that of 60°C conductors and refers to 310.15.

▶ 3. Section 310.15(B) requires the ampacities to be as specified in Tables 310.15(B)(16) through 310.15(B)(19).

▶ 4. Scan the titles of the tables; Table 310.15(B)(16) applies to the ampacities for insulated conductors in raceways, cables or directly buried in the earth so it is applicable to this question.

▶ 5. In the 60°C column of Table 310.15(B)(16), the allowable ampacity of 6 AWG copper is 55 amperes.

▶ 6. The correct answer is B.

QUESTION 6.
Where a 100 mm x 100 mm (4 in. x 4 in.) nonmetallic box is used with nonmetallic-sheathed cable, the *Code* requires the cable to be:

A. extended into the box not less than 6 mm (¼ in.) inside the box and beyond any cable clamp
B. stapled within 150 mm (6 in.) of the box
C. stapled within 250 mm (10 in.) of the box
D. extended into the box not less than 10 mm (⅜ in.)

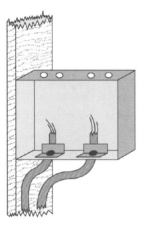

ANSWER _____

PROCEDURE TO ESTABLISH ANSWER
The question is about securing of nonmetallic-sheathed cables to nonmetallic boxes.

▶ 1. In Index, find "Boxes" under which find "Nonmetallic, 314.3, 314.17(C), 314.43, 334.40."

▶ 2. Section 314.17(C) is applicable to nonmetallic boxes, and requires the nonmetallic-sheathed cable to be extended into the box not less than 6 mm (¼ in.) inside the box and beyond any cable clamp.

▶ 3. To check stapling requirements, in Index, find "Nonmetallic-sheathed cable, etc." under which find "Supports, 334.30."

▶ 4. Section 334.30, Securing and Supporting, requires NM cable to be stapled within 300 mm (12 in.) of a junction or outlet box, cabinet or fitting.

▶ 5. The correct answer is A.

QUESTION 7. A nonmetallic-sheathed cable with a 13 mm (½ in.) diameter shall be installed so that the inner edge of any bend in the cable is not less than:

A. 13 mm (½ in.)
B. 50 mm (2 in.)
C. 65 mm (2-½ in.)
D. 125 mm (5 in.)

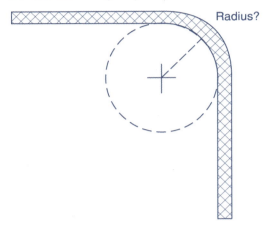

ANSWER _____

PROCEDURE TO ESTABLISH ANSWER
The question is about bends in nonmetallic-sheathed cable.

▶ 1. In Index, find "Nonmetallic-sheathed cable" under which find "Bends, 334.24."

▶ 2. Section 334.24 requires that the radius of the curve of the inner edge of any bend shall not be less than five times the diameter of the cable.

▶ 3. Our stated cable diameter is 13 mm (½ in.). 13 mm (½ in.) x 5 = 65 mm (2½ in.)

▶ 4. The correct answer is C.

QUESTION 8. Where installed in a 19 mm (¾ in.) groove and covered with wallboard, paneling, or carpeting, which one of the following wiring methods is not required to be protected by a 1.6 mm (¹⁄₁₆ in.) thick steel plate or sleeve?

A. Type NM cable
B. Type SE cable
C. Type UF cable
D. Schedule 40 PVC conduit

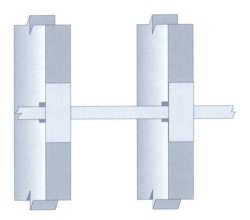

ANSWER _____

PROCEDURE TO ESTABLISH ANSWER
The question is about protection of wiring methods against physical damage.

▶ 1. In Index, find "Cables" under which find "Protection against physical damage, 300.4."

▶ 2. Section 300.4(F) requires all cables run in shallow grooves with less than 32 mm (1¼ in.) free space to be protected by a 1.6 mm (¹⁄₁₆ in.) thick steel plate, sleeve, or equivalent.

▶ 3. Exception No. 1 to Section 300.4(F) does not require this protection for rigid nonmetallic conduit (Schedule 40 PVC conduit).

▶ 4. The correct answer is D.

QUESTION 9. Service-entrance cable shall be supported by straps or similar means within 300 mm (12 in.) of the service head or gooseneck and at intervals NOT to exceed:

A. 750 mm   (30 in.)
B. 900 mm   (36 in.)
C. 1.4 m   (4 ½ ft)
D. 1.8 m   (6 ft)

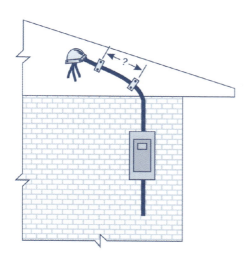

ANSWER _____

PROCEDURE TO ESTABLISH ANSWER
The question is about mounting supports for Type SE service-entrance cables.

▶ 1. In Index, find "Service-entrance cable" under which find "Mounting Supports, 230.51."

▶ 2. Section 230.51(A) requires Type SE cables to be supported at intervals not exceeding 750 mm (30 in.).

▶ 3. The correct answer is A.

QUESTION 10. Which one of the following statements about fastening nonmetallic-sheathed cable to nonmetallic boxes is NOT true?

A. Where the cable sheath extends 6 mm (¼ in.) into a 100 mm x 100 mm (4 in. x 4 in.) box and the cable is strapped within 200 mm (8 in.) of the box measured along the sheath, securing the cable to the box is not necessary.
B. Where the cable sheath extends 6 mm (¼ in.) into a 57 mm x 100 mm (2¼ in. x 4 in.) box and the cable is secured within 200 mm (8 in.) of the box, securing the cable to the box is not necessary.
C. Where the cable is not required to be secured to the box, the box may be mounted in walls or ceilings.
D. Where the cable is not required to be secured to the box, multiple cables are permitted in a single cable knockout opening.

ANSWER _____

PROCEDURE TO ESTABLISH ANSWER
The question is about securing of nonmetallic-sheathed cables to nonmetallic boxes.

▶ 1. In Index, find "Boxes" under which find "Nonmetallic, 314.3, 314.17(C), 314.43, 334.40."

▶ 2. Section 314.17(C) is applicable and in part requires all wiring methods to be secured to the boxes. The exception, however, exempts under specific conditions, nonmetallic cables from being secured to nonmetallic boxes mounted in walls or ceilings only where the boxes are no larger than 57 mm x 100 mm (2 ¼ in. x 4 in.) and the cable is secured within 200 mm (8 in.) of the box. The 100 mm x 100 mm (4 in. x 4 in.) box does not meet the permitted exception.

▶ 3. The exception to 314.17(C) also permits multiple cables in a single cable knockout.

▶ 4. The correct answer is A.

32 | 1- and 2-Family Study Guide | Cables

QUESTION 11.
Where installing nonmetallic-sheathed cable in a new two-story dwelling, the cable shall be supported and secured in place at intervals not exceeding which one of the following?

A. 450 mm (18 in.)
B. 900 mm (3 ft)
C. 1.4 m (4½ ft)
D. 1.8 m (6 ft)

ANSWER _____

PROCEDURE TO ESTABLISH ANSWER
The question is about the support of nonmetallic-sheathed cables.

▶ 1. In Index, find "Nonmetallic-sheathed cable" under which find "Supports, 334.30."

▶ 2. Section 334.30 requires Type NM cable to be supported and secured by staples, cable ties, straps, hangers, etc., every 1.4 m (4½ ft), and within 300 mm (12 in.) of every cabinet, box or fitting.

▶ 3. The correct answer is C.

QUESTION 12.
In unfinished basements, Type NM nonmetallic-sheathed cable is required to be run through bored holes in joists or on running boards if smaller than:

A. Two 4 AWG or three 6 AWG
B. Two 6 AWG or three 8 AWG
C. Two 8 AWG or three 6 AWG
D. Two 8 AWG or three 10 AWG

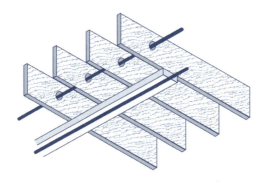

ANSWER _____

PROCEDURE TO ESTABLISH ANSWER
The question is about the support of nonmetallic-sheathed cables in unfinished basements.

▶ 1. In Index, find "Nonmetallic-sheathed cable" under which find "Unfinished basements, 334.15(C)."

▶ 2. Section 334.15(C) requires cables smaller than two 6 AWG or three 8 AWG to be run through bored holes in joists or on running boards.

▶ 3. The correct answer is B.

QUESTION 13.
The insulated conductors for Type NM cable shall be rated at:

A. 140°F
B. 167°F
C. 194°F
D. 120°F

ANSWER _____

PROCEDURE TO ESTABLISH ANSWER
The question is about the minimum temperature rating of insulated conductors in Type NM cable.

▶ 1. In Index, find "Nonmetallic-sheathed cable" under which find "Insulation, 334.112."

▶ 2. Section 334.112 requires Type NM cable to be constructed of conductor insulation rated at 90°C (194°F).

▶ 3. The correct answer is C.

QUESTION 14.
Type UF cable assemblies shall be permitted for all of the following applications EXCEPT:

A. a branch-circuit cable embedded in poured concrete
B. underground between a dwelling and garage
C. installed in insulation in a dwelling attic
D. for solar photovoltaic systems

ANSWER _____

PROCEDURE TO ESTABLISH ANSWER
The question is about the uses of Type UF cable.

▶ 1. In Index, find "Underground feeder and branch-circuit cable (Type UF)" under which find "Uses not permitted, 340.12" and "Uses permitted, 340.10."

▶ 2. Section 340.10(1) permits the use of Type UF cable underground.

▶ 3. Section 340.10(4) permits the use of Type UF cable for interior wiring.

▶ 4. Section 340.10(5) permits the use of Type UF cable for solar photovoltaic systems.

▶ 5. Section 340.12(8) prohibits the use of Type UF cable embedded in poured concrete.

▶ 6. The correct answer is A.

QUESTION 15.
Type UF cable used on a 120/240-volt circuit emerging from the ground and routed up the side of a pole where it is subject to physical damage is protected by Schedule 80 PVC conduit. What is the minimum total length of the PVC conduit required for the aboveground portion of this installation?

A. 2.5 m (8 ft)
B. 2.7 m (9 ft)
C. 3.0 m (10 ft)
D. 3.7 m (12 ft)

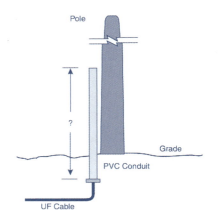

ANSWER _____

PROCEDURE TO ESTABLISH ANSWER
The question is about underground wiring and the protection of Type UF cable where it emerges from the ground.

▶ 1. In Index, find "Underground feeder and branch circuit cable (Type UF), Art. 340" under which, find "Uses Permitted, 340.10."

▶ 2. Section 340.10(1), Uses Permitted, refers us to 300.5 for underground and direct burial requirements.

▶ 3. Section 300.5(D)(1) requires direct buried cables emerging from grade to be protected from the minimum cover distance below grade required by 300.5(A) to a point at least 2.5 m (8 ft) above finished grade. This question asks only for the length of conduit from where the UF cable emerges from the ground.

Note: Protection for the underground portion is not included in this question. (The below grade conduit is not required to exceed 450 mm (18 in.) below grade, but may be longer).

▶ 4. The correct answer is A.

QUESTION 16. How many inches under a landscaped yard shall a 50-ampere, 240-volt circuit of Type UF cable on one- or two-family dwelling property be buried?

A. 150 mm (6 in.)
B. 300 mm (12 in.)
C. 450 mm (18 in.)
D. 600 mm (24 in.)

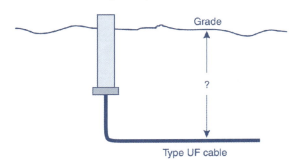

ANSWER _____

PROCEDURE TO ESTABLISH ANSWER
The question is about the minimum burial depth of Type UF cable on residential property.

▶ 1. In Index, find "Underground wiring" under which find "Minimum cover requirements, 300.5(A)."

▶ 2. Section 300.5(A) requires depths to comply with Table 300.5.

▶ 3. Column 1 of Table 300.5 fits our described situation since we are dealing with a 50-ampere branch circuit or feeder installed under a one- and two-family dwelling yard. Since the described situation does not fit any of the specified locations, we would use the first row, Column 1.

▶ 4. We would need a minimum burial depth of 600 mm (24 in.) in this situation.

▶ 5. The correct answer is D.

QUESTION 17. Type NM cable is required to have all of the following markings EXCEPT:

A. maximum rated voltage
B. manufacturers name, trademark, or distinctive marking
C. maximum rated ampacity
D. AWG size or circular mil area

ANSWER _____

PROCEDURE TO ESTABLISH ANSWER
The question is about markings on Type NM cable.

▶ 1. In Index, find "Nonmetallic-sheathed cable," under which find "Marking, 310.120."

▶ 2. Section 310.120(A) requires all of the above markings except the maximum rated ampacity.

▶ 3. The correct answer is C.

QUESTION 18. Type NM cable is permitted to be used in which one of the following applications?

A. In one- and two-family dwellings of any height
B. In damp locations
C. As service-entrance cable
D. Embedded in poured concrete

ANSWER _____

PROCEDURE TO ESTABLISH ANSWER
The question is about the permitted and non-permitted uses of Type NM Cables.

▶ 1. In Index, find "Nonmetallic-sheathed cable," under which find "Uses permitted, 334.10" and "Uses not permitted, 334.12."

▶ 2. Section 334.10(1) permits Type NM cable to be used in one- and two-family dwellings, with no height restriction indicated.

▶ 3. Section 334.12(B)(4) prohibits Type NM cable to be used in damp or wet locations.

▶ 4. Section 334.12(A)(3) prohibits Type NM cable to be used as service-entrance cable.

▶ 5. Section 334.12(A)(9) and (B)(2) prohibit Type NM cable to be embedded in poured concrete.

▶ 6. The correct answer is A.

QUESTION 19.
Type SE cable supplying 240-volt circuits is permitted for all but which one of the following applications?

A. Feeders only
B. Interior wiring
C. Underground wiring
D. Services only

ANSWER _____

PROCEDURE TO ESTABLISH ANSWER
The question is about the permitted use of Type SE cable.

▶ 1. In Index, find "Service-entrance cable" under which find "Uses permitted, 338.10."

▶ 2. Section 338.10(B) allows Type SE to be used as a feeder, but does not limit its use to feeders.

▶ 3. Section 338.10(B)(4)(a) permits Type SE cable to be used as interior wiring under specific conditions.

▶ 4. Section 338.12(2) prohibits Type SE cables from being installed underground with or without a raceway.

▶ 5. Section 338.10(A) allows Type SE to be used as service conductors, but does not limit its use to services.

▶ 6. The correct answer is C.

QUESTION 20.
For which one of the following applications may Type SE cable without individual insulation on the grounded conductor be used?

A. As a new branch circuit supplying ranges and dryers
B. As a branch circuit to a 120/240-volt heat pump, where the uninsulated conductor is used only for equipment grounding
C. Service-entrance conductors
D. B and C

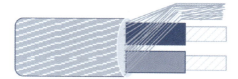

ANSWER _____

PROCEDURE TO ESTABLISH ANSWER
The question is about the use of Type SE cable without insulation on the grounded conductor.

▶ 1. In Index, find "Service-entrance cable" under which find "Uses permitted, 338.10."

▶ 2. In 338.10(B)(2) permits the use of Type SE cable where the uninsulated conductor is used as the equipment grounding conductor. Answer B is true.

▶ 3. Section 338.10(B)(2), Exception, refers to 250.140, which prohibits the use of a Type SE uninsulated grounded conductor in new installations, but does allow its use in existing installations. This section also allows existing installations of branch circuits to ranges and dryers that do not contain an equipment grounding conductor, but use the grounded conductor to ground the metal frames of equipment and outlets or junction boxes for these circuits. Since these are new circuits to the ranges and dryers, Answer A is not true.

▶ 4. Section 338.10(A) allows Type SE cable to be used as service-entrance conductors.

▶ 5. The correct answer is D.

36 | 1- and 2-Family Study Guide | Cables

QUESTION 21. How many inches of free conductor shall extend beyond the opening of an outlet box that measures less than 200 mm (8 in.) in any dimension? The conductors are intended to either be spliced or terminated at the outlet box.

A. 75 mm   (3 in.)
B. 150 mm (6 in.)
C. 200 mm (8 in.)
D. 300 mm (12 in.)

ANSWER _____

PROCEDURE TO ESTABLISH ANSWER
The question is about the length of free conductor at each outlet box.

▶ 1. In Index, find "Conductors" under which find "Length in boxes, 300.14."

▶ 2. Section 300.14 requires 75 mm (3 in.) of free conductor extending outside the outlet, junction, or switch box with openings of less than 200 mm (8 in.) in any dimension.

▶ 3. The correct answer is A.

QUESTION 22. Which one of the following characteristics is not required for the overall covering on Type UF cable in sizes 14 through 4/0 AWG?

A. Flame-retardant
B. Moisture-resistant
C. Fungus-resistant and corrosion-resistant
D. Sunlight-resistant

ANSWER _____

PROCEDURE TO ESTABLISH ANSWER
The question is about the construction of a cable as it is concerned with the requirements for the outer covering, or sheath, of Type UF cable.

▶ 1. In Index, find "Underground feeder and branch-circuit cable (Type UF)" under which find "Construction specifications, 340–Part III."

▶ 2. Scan Part III of Article 340 to find "340.116, Sheath," which requires the overall covering to be flame-retardant; moisture-, fungus-, and corrosion-resistant; and suitable for direct burial in the earth. This cable is not specifically required to be sunlight-resistant although that marking would be necessary if the cable were used where exposed to the sunlight.

▶ 3. The correct answer is D.

QUESTION 23. Where several Type NM cables are bundled together and the ampacity is required to be adjusted due to the number of current-carrying conductors (derated), what is the maximum temperature rating permitted to be used for the conductor ampacity adjustment?

A. 60°C
B. 75°C
C. 90°C
D. 105°C

ANSWER _____

PROCEDURE TO ESTABLISH ANSWER
The question is about temperature rating associated with the ampacity adjustment of Type NM cable.

▶ 1. In Index, find "Nonmetallic-sheathed cable" under which find "334.80, Ampacity.

▶ 2. Section 334.80 permits the 90°C rating to be used for ampacity adjustment or correction (derating) calculations.

▶ 3. The correct answer is C.

Note: What is commonly called *derating* in the electrical trade is actually *ampacity adjustment and correction factors* in the *NEC*. We "adjust" conductor ampacity for the number of conductors and we "correct" conductor ampacity for ambient temperature. See 310.15(B)(3)(a) and 310.15(B)(2)(a) respectively.

QUESTION 24. Type NM cable shall be permitted to be used in one- or two-family dwellings for all of the following applications EXCEPT:

A. enclosed in flexible metal conduit outside to feed an A/C unit
B. in air voids of a concrete block wall not subject to excessive moisture
C. embedded in foam insulation in walls
D. in a one- and two-family dwelling of any height

ANSWER _____

PROCEDURE TO ESTABLISH ANSWER
The question is about the use of Type NM cable in one- and two-family dwellings.

▶ 1. In Index, find "Nonmetallic-sheathed cable," under which find "Uses permitted, 334.10" and "Uses not permitted, 334.12."

▶ 2. Section 334.10(1) permits Type NM cable to be installed in one- and two-family dwellings, regardless of the height of the structure. Answer D is true.

▶ 3. Section 334.10(A)(1) permits Type NM cable to be used for both exposed and concealed work in dry locations. Answer C is true.

▶ 4. Section 334.10(A)(2) permits Type NM cable to be installed or fished in air voids of masonry block or tile walls. Section 334.12(B)(4) does not allow NM cable to be installed in damp or wet locations. Answer B is true.

▶ 5. The wiring method using flexible metal conduit feeding an outside air-conditioning unit can be considered a damp or wet location, because it is located outdoors. Section 334.12(B)(4) prohibits the use of Type NM cable in damp or wet locations. Answer A is not true.

▶ 6. Type NM cable is not allowed to be installed in a complete raceway system unless it is permitted by the respective cable article. Article 334 does not specifically permit Type NM cable to be installed in a raceway system. However, 334.15 permits it to be protected from physical damage by rigid metal conduit, intermediate metal conduit, electrical metallic tubing, Schedule 80 PVC and RTRC with an XW suffix.

▶ 7. The correct answer is A.

QUESTION 25. Type NM nonmetallic-sheathed cable installed in an attic accessible by a scuttle hole but not by permanent stairs shall be protected by guard strips in which one of the following locations?

A. Across the top of floor joists 3.0 m (10 ft) from a scuttle hole
B. Across the top of floor joists 1.8 m (6 ft) from a scuttle hole
C. Parallel to the sides of rafters or floor joists within 900 mm (3 ft) of a scuttle hole
D. Across the face of rafters or studding 3.0 m (10 ft) from the scuttle hole

ANSWER _____

PROCEDURE TO ESTABLISH ANSWER
The question is about protection of Type NM cable in an accessible attic.

▶ 1. In Index, find "Nonmetallic-sheathed cable" under which find "Accessible attics, 334.23."

▶ 2. Section 334.23 refers to 320.23.

▶ 3. Section 320.23(A) only requires protection within 1.8 m (6 ft) of a scuttle hole where not accessible by permanent stairs or ladders.

▶ 4. The correct answer is B.

QUESTION 26. When nonmetallic-sheathed cable is installed through metal studs, all of the following requirements apply EXCEPT:

A. the holes or slots in the metal studs must be factory-cuts
B. the cable must be protected as it passes through the metal hole by a *listed* bushing or grommet
C. the bushing or grommet must cover the entire

metal edge, remain in place, and be securely fastened in the opening
D. the bushing or grommet must be installed prior to the installation of the cable

ANSWER _____

PROCEDURE TO ESTABLISH ANSWER
The question is about the Type NM cable installed through metal framing members.

▶ 1. In Index, find "Nonmetallic-sheathed cable" under which find "Through or parallel to framing members, 300.4, 334.17."

▶ 2. Section 334.17 refers to 300.4.

▶ 3. Section 300.4(B)(1) permits the hole or slot in the metal stud to be either factory or field punched, cut or drilled. Answer A is not true.

▶ 4. Section 300.4(B)(1) requires listed bushings or grommets to be used with metal studs.

▶ 5. Section 300.4(B)(1) also requires the listed bushing or grommet to cover the entire metal edge and be securely fastened in the opening.

▶ 6. Section 300.4(B)(1) requires the bushing or grommets to be installed prior to the installation of the cable.

▶ 7. The correct answer is A.

QUESTION 27. In a new dwelling where 57 mm x 100 mm (2¼ in. x 4 in.) metal outlet boxes are installed with Type NM cable, which one of the following statements is NOT true?

A. The cable is not required to be secured to the box if it is stapled within 200 mm (8 in.) of the box.
B. A cable clamp or connector is required to secure the cable to the box.
C. The cable must be secured not more than 300 mm (12 in.) from the box.
D. The cable is not permitted to be stapled on edge.

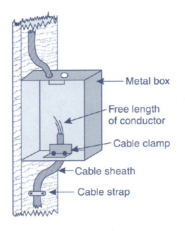

ANSWER _____

PROCEDURE TO ESTABLISH ANSWER
The question is about securing of cable to boxes.

▶ 1. In Index, find "Boxes" under which find "Conductors, number in box" under which find "Entering boxes, conduit bodies or fittings, 314.17."

▶ 2. Section 314.17(B), Metal Boxes and Conduit Bodies, requires that where conduit or cable is installed with metal boxes, they shall be secured to such boxes. Note that the exception to 314.17(C) permits the cable not to be secured to the box only when the box is nonmetallic. Answer B is true.

▶ 3. In Index, find "Nonmetallic-sheathed cable" under which find "Supports, 334.30."

▶ 4. Section 334.30 requires the cable to be secured within 300 mm (12 in.) of every box. Also, two-conductor (flat) cable is not permitted to be stapled on edge. Answers C and D are true.

▶ 5. The correct answer is A.

QUESTION 28. What is the largest permitted size Type UF cable?

A. 8 AWG
B. 1 AWG
C. 4/0 AWG
D. 500 kcmil

ANSWER _____

PROCEDURE TO ESTABLISH ANSWER
The question is about the largest size Type UF cable recognized or described by the *Code*, which we know is determined by the conductor size.

▶ 1. In Index, find "Underground feeder and branch-circuit cable (Type UF), Art. 340" under which, find "Conductors," 340.104."

▶ 2. Section 340.104 recognizes a maximum of 4/0 AWG for Type UF cable.

▶ 3. The correct answer is C.

QUESTION 29. Where a nonmetallic 57 mm x 100 mm (2¼ in. x 4 in.) box is used with Type UF cable that is not secured to the box, the cable shall be fastened within how many inches of the box?

A. 200 mm (8 in.)
B. 300 mm (12 in.)
C. 450 mm (18 in.)
D. 600 mm (24 in.)

ANSWER _____

PROCEDURE TO ESTABLISH ANSWER
The questions is about securing Type UF cable where entering a nonmetallic box without clamps.

▶ 1. In Index, find "Boxes" under which find "Conductors, number in box" under which find "Entering boxes, conduit bodies or fittings, 314.17."

▶ 2. Section 314.17(C), Exception, permits securing Type UF cable to be installed without a clamp where secured within 200 mm (8 in.) of a nonmetallic box not larger than nominal 57 mm x 100 mm (2¼ in. x 4 in.).

▶ 3. The correct answer is A.

QUESTION 30. Where cables are installed parallel to framing members, the outside surface of the cable shall be a minimum of how many inches from the nearest edge of the studs or joists unless protected by either a steel plate or sleeve?

A. 6 mm (¼ in.)
B. 25 mm (1 in.)
C. 32 mm (1¼ in.)
D. 38 mm (1½ in.)

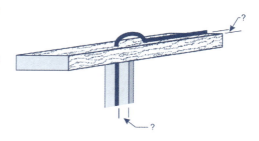

ANSWER _____

PROCEDURE TO ESTABLISH ANSWER
The question is about the physical protection required where cables run parallel to framing member of a building.

▶ 1. In Index, find "Cables" under which find "Protection against physical damage, 300.4."

▶ 2. Section 300.4(D) requires protection of cables when installed parallel to framing members is not less than 32 mm (1¼ in.) from the edge of a framing member. This protection shall be at least a 1.6 mm (ⁱ⁄₁₆ in.) thick steel plate, sleeve or equivalent.

▶ 3. The correct answer is C.

QUESTION 31. Which one of the following statements about requirements for securing cables with nonmetallic sheaths that enter a panelboard through a raceway provided for physical protection is not true?

A. Cables must be secured to the structure within 300 mm (12 in.) of the point where they enter the raceway.
B. A fitting is required on each end of the raceway to protect the cable from abrasion.
C. The outer sheath of the cable must be continuous through the raceway.
D. For lengths up to 1.2 m (4 ft), the raceway is permitted to be filled to 60 percent with the cables.

ANSWER _____

PROCEDURE TO ESTABLISH ANSWER
The question is about rules under which it is not required to secure cables to panelboard cabinets.

▶ 1. In Index, find "Cabinets, cutout boxes, and meter socket enclosures, Art. 312" under which, find "Installation, 312–Part I."

▶ 3. Scan Part I of Article 312 and find "312.5(C), Cables."

▶ 4. Section 312.5(C) Exception (a) confirms that nonmetallic sheath cables are to be secured within 300 mm (12 in.) of the outer end of the raceway. Answer A is true.

▶ 5. Section 312.5(C) Exception (c) requires a fitting to be installed on each end of the raceway to protect the cables. Answer B is true.

▶ 6. Section 312.5(C) Exception (e) requires the cable sheath to be continuous through the entire raceway. Answer C is true.

▶ 7. Section 312.5(C) Informational Note refers to Table 1 in Chapter 9, including Note 9, for allowable cable fill in circular raceways. Reviewing Note 9, a fill of 60 percent is permitted for nipples no longer than 600 mm (24 in.).

▶ 8. The correct answer is D.

QUESTION 32. All of the following statements about Type NM cable are true EXCEPT:

A. When more than two NM cables containing more than two current-carrying conductors are installed without maintaining spacing between the cables and are installed through the same opening in wood framing that is to be sealed with thermal insulation, caulk or sealing foam, the allowable ampacity must be adjusted per Table 310.15(B)(3)(a).
B. NM cable shall be secured by staples, cable ties, straps, hangers, or similar fittings designed and installed so as not to damage the cable.
C. NM cable shall be supported and secured by staples, cable ties, straps, hangers, or similar fittings designed and installed so as not to damage the cable.
D. Communication conductors included in NM cable must comply with Part V of Article 800.

ANSWER _____

PROCEDURE TO ESTABLISH ANSWER
The question is about the installation, construction, and ampacity of Type NM cable.

▶ 1. In Index, find "Nonmetallic-sheathed cable (Types NM, NMC, and NMS), Art. 334" under which, find "Construction, 334–Part III," "Supports, 334.30," and "Ampacity, 334.80."

Cables | 1- and 2-Family Study Guide | 41

▶ 2. Scan Part III of Article 334 and find "334.104, Conductors." Answer D is true.

▶ 3. Next, find "334.30, Securing and Supporting."

▶ 4. Section 334.30 requires NM cable to be supported and secured. Answer C is true; Answer B is not true as it only addresses securing the cable.

▶ 5. Find "334.80, Ampacity." In the second paragraph of this section, we find that Answer A is true.

▶ 6. Answer B is correct.

QUESTION 33. Where Type UF cable is used as a substitute for Type NM cable, the conductor insulation is required to be rated at:

A. 60°C (140°F)
B. 75°C (167°F)
C. 90°C (194°F)
D. 30°C (86°F)

ANSWER _____

PROCEDURE TO ESTABLISH ANSWER
The question is about the required insulation rating of Type UF cable.

▶ 1. In Index, find "Underground feeder and branch-circuit cable (Type UF), Art. 340" under which, find 'Insulation, 340.112."

▶ 2. In 340.112, we find that where Type UF cable is installed as a substitute wiring method for Type NM cable, the conductor insulation is required to be rated at 90°C (194°F).

▶ 3. The correct answer is C.

QUESTION 34. All of the following statements about rigid polyvinyl chloride conduit (PVC) are true EXCEPT:

A. Cables are permitted in PVC provided they are not prohibited by the respective cable article nor exceed the percentage fill requirements in Table 1 of Chapter 9.
B. For installations of PVC, expansion fittings are required when thermal expansion is expected to be greater than 6 mm (¼ in.) in a straight run between boxes.
C. Rigid nonmetallic conduit is permitted to support any size conduit body or luminaire (fixture) when properly supported per 352.30.
D. Rigid nonmetallic conduit, factory elbows, and associated fittings must be listed.

ANSWER _____

PROCEDURE TO ESTABLISH ANSWER
The question is about rigid polyvinyl chloride conduit (Type PVC).

▶ 1 In Index, find "Rigid polyvinyl chloride conduit (Type PVC), Art. 352" under which, find "Expansion fittings, 300.7(B), 352.44, etc.," "Installation, Article 352–Part III," "Listing, 352.6," and "Number of conductors, 352.22."

▶ 2 In 352.44, we find that expansion fittings are required when thermal expansion is expected to be greater than 6 mm (¼ in.) in a straight run between boxes. Answer B is true.

▶ 3. Scan Part II of Article 352, and find that in 352.10(H), rigid nonmetallic conduit is only permitted to support conduit bodies that are no larger than the largest trade size of an entering raceway. These nonmetallic conduit bodies are not permitted to support luminaires (fixtures). Answer C is not true.

▶ 4. Section 352.6 requires PVC, factory elbows, and associated fittings to be listed. Answer D is true.

▶ 5. In 352.22, Number of Conductors, we find that cables are permitted in PVC provided it is not prohibited by the respective cable article nor exceed the percentage fill requirements in Table 1 of Chapter 9.

▶ 6. The correct answer is C.

5 Conductors

QUESTION 1. How many 14 AWG conductors are permitted in a 75 mm x 50 mm x 90 mm (3 in. x 2 in. x 3½ in.) metal device box that includes a cable clamp for connecting the NM cable to the box and a duplex receptacle is installed?

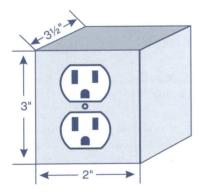

ANSWER _____

PROCEDURE TO ESTABLISH ANSWER
The question is about the number of conductors allowed in a device box. However, careful review of the question is required because the volume allowances for the cable clamp and device have to be considered before the number of actual 14 AWG conductors permitted can be determined.

▶ 1. In Index, find "Boxes (outlet, device, pull, and junction)" under which find "Conductors, number in box, 314.16."

▶ 2. Section 314.16(A) applies to standard boxes not marked with their volume and refers to Table 314.16(A), Metal Boxes.

▶ 3. Table 314.16(A) permits nine 14 AWG conductors in a 75 mm x 50 mm x 90 mm (3 in. x 2 in. x 3½ in.) device box.

▶ 4. Section 314.16(B), Box Fill Calculations, provides for the volumes in paragraphs 314.16(B)(1) through (B)(5) to be added together. In our case, because we are dealing with Table 314.16(A) each volume calculated under 314.16(B)(1) – (5) represents one conductor.

▶ 5. Section 314.16(B)(4) covers cable clamps and requires one volume allowance.

▶ 6. Devices or equipment fill are covered in 314.16(B)(4) and two volume allowances are required for a device.

Conductors | 1- and 2-Family Study Guide | 43

► 7. Section 314.16(B)(5) requires one volume allowance to be taken for the equipment grounding conductors.

► 8. The volume allowances required in steps 5 – 7 add up to four volumes or conductors, leaving five volume allowances or conductors remaining.

► 9. The correct answer is B.

QUESTION 2. Branch circuits supplying ranges and clothes dryers in an existing dwelling may be supplied with cables containing an uninsulated grounded conductor which may be used to ground the frames provided all of the following conditions are met EXCEPT:

A. the grounded conductor is no smaller than 10 AWG aluminum
B. the grounded conductor is no smaller than 10 AWG copper
C. the grounded conductor is part of Type SE service-entrance cable
D. the Type SE cable originates at the service equipment

ANSWER _____

PROCEDURE TO ESTABLISH ANSWER
The question is about grounding of ranges and clothes dryers.

► 1. In Index, find "Ranges" under which find "Grounding, 250.140."

► 2. In Index, find "Clothes dryers" under which, find "Grounding, 250.114(3), 250.140."

► 3. Section 250.140 Exception (2) requires the grounded conductor to be not smaller than 10 AWG copper or 8 AWG aluminum. Answer A is correct. However, answer (B) is not correct as aluminum conductors must be a minimum of 8 AWG.

► 4. Section 250.140 Exception (3) requires the uninsulated grounded conductor to be part of a Type SE service-entrance cable and the branch circuit is required to originate at the service equipment.

Note: Permission to ground frames of ranges and dryers to the grounded conductor (neutral) is only permitted for existing installations.

► 5. The correct answer is A.

QUESTION 3. Which one of the following statements about an aluminum grounding electrode conductor is true?

A. A bare aluminum grounding electrode conductor that is physically protected can be connected to an outside buried ground rod.
B. An insulated aluminum grounding electrode conductor can be connected to an outside buried ground rod if physically protected.
C. A bare aluminum grounding electrode conductor is permitted to be installed in a basement on a masonry wall.
D. An insulated aluminum grounding electrode conductor is permitted to be installed in a basement on a masonry wall.

ANSWER _____

PROCEDURE TO ESTABLISH ANSWER
The question is about the installation of an aluminum grounding electrode conductor.

► 1. In Index, find "Grounding electrode conductors" under which find "Installation, 250.64."

► 2. Section 250.64(A) provides that bare aluminum grounding conductors shall not be used where in direct contact with masonry or the earth. Aluminum conductors that come with insulation listed as suitable for direct burial (such as USE) are readily available and would allow this type insulated aluminum grounding electrode conductor to be installed in a basement on a masonry wall.

► 3. Section 250.64(A) also states that an aluminum grounding conductor used outside shall not be terminated within 450 mm (18 in.) of the earth, which would prohibit both bare and insulated aluminum conductors from being connected directly to a buried ground rod.

▶ 4. The correct answer is D.

QUESTION 4. Where a feeder consisting of three 4/0 AWG Type THW aluminum conductors and an insulated equipment grounding conductor are installed in a nonmetallic conduit and serve as the main power feeder to a dwelling unit, the rating of the feeder is how many amperes?

A. 150
B. 180
C. 200
D. 230

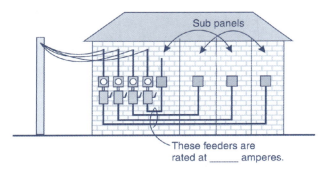

ANSWER _____

PROCEDURE TO ESTABLISH ANSWER
This question is about the rating of feeders to a dwelling unit.

▶ 1. In Index, find "Ampacities" under which find "Conductors, 310.15."

▶ 2. Scan 310.15 and find 310.15(B)(7), which states that 120/240 single phase dwelling unit service or feeder conductors shall be as in 310.15(B)(7)(1)-(4).

▶ 3. For a feeder rated 100 through 400 amperes, the feeder conductors supplying the entire load associated with a one-family dwelling or the feeder conductors supplying the entire load associated with an individual dwelling unit in a two-family or multifamily dwelling shall be permitted to have an ampacity not less than 83% of the feeder rating.

▶ 4. The question uses Type THW aluminum conductors. Scan Table 310.15(B)(16), and note that 4/0 AWG Type THW aluminum conductors have an allowable rating of 180 amperes at 75°C. It appears the appropriate feeder rating for these conductors would be 200 amperes.

▶ 5. To verify the 200 ampere feeder rating: 200 x .83 = 166 amperes. The 4/0 aluminum conductors are sufficient for a 200 ampere rated feeder that supplies the entire load associated with the individual dwelling unit.

▶ 6. The correct answer is C.

QUESTION 5. What service rating may be used where there is a bare 4 AWG copper neutral conductor installed with two 4 AWG Type THWN insulated conductors in a single-phase 3-wire residential service? All terminations are made with lugs rated 75°C.

A. 60 amperes
B. 85 amperes
C. 150 amperes
D. 100 amperes

ANSWER _____

PROCEDURE TO ESTABLISH ANSWER
The question is about the ampacity of a bare service conductor at a dwelling.

▶ 1. In Index, find "Bare conductors" under which find "Ampacities, 310.15(B)(4)."

▶ 2. Section 310.15(B)(4), Bare Conductors, states that where bare conductors are used with insulated conductors, their allowable ampacities shall be limited to those permitted for the adjacent insulated conductors.

▶ 3. In Index, find "Ampacities" under which find "Conductors, 310.15."

▶ 4. Scan Section 310.15 to 310.15(B)(7), which states that 120/240 single phase dwelling unit service or feeder conductors shall be as in 310.15(B)(7)(1)-(4).

Conductors | 1- and 2-Family Study Guide | 45

▶ 5. Section 310.15(B)(7)(a) notes a 120/240 volt single phase service rated 100 through 400 amperes and associated with an individual dwelling unit shall be permitted to have service conductors with an ampacity not less than 83% of the service rating.

▶ 6. To determine the size conductors permitted: 100 amperes x .83 = 83 amperes. The 100 ampere rated service could be supplied by conductors rated not less than 83 amperes.

▶ 7. Scanning Table 310.15(B)(16), we find that a 4 AWG, THWN, copper conductor can carry up to 85 amperes at 75°C.

▶ 8. The correct answer is D.

QUESTION 6. The conductor used to connect equipment grounding conductors and the grounded circuit conductor of the wiring system to the grounding electrode is which one of the following conductors?

A. Main bonding jumper
B. Grounding electrode conductor
C. Equipment grounding conductor
D. Grounded conductor

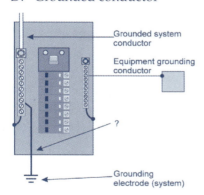

ANSWER _____

PROCEDURE TO ESTABLISH ANSWER
The question is about definitions and is asking us to identify the conductor that connects the equipment grounding conductors and or the grounded conductor to the grounding electrode. From experience, we know this is the "grounding electrode conductor." To verify this is correct:

▶ 1. In Index, find "Definitions, Art. 100."

▶ 2. In Article 100, review the terms listed and find "Grounding electrode conductor."

▶ 3. The correct answer is B.

QUESTION 7. A small appliance branch circuit in a dwelling unit shall comply with which one of the following?

A. Have no lighting outlets supplied by it
B. Be limited to four outlets and four lights
C. Be protected with a 15-ampere overcurrent device
D. Be permitted in the living room

ANSWER _____

PROCEDURE TO ESTABLISH ANSWER
The question is about dwelling unit branch-circuit requirements.

▶ 1. In Index, find "Dwellings" under which find "Receptacle circuits required, 210.11."

▶ 2. Section 210.11(C)(1) states that two or more 20-ampere small appliance branch circuits shall be provided for all receptacle outlets specified by 210.52(B) for the small appliance loads.

▶ 3. Section 210.52(B)(1) provides that two or more small appliance branch circuits are limited to receptacle outlets in the kitchen, pantry, breakfast room, dining room or similar area.

▶ 4. Section 210.11(C)(1) and 210.52(B)(1) require the small appliance branch circuits be rated at 20-ampere.

▶ 5. Section 210.52(B)(2) provides that the small appliance circuits shall have no other outlets.

▶ 6. The correct answer is A.

QUESTION 8. Which one of the following statements about splicing ungrounded conductors is NOT true?

46 | 1- and 2-Family Study Guide | Conductors

A. They may be spliced with a splicing device identified for the use.
B. They may be spliced by brazing or welding.
C. They are not permitted to be spliced by soldering.
D. They shall be covered with insulation equivalent to that of the conductors or with an insulating device identified for the purpose.

ANSWER _____

PROCEDURE TO ESTABLISH ANSWER
The question is about splicing conductors.

▶ 1.   In Index, find "Splices and taps" under which find "General provisions, 110.14."

▶ 2.   Section 110.14(B) specifies permitted methods of splicing conductors, one of which is by soldering, if the conductors are mechanically and electrically secure before the solder is applied. Answer C is not true.

▶ 3.   Section 110.14(B) also notes that splicing may be by brazing, welding or by connectors identified for the use and that splices and joints must be covered with insulation equivalent to that of the conductors or by an insulating device. Answers A, B and C are true.

▶ 4.   The correct answer is C.

QUESTION 9. The grounding electrode conductor to a metal water pipe grounding electrode for alternating-current systems shall be sized in accordance with which one of the following?

A. Size of the ungrounded service-entrance conductors
B. Rating of service disconnecting means
C. Size of conduit supplying the service disconnect
D. Size of grounding electrode

ANSWER _____

PROCEDURE TO ESTABLISH ANSWER
The question is about the size of the grounding electrode conductor.

▶ 1.   In Index, find "Grounding electrode conductors" under which find "Sizing, 250.30(A)(6)(a), 250.66, 250.166."

▶ 2.   Section 250.66 provides that the size of the grounding electrode conductor is to be not less than given in Table 250.66, which is based on the size of the ungrounded service-entrance conductors.

▶ 3.   The correct answer is A.

QUESTION 10. A branch circuit's equipment grounding conductor shall be permitted to be connected to a metal box by which one of the following?

A. A coarse treaded sheet metal screw (only one thread engaged in the enclosure)
B. A solder connection
C. Connection to the grounding terminal on the receptacle
D. A listed grounding clip on the box

ANSWER _____

PROCEDURE TO ESTABLISH ANSWER
The question is about connecting equipment grounding conductors to boxes.

▶ 1.   In Index, find "Boxes (outlet, device, pull, and junction)" under which find "Grounding, 250.148, 250–Part VI."

▶ 2.   Sections 250.148(E) and 250.8(B) prohibit connection solely by solder. Section 250.8(A)(5) & (6) permit connecting equipment grounding conductors with machine screw-type fasteners or thread-forming machine screws; however, there must be a minimum of 2 threads fully engaged.

▶ 3.   Section 250.148(C) requires connection between the equipment grounding conductor and metal box by means of a grounding screw used for no other purpose, or a device suitable for the use. This could be a listed grounding clip that connects the equipment grounding conductors to the box.

▶ 4. The correct answer is D.

QUESTION 11.
The ampacity of the conductors in Type NM nonmetallic-sheathed cable is based on:

A. 60°C column in Table 310.15(B)(16)
B. 75°C column in Table 310.15(B)(16)
C. 90°C column in Table 310.15(B)(16)
D. None of the above

ANSWER _____

PROCEDURE TO ESTABLISH ANSWER
The question is about the allowable ampacity of conductors in Type NM cable.

▶ 1. In Index, find "Nonmetallic-sheathed cable (Types NM, NMC, and NMS)" and find "334.80, Ampacity."

▶ 2. Section 334.80 requires the ampacity of conductors of Type NM cables to be determined in accordance with the 60°C conductor temperature rating.

▶ 3. The correct answer is A.

Note: Section 334.112 requires the conductor insulation to have a 90°C rating. However, our question deals with the ampacity of the conductor, not the insulation rating.

QUESTION 12.
What is the minimum size copper equipment grounding conductor required for a water heater connected to a circuit protected by a 40-ampere overcurrent device?

A. 14 AWG
B. 12 AWG
C. 10 AWG
D. 8 AWG

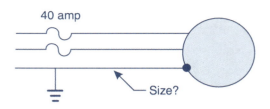

ANSWER _____

PROCEDURE TO ESTABLISH ANSWER
The question is about the sizing of equipment grounding conductors.

▶ 1. In Index, find "Equipment grounding conductors," under which find "Sizing, 250.122."

▶ 2. Section 250.122 refers to Table 250.122, which shows a minimum 10 AWG copper equipment grounding conductor for overcurrent devices rated more than 20 amperes and not more than 60 amperes.

▶ 3. The correct answer is C.

Note: The 30, 40 and 50 ampere references were removed from Table 250.122 in the 2011 *NEC*. The equipment grounding conductors for these circuits were, and still are, all required to be 10 AWG as they lay between 20 and 60 amperes.

QUESTION 13.
The minimum size Type NM cable with two insulated and one uninsulated conductor that may be used in a dwelling to supply a 240-volt, 4.5-kVA, 60-gallon storage-type electric water heater is:

A. 14 AWG
B. 12 AWG
C. 10 AWG
D. 8 AWG

ANSWER _____

PROCEDURE TO ESTABLISH ANSWER

The question is about the sizing of branch-circuit conductors for a storage type (60-gallon) water heater.

▶ 1. In Index, find "Branch circuits" under which find "Appliances, 210.23, 422–Part II"

▶ 2. Scan Article 422, Part II, and find "422.10, Branch-circuit Sizing." Section 422.10(A) requires that the branch-circuit rating for a single non-motor appliance shall not be less than 125 percent of the marked rating. Appliances rated for continuous duty may have their circuits rated at 100 percent of the marked rating.

▶ 3. To find the branch-circuit load, use the formula
$I\ (current) = P\ (power) / E\ (voltage)$
to determine the load on the circuit.

▶ 4. Nameplate rating: 4.5 KW or 4.5 × 1,000 = 4500 VA

$I = P/E$
$I = 4500 VA / 240V$
$I = 18.75$ amperes
1.25×18.75 amperes
$= 23.48$ or 23 amperes

▶ 5. In Index, find "Conductors" under which find "Copper" under which find "Ampacity Tables 310.15(B)(16) through 310.15(B)(21)..."

▶ 6. Observe the "**" next to conductors 14, 12 and 10 AWG and the reference at the bottom of the table to 240.4(D).

▶ 7. Section 240.4(D)(7) requires that 10 AWG 60°C conductors to have overcurrent protection not exceeding 30 amperes.

▶ 8. Section 334.80 requires the 60°C ampacity to be used for Type NM cable. As a result a 30-ampere overcurrent device with 10 AWG conductors would be required.

▶ 9. The correct answer is C.

QUESTION 14. Which of the following conductor types is NOT permitted to be installed in flexible metal conduit on the outside of a dwelling extending from the dwelling to a central air-conditioning unit?

A. Type TW
B. Type THW
C. Type THHN
D. None of the above.

ANSWER _____

PROCEDURE TO ESTABLISH ANSWER

The question is about conductors in flexible metal conduit outdoors.

▶ 1. In Index, find "Flexible metal conduit (Type FMC)" under which find "Uses not permitted, 348.12."

▶ 2. Section 348.12(1) provides that flexible metal conduit is not permitted in a wet location.

▶ 3. The correct answer is D.

QUESTION 15. Which one of the following statements regarding circuits supplying dwelling unit bathrooms is true?

A. A 20-ampere circuit is required to supply only bathroom lights.
B. A 20-ampere circuit may supply both bathroom receptacles and lights in the same bathroom.
C. A 15-ampere circuit may supply only bathroom receptacles.
D. A 15-ampere circuit may supply both bathroom receptacles and lights.

ANSWER _____

PROCEDURE TO ESTABLISH ANSWER
The question is about branch circuits for bathroom receptacles and lights.

▶ 1. In Index, find "Dwellings" under which find "Receptacle circuits required, 210.11."

▶ 2. Section 210.11(C)(3), Bathroom Branch Circuits, requires bathroom receptacle outlets in dwellings to be supplied by at least one 20-ampere branch circuit.

▶ 3. Section 210.11(C)(3) also requires that the 20-ampere bathroom receptacle circuit has no other outlets, which prohibits lights on the same circuit unless the circuit supplies a single bathroom per the exception to 210.11(C)(3).

▶ 4. This exception would allow receptacles and lighting outlets within the same bathroom to be supplied by the same 20-ampere circuit per 210.23(A)(1) and (A)(2), as long as the circuit is limited to that particular bathroom.

▶ 5. The correct answer is B.

QUESTION 16. Where four current-carrying conductors are installed in a raceway, it is necessary to reduce the allowable ampacity of the conductors to which one of the following?

A. 60 percent
B. 70 percent
C. 80 percent
D. 90 percent

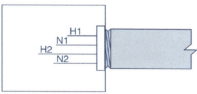

Two 2-wire branch circuits

ANSWER _____

PROCEDURE TO ESTABLISH ANSWER
The question is about the allowable ampacity of conductors, specifically more than three in a raceway as indicated in the drawing.

▶ 1. In Index, find "Ampacities" under which find "Conductors, 310.15, Tables 310.15(B)(16) through 310.15(B)(21), etc."

▶ 2. Section 310.15(B) states that the ampacities for conductors shall be as specified in Tables 310.15(B)(16) through 310.15(B)(19), and Ampacity Table 310.15(B)(20) and Table 310.15(B)(21) as modified by (B)(1) through (B)(7).

▶ 3. Scan 310.15(B)(3)(a), which refers to Table 310.15(B)(3)(a).

▶ 4. Table 310.15(B)(3)(a) establishes the adjustment factors for more than three current-carrying conductors in a raceway. Four to six conductors that are current-carrying require 80 percent correction factor.

▶ 5. The correct answer is C.

QUESTION 17. Where the conductor material (i.e., copper or aluminum) is not specified in the *National Electrical Code*, it must apply to what type conductor?

A. Aluminum
B. Copper-clad aluminum
C. Copper
D. Magnesium

ANSWER _____

PROCEDURE TO ESTABLISH ANSWER
Our question is asking what material a conductor would have to be made of, if copper or aluminum is not specified in the applicable *NEC* requirement.

▶ 1. In Index, find "Conductors" under which find "Aluminum conductor material, 250.120(B)." Section 250.120(B) is regarding equipment grounding conductors and is not applicable to this question.

► 2. In Index, find "Conductors" under which find "Copper, 110.5, etc." Section 110.5 states; "Where the conductor material is not specified, the material and the sizes given in this *Code* shall apply to copper conductors."

► 3. The correct answer is C.

QUESTION 18.
Unless permitted by exception, which one of the following conductors is the minimum size permitted for a kitchen small appliance branch circuit in a dwelling unit?

A. 14 AWG Copper
B. 12 AWG Copper
C. 12 AWG Aluminum
D. 10 AWG Aluminum

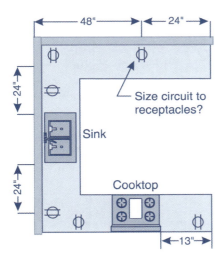

ANSWER _____

PROCEDURE TO ESTABLISH ANSWER
The question is about the small appliance circuits in dwelling unit kitchens.

► 1. In Index, find "Dwellings" under which find "Receptacle circuits required, 210.11."

► 2. Section 210.11(C)(1) requires at least two 20-ampere branch circuits to supply the small appliance circuits in the kitchen area.

► 3. Scan Table 310.15(B)(16) for a 20-ampere rated conductor and find that 12 AWG copper wire has an ampacity of 20 amperes and 10 AWG aluminum wire has an allowable ampacity of 25 amperes.

► 4. Observe the "*" next to conductors 14, 12 and 10 AWG and the reference at the bottom of the Table to 240.4(D).

► 5. Section 240.4(D) requires that 12 AWG 60°C copper conductors, having an ampacity of 20 amperes, must have overcurrent protection not exceeding 20 amperes.

► 6. Although 10 AWG aluminum has an acceptable ampacity, it is a larger size than the 12 AWG copper.

► 7. The correct answer is B.

QUESTION 19.
What percentage of the ampere rating of the service is permitted for determining the ampacity of service conductors supplying a single family dwelling with a 400 ampere 120/240 volt single phase service?

A. 98%
B. 83%
C. 50%
D. 75%

ANSWER _____

PROCEDURE TO ESTABLISH ANSWER
The question is about the percentage of the service rating allowed for conductors for a residential 400 ampere service.

► 1. In Index, find "Conductors," under which find "Ampacities of, 310.15, Tables 310.15(B)(16) through 310.15(B)(21)…"

► 2. Section 310.15(B) states that the ampacities for conductors shall be as specified in Tables 310.15(B)(16) through 310.15(B)(19) and Ampacity Tables 310.15(B)(20) and 310.15(B)(21) as modified by (B)(1) through (B)(7).

Scan Section 310.15 to 310.15(B)(7) which states that 120/240 single phase dwelling unit service or feeder conductors shall be as in 310.15(B)(7)(1)-(4).

▶ 3. Section 310.15(B)(7)(1) permits 3-wire dwelling unit service and feeder conductors that carry all the load of the dwelling unit to be sized at 83% of the rating.

▶ 4. The correct answer is B.

QUESTION 20. The area in square inches of four 8 AWG Type THW conductors is:

A. .1040
B. .1332
C. .1748
D. .2904

ANSWER _____

PROCEDURE TO ESTABLISH ANSWER
The question is about the dimensions of Type THW conductors.

▶ 1. In Index find "Conductors" under which find "Sizes, 110.6, Chap. 9, Tables 5 and 5A."

▶ 2. Chapter 9, Table 5, Dimensions of Insulated Conductors, shows one size 8 AWG Type THW to have a square inch area of 0.0437

▶ 3. Four conductors x 0.0437 sq. in. = 0.1748 square inches

▶ 4. The correct answer is C.

QUESTION 21. Two 12 AWG Type TW aluminum conductors may be installed in a raceway as a branch circuit with which one of the following ratings?

A. 15 amperes
B. 20 amperes
C. 25 amperes
D. 30 amperes

ANSWER _____

PROCEDURE TO ESTABLISH ANSWER
The question is about the ampacity rating of 12 AWG Type TW aluminum conductors.

▶ 1. In Index, find "Ampacities," under which find "Conductors, 310.15, Tables 310.15(B)(16) through 310.15(B)(21), etc."

▶ 2. Section 310.15(B) requires conductor ampacities to be as shown in Tables 310.15(B)(16) through 310.15(B)(19), etc.

▶ 3. Table 310.15(B)(16) shows 12 AWG aluminum Type TW conductors to have a 15-ampere rating. The "*" note, however, refers to 240.4(D). Section 240.4(D) limits the 12 AWG aluminum conductor to 15 amperes, so our answer is not changed.

▶ 4. The correct answer is A.

QUESTION 22. Which one of the following items determines the minimum size of a branch-circuit equipment grounding conductor?

A. The nameplate rating of the equipment
B. The size of the conductors feeding the equipment
C. The size of the raceway enclosing the branch-circuit conductors
D. The ampere rating of the overcurrent device protecting the equipment

ANSWER _____

PROCEDURE TO ESTABLISH ANSWER
The question is about the size of branch-circuit equipment grounding conductors.

▶ 1. In Index, find "Equipment grounding conductors," under which find "Sizing, 250.122."

▶ 2. Section 250.122 refers to Table 250.122, which bases the minimum size of equipment grounding conductors on the ampere rating of the overcurrent device in the circuit ahead of the equipment.

▶ 3. The correct answer is D.

QUESTION 23. What are the minimum size Type THWN copper service-entrance conductors for a 100-ampere, 3-wire, single-phase dwelling service?

A. 6 AWG
B. 4 AWG
C. 3 AWG
D. 2 AWG

ANSWER _____

PROCEDURE TO ESTABLISH ANSWER
The question is about the ampere rating of conductors for a 3-wire dwelling service.

▶ 1. In Index, find "Ampacities" under which find "Conductors, 310.15, etc."

▶ 2. Section 310.15(B) states that the ampacities of conductors rated 0 to 2000 volts to be as shown in Tables 310.15(B)(16) through 310.15(B)(19), and Ampacity Tables 310.15(B)(20) and 310.15(B)(21) as modified by (B)(1) through (B)(7).

▶ 3. Scan 310.15 and find 310.15(B)(7) states that 120/240 single phase dwelling unit service or feeder conductors shall be as in 310.15(B)(7)(1)-(4).

▶ 4. Section 310.15(B)(7)(1) permits 3-wire dwelling unit service and feeder conductors that carry the entire load of the dwelling unit to be sized at 83% of the rating of the service.

▶ 5. To determine the size conductors permitted: 100 amperes x .83 = 83 amperes. The 100 ampere rated dwelling unit service can be supplied by conductors rated not less than 83 amperes.

▶ 6. Scanning Table 310.15(B)(16) we find that a 4 AWG, THWN, copper conductor can carry up to 85 amperes at 75°C. However, with no information given in the question regarding termination temperature ratings 110.14(C)(1) would require the use of the 60C temperature rating for the terminations. A 4 AWG copper conductor at 60C would only provide a maximum ampacity of 70 amperes so a 3 AWG copper conductor would be required which is permitted to be a maximum of 85 amperes.

Section 110.14(C), Temperature Limitations, states the termination provisions of equipment for circuits rated 100 amperes or less, or marked for 14 AWG through 1 AWG conductors, shall be used only for one of the following: (1) Conductors rated 60°C (140°F).

▶ 7. The correct answer is C.

QUESTION 24. In general, what is the minimum horizontal clearance (conductors to building) requirement for insulated feeder conductors of voltages not over 600 volts nominal that are installed next to a building?

A. 900 mm   (3 ft)
B. 1.5 m   (5 ft)
C. 1.8 m   (6 ft)
D. 3.0 m   (10 ft)

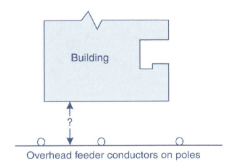

ANSWER _____

Conductors | 1- and 2-Family Study Guide | 53

PROCEDURE TO ESTABLISH ANSWER
The question is about clearances of outside overhead feeder conductors from a building.

▶ 1. In Index, find "Outside branch circuits and feeders, Article 225 under which find "Conductors.

Under "Conductors" find "Clearances" under which find "From buildings, 225.19."

▶ 2. Section 225.19(C) requires a minimum of a 900 mm (3 ft) horizontal clearance.

▶ 3. The correct answer is A.

QUESTION 25. All of the following insulation types are permitted for the exterior portion of a 200-ampere, single-phase, 3-wire, dwelling service EXCEPT:

A. Type TW.
B. Type THW
C. Type THHN
D. Type THWN

ANSWER _____

PROCEDURE TO ESTABLISH ANSWER
The question is about the ampere rating and type of conductors for a dwelling service.

▶ 1. In Index, find "Ampacities" under which find "Conductors" under which find "Wet locations," 225.4, 310.10(C), Table 310.104(A)."

▶ 2. Section 225.4 applies to outside branch circuits and feeders so it is not relevant to the question. However, it does reference 310.10(C) where conductors are installed in a wet location which was also one of the choices from the Index.

▶ 3. Section 310.10(C) requires conductors to be types MTW, RHW, RHW-2, TW, THW, THW-2, THHW, THWN, THWN-2, XHHW, XHHW-2, ZW when installed in a wet location. Answers A, B and D are permitted in wet locations.

▶ 4. The Index also referenced Table 310.104(A) which can be used to verify the permitted application for conductors. Scanning the Table we find the conductors listed in Answers A, B, and D are permitted for wet locations and Answer C is not. THHN conductors are only permitted for dry and damp locations.

▶ 5. The correct answer is C.

QUESTION 26. Fixture wires shall not be smaller than

A. 24 AWG
B. 22 AWG
C. 20 AWG
D. 18 AWG

ANSWER _____

PROCEDURE TO ESTABLISH ANSWER
The question is about the minimum size of fixture wires.

▶ 1. In Index, find "Fixture wires" under which find "Minimum size, 402.6."

▶ 2. Section 402.6 states that the minimum size is 18 AWG.

▶ 3. The correct answer is D.

QUESTION 27. Equipment grounding conductors are permitted to be any of the following EXCEPT:

A. a stranded bare wire
B. a bare circular busbar
C. a surface metal raceway listed for grounding
D. 2.0 m (6½ ft) of listed flexible metal conduit

ANSWER _____

54 | 1- and 2-Family Study Guide | Conductors

PROCEDURE TO ESTABLISH ANSWER

The question is about the type of conductors recognized for equipment grounding use.

▶ 1. In Index, find "Equipment grounding conductors" under which find "Types recognized, 250.118, 250.120, 250.134."

▶ 2. Section 250.134(A) refers to 250.118, which permits the conductor to be: (1) a stranded bare wire or a busbar of any shape or (14) a surface metal raceway listed for grounding.

▶ 3. 250.118(5)(c) allows listed flexible conduit to be used as an equipment grounding conductor, but limits its length to 1.8 m (6 ft).

▶ 4. The correct answer is D.

QUESTION 28. What is the ampacity of 10 AWG copper Type UF cable?

A. 25 amperes
B. 30 amperes
C. 35 amperes
D. 40 amperes

ANSWER _____

PROCEDURE TO ESTABLISH ANSWER

The question is about the ampacity of Type UF cable.

▶ 1. In Index, find "Underground feeder and branch-circuit cable (Type UF)" under which find "Ampacity, 340.80."

▶ 2. Section 334.80 requires the ampacity of Type UF cable to be that of 60°C (140°F) conductors in accordance with 310.15.

▶ 3. Section 310.15(B) provides that the ampacities of conductors rated 0 to 2000 volts are to be as shown in Tables 310.15(B)(16) through 310.15(B)(19), and Ampacity Tables 310.15(B)(20) and 310.15(B)(21) and as modified by (B)(1) through (B)(7).

▶ 4. The ampacity of 10 AWG copper conductors in Table 310.15(B)(16) is 30 amperes.

▶ 5. The correct answer is B.

QUESTION 29. Which of the following statements about insulation of conductors is true?

A. Insulation must be suitable for wet locations.
B. Insulation that is exposed to direct rays of the sun must be listed, or listed and marked "sunlight resistant," or be covered with insulating material that is sunlight resistant.
C. Type XHHW insulation is suitable for direct burial.
D. A suffix "2" on the insulation means the wire can be installed in parallel.

ANSWER _____

PROCEDURE TO ESTABLISH ANSWER

The question is about insulation on conductors.

▶ 1. In Index, find "Insulation" under which find "Conductors see Conductors, insulation." In Index, find "Conductors, Insulation, Art. 310," and "Conductors, Applications, 310.104."

▶ 2. In the Index find "Conductors" under which find "Wet locations, 225.4, 310.10(C), Table 310.104(A)." Section 310.10 permits insulation to be suitable for dry, damp or wet locations respectively. It is required to be suitable for wet locations only where used in that location. Answer A is not true for all installations, and therefore is not true.

▶ 3. Section 310.10(D) requires that insulation exposed to direct rays of the sun be listed; or listed and marked as being sunlight-resistant, or be covered with insulating material that is sunlight-resistant. Answer B is true.

▶ 4. Table 310.104(A) indicates Type XHHW insulation is suitable for dry, damp and wet locations but is silent with regard to being suitable for direct-buried installations. Answer C is not true.

▶ 5. Footnote 4 to Table 310.104(A) states the suffix "2" indicates the insulation is suitable for 90°C (194°F) wet or dry. In example, THWN – 2 is rated for 90°C, and THWN is rated for 75°C. Answer D is not true.

▶ 6. The correct answer is B.

QUESTION 30. Which one of the following statements about the ampacity adjustment or correction (derating) conductors in six 12/2 W/G Type NM cables operating at 120 volts and installed in an attic in a bundled fashion and an ambient attic temperature of 120°F is true?

A. The allowable ampacity of Table 310.15(B)(16) must be corrected to 82 percent for the 120° temperature and adjusted to 50 percent for the bundling of the cables.
B. The allowable ampacity of Table 310.15(B)(16) must be corrected to 82 percent for the high temperature only.
C. The allowable ampacity of Table 310.15(B)(16) must be adjusted to 50 percent for the bundling only.
D. The allowable ampacity of Table 310.15(B)(16) is not required to be corrected for the high temperature or adjusted for the bundling since the cables have conductors with 90°C insulation.

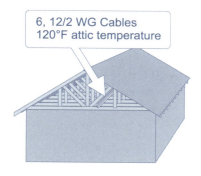

ANSWER _____

PROCEDURE TO ESTABLISH ANSWER
The question is about the ampacity of conductors.

▶ 1. In Index, find "Conductors" under which find "Ampacities of, 310.15, Tables 310.15(B)(16) through 310.15(B)(21), etc."

▶ 2. Section 310.15(A)(1) permits the ampacities for conductors to be determined by tables as provided in 310.15(B) or under engineering supervision. Since conductor ampacity for one- and two-family dwellings is not normally determined under engineering supervision, the ampacity will be determined by the tables.

▶ 3. Section 310.15(B) provides that the ampacities of conductors rated 0 to 2000 volts are to be as shown in Tables 310.15(B)(16) through 310.15(B)(19), and Ampacity Tables 310.15(B)(20) and 310.15(B)(21) and as modified by (B)(1) through (B)(7).

▶ 4. Scan through the subsections and find "310.15(B)(3)(a), Adjustment Factors," which refers to Table 310.15(B)(3)(a). Note that the column heading of Table 310.15(B)(3)(a) reads "Percent of Values in Tables 310.15(B)(16) through 310.15(B)(19) as Adjusted for Ambient Temperature if Necessary."

▶ 5. The ampacity adjustment (derating) for 12 current-carrying conductors in Table 310.15(B)(3)(a) is 50 percent. Note that a 120-volt circuit has an ungrounded and grounded conductor (hot and neutral), and both carry current, therefore requiring both of them to be counted for ampacity adjustment).

▶ 6. The ampacity correction factor (derating) for high ambient temperature shown in Table 310.15(B)(2)(a) is .82 or 82 percent.

▶ 7. Since both conditions are present, an adjustment for the number of current-carrying conductors and a correction for the higher ambient temperature must be made.

▶ 8. Section 334.80 permits the 90°C (194°F) rating to be used for ampacity adjustment or correction (derating) purposes.

▶ 9. The correct answer is A.

56 | 1- and 2-Family Study Guide | Conductors

QUESTION 31. All of the following are true when protecting conductors from physical damage EXCEPT:

A. When run through holes in metal framing or studs, Type NM cable must be protected by listed bushings or grommets.

B. Generally, where installed in notches of wood framing, Type NM cable and electrical nonmetallic tubing shall be protected from physical damage by nails or screws by a steel plate at least 1.6 mm (1/16 in.) thick.

C. Generally, where installed in wood framing, rigid metal conduit, intermediate metal conduit, rigid polyvinyl chloride conduit (PVC), and electrical metallic tubing do not require nailplates to be installed to protect them from physical damage.

D. Nailplates are required to be at least 1.6 mm (1/16 in.) thick in all installations.

ANSWER _____

PROCEDURE TO ESTABLISH ANSWER

The question is about physical protection of conductors.

▶ 1. In Index, find "Protection" under which find "Physical Damage" under which find "Conductors, 250.64(B), 300.4, 300.50(B)."

▶ 2. Section 300.4 states that where subject to physical damage, conductors, raceways and cables shall be protected. Section 300.4(B)(1) requires listed bushings or grommets to protect NM cable and ENT where installed through holes in metal framing. Answer A is true.

▶ 3. Section 300.4(A)(2) generally requires nailplates to protect NM cables and conductors that are laid in notches in wood. Answer B is true.

▶ 4. Section 300.4(A)(1), Exception No. 1, does not require nailplates to be installed to protect, rigid metal conduit, intermediate metal conduit, rigid polyvinyl chloride conduit (PVC), and electrical metallic tubing where installed in wood framing. Answer C is true.

▶ 5. Section 300.4(A)(1), Exception No. 2, now allows listed and marked nailplates less than 1.6 mm (1/16 in.) thick that provide equal or better protection to standard 1/16 in. thick nailplates to be installed to protect cables, conductors, etc., from physical damage. Answer D is not true.

▶ 6. The correct answer is D.

QUESTION 32. All of the following statements are true of conductor fill in boxes EXCEPT:

A. A looped, unbroken conductor not less than twice the minimum length required for free conductors in 300.14 must be counted twice.

B. The minimum length of conductors from where they enter a 4 in. x 4 in. x 2 1/8 in. box is 8 inches.

C. Where the opening to an outlet, junction, or switch point is less than 200 mm (8 in.) in any dimension, each conductor shall be long enough to extend at least 75 mm (3 in.) outside the opening.

D. No allowance for fill is required for locknuts and bushings.

ANSWER _____

PROCEDURE TO ESTABLISH ANSWER

The question is about conductor fill in boxes.

▶ 1. In the Index, find "Boxes (outlet, device, pull, and junction)" under which find "Fill calculations, 314.16(B)." In Index, also find "Conductors" under which find "Length in boxes, 300.14."

▶ 2. In 314.16(B)(1), we find that Answer A is true. If a 300 mm (12 in.) or more loop of conductor is left in a box, it must be counted as two conductors [2 x 150 mm (6 in.)] for box fill calculation purposes.

▶ 3. 314.16(B) states that no allowance for fill is required for small fittings such as locknuts and bushings. Answer D is true.

Conductors | 1- and 2-Family Study Guide | 57

▶ 4. Section 300.14 requires a minimum of 150 mm (6 in.) of conductor in a box. Answer B is not true. The same section also requires that where the opening to an outlet, junction, or switch point is less than 200 mm (8 in.) in any dimension, each conductor shall be long enough to extend at least 75 mm (3 in.) outside the opening. Answer C is true.

▶ 5. The correct answer is B.

QUESTION 33. All of the following statements regarding conductor fill and clamp assemblies in boxes are true EXCEPT:

A. A clamp assembly that incorporates a cable termination for the cable conductors shall be listed and marked for use with specific nonmetallic boxes.
B. The Conductors that originate within the clamp assembly shall be included in conductor fill calculations as though they entered from outside the box.
C. The clamp assembly shall require a single fill allowance based on the largest conductor in the box
D. the marked volume on box shall be reduced by the volume of the portion of the assembly that remains within the box after installation shall be excluded from the box volume as marked in 314.16(A)(2).

ANSWER _____

PROCEDURE TO ESTABLISH ANSWER
The question is about the fill allowance for a "clamp assembly" in nonmetallic boxes.

▶ 1. In the Index, find "Boxes (outlet, device, pull, and junction)" under which find "Fill calculations, 314.16(B)."

▶ 2. In 314.16(B)(2), we find that a clamp assembly must be listed and marked for the specific nonmetallic box. Answer A is true.

▶ 3. 314.16(B)(2) also notes no fill allowance is required for the clamp assembly but the volume of the portion of the assembly that remains within the box after installation shall be excluded from the marked box volume. Answer D is true and Answer C is not true.

▶ 4. Section 314.16(A)(2) further specifies the conductors that originate within the clamp assembly must be included in the conductor fill calculations covered in 314.16(B)(1) as though they entered from outside the box. Answer B is true.

▶ 5. The correct answer is C.

QUESTION 34. All of the following are required to be provided with ground fault circuit-interrupter (GFCI) protection when located in a dwelling unit EXCEPT:

A. A 15 ampere, 125 volt, single phase locking type (Twistlock) receptacle located on the kitchen counter.
B. A 15 or 20 ampere, 125 volt, single phase, receptacle installed in the laundry room.
C. A 15 ampere, 125 volt, single phase nonlocking type (standard) receptacle located on the kitchen counter.
D. A 15 ampere, 125 volt, single phase nonlocking type receptacle installed on the kitchen wall next to, but not serving the kitchen counter and located 2.5 m (8 ft) from the kitchen sink.

ANSWER _____

PROCEDURE TO ESTABLISH ANSWER
The question is about ground fault circuit-interrupter protection.

▶ 1. In Index, find "Ground-fault circuit-interrupters" under which find "Receptacles, 210.8."

▶ 2. In 210.8(A) find 210.8(A)(6) which requires that GFCI protection be provided for all 15 or 20 ampere, 125 volt receptacles installed to serve kitchen counters. Note that 210.8(A) does not distinguish between locking and nonlocking type receptacles. Therefore GFCI protection is required for both the locking and nonlocking type receptacles installed on the kitchen counter. Answers A and C require GFCI protection..

▶ 3. Section 210.8(A)(10) requires that GFCI protection be provided for 15 and 20 ampere, 125 volt, single phase receptacles installed in the laundry rooms. Answer B requires GFCI protection.

58 | 1- and 2-Family Study Guide | Conductors

▶ 4. Section 210.8(A)(6) requires GFCI protection be provided for 15 or 20 ampere, 125 volt, single phase receptacles installed for a kitchen counter. GFCI protection is not required for a kitchen wall receptacle that is not serving a countertop or is not located within 1.8 m (6 ft) for the kitchen sink. Answer D does not require GFCI protection.

▶ 5. The correct answer is D.

6 Service Equipment

QUESTION 1. A set of service-entrance conductors for a 120/240 service for a single-family dwelling are installed on the outside wall of the dwelling up to the point of connection to the service drop. This service drop is supported on and cabled together with a grounded bare messenger over a level yard from a 9.0 m (30 ft.) high utility pole. There is no driveway. The lowest point of the drip loop at the building electrical entrance shall be at least _____ above final grade.

A. 2.5 m (8 ft.)
B. 3.0 m (10 ft.)
C. 3.7 m (12 ft.)
D. 4.5 m (15 ft.)

ANSWER _____

PROCEDURE TO ESTABLISH ANSWER
This question is about clearance of a drip loop for overhead service-entrance conductors from grade..

▶ 1. In Index, find "Overhead service conductors" under which find "Clearances, 230.24."

▶ 2. Section 230.24(B)(1) requires a minimum 3.0 m (10 ft) clearance for the drip loop of the building electric entrance.

▶ 3. The correct answer is B.

QUESTION 2. What is the minimum working space depth in front of residential service equipment rated at 120/240-volt?

A. 762 mm (30 in.)
B. 610 mm (24 in.)
C. 914 mm (36 in.)
D. 1 m (42 in.)

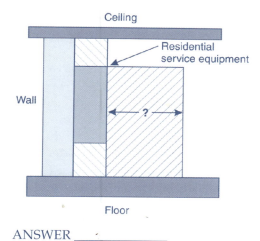

ANSWER _____

PROCEDURE TO ESTABLISH ANSWER
This question is about working space at service equipment.

▶ 1. In Index, find "Working space" under which find "About electrical equipment, 110.26, 110.32 through 110.34, 110.72, 110.73."

▶ 2. Table 110.26(A)(1) indicates a 900 mm (3 ft) minimum clear distance at 0–150 volts to ground for all three conditions.

▶ 3. The correct answer is C.

QUESTION 3. All the following wiring methods are permitted for service-entrance conductors under 1000 volts EXCEPT:

A. nonmetallic-sheathed cable (NM cable)
B. intermediate metal conduit (IMC)
C. flexible metal conduit (FMC) not more than 2 m (6 ft) in length between raceways
D. rigid metal conduit (RMC)

ANSWER _____

PROCEDURES TO ESTABLISH ANSWER
This question is about wiring methods for service-entrance conductors.

▶ 1. In Index, find "Service-entrance conductors" under which find "Wiring methods, 230.43."

▶ 2. Section 230.43, which lists 19 different wiring methods recognized for services under 1000 volts, does not include nonmetallic-sheathed cable.

▶ 3. The correct answer is A.

QUESTION 4. A ferrous metal raceway is used as physical protection for a grounding electrode conductor run to the service grounding electrode. The metal raceway is mechanically connected to the service equipment enclosure using standard locknuts but terminates one foot from the grounding electrode. Which one of the following statements is NOT true?

A. The raceway shall be bonded to the grounding electrode conductor where it terminates at the electrode.
B. The raceway is required to be bonded to the service equipment enclosure.
C. The raceway is required to be bonded to all intervening boxes between the service equipment and the electrode.
D. A metal raceway is required to protect the grounding electrode conductor where it is smaller than 6 AWG in size.

ANSWER _____

PROCEDURES TO ESTABLISH ANSWER
This question is about the installation of grounding electrode conductors.

▶ 1. In Index, find "Grounding electrode conductors" under which find "Installation, 250.64."

▶ 2. To verify that A, B and C are correct 250.64(E) requires:

Ferrous metal raceways and enclosures to be electrically continuous from the point of attachment to cabinets or equipment to the grounding electrode.

Ferrous metal raceways and enclosures that are not physically continuous from the cabinet or equipment to the electrode shall be made continuous by bonding both ends of

Service Equipment | 1- and 2-Family Study Guide | 61

the enclosure to the grounding electrode conductor.

The bonding methods shall apply at each end and to all intervening ferrous metal raceways, boxes, and enclosures.

▶ 3. Section 250.64(B) provides that conductors smaller than 6 AWG are permitted to be protected by enclosing them in PVC or RTRC nonmetallic, conduit as well as metal raceways, and cable armor. The protection is not limited to metal raceways so Answer D is not true.

▶ 4. The correct answer is D.

QUESTION 5. A main disconnect circuit breaker for a grounded AC service is installed outdoors in a weatherproof enclosure below the meter and supplies a distribution panel in the basement of a residence. Which one of the following statements is NOT true?

A. The grounding electrode conductor may be connected to the grounded service conductor (neutral) at the service disconnecting means.
B. The grounding electrode conductor may be connected to the grounded circuit conductor (neutral) in the distribution panel.
C. The grounded service conductor bus (neutral bar) in the service disconnecting means must be connected to the disconnecting means enclosure.
D. The grounded circuit conductor bus (neutral bar) in the distribution panel is not permitted to be connected to the panel enclosure.

ANSWER _____

PROCEDURES TO ESTABLISH ANSWER
The questions are related to connection of the grounding electrode conductor at services (supply side equipment) and feeder distribution (load side) equipment and the use of the grounded conductor (neutral) for grounding equipment. .

▶ 1. In Index, find "Grounding" under which find "AC systems, 250.20, 250.24, 250.26."

▶ 2. Section 250.24(A), System Grounding Connections" specifically provides that the grounding electrode conductor be connected to the grounded service conductor at each service disconnecting means. Section 250(24(A)(1) verifies that (A) above is a correct statement as it permits the grounding electrode conductor connection to be made at any point from the load end of the overhead service conductors, service drop, underground service conductors or service lateral to the bus to which the grounded service conductor is connected to at the service disconnecting means.

250.24(A)(5) provides that a grounding connection shall not be made to any grounded circuit conductor on the load side of the service disconnecting means. Section 250.24(A)(5)confirms that (B) above is an incorrect statement. Further, the Informational Note following 250.24(A)(5) refers to 250.30(A), 250.32, and 250.142 for the use of the grounded conductor for grounding equipment.

▶ 3. In 250.142(A) and (B), Use of Grounded Circuit Conductor for Grounding Equipment, it is permitted to ground equipment on the supply side or within the enclosure of the AC service disconnecting means to the grounded conductor (neutral) in accordance with (A) but not on the load side of the service disconnecting means in accordance with (B).

▶ 4. The correct answer is B.

QUESTION 6. Which of the following single-family dwelling 3-wire installations require the ungrounded service-entrance conductors to have an ampacity of not less than 100 amperes?

A. One with six or more 2-wire branch circuits
B. One with an initial net computed load of 10 kVA
C. One with five or more 2-wire branch circuits and 10 kVA of initial net computed load
D. All of the above

ANSWER _____

PROCEDURES TO ESTABLISH ANSWER
The question is about sizing of service-entrance conductors for dwellings.

▶ 1. In Index, find "Service-entrance conductors" under which find "Size, 230.42."

▶ 2. Section 230.42(B) requires that the ungrounded conductors have an ampacity of not less than the minimum rating of the disconnecting means specified in 230.79(A) through (D).

▶ 3. 230.79(C) requires a rating of not less than 100 amperes for a single-family dwelling service disconnect, therefore none of the conditions above would change the basic requirement of 100-amp rating.

▶ 4. The correct answer is D.

QUESTION 7. What is the minimum permitted rating for mobile home service equipment in mobile home parks?

A. 50 amperes
B. 70 amperes
C. 100 amperes
D. 150 amperes

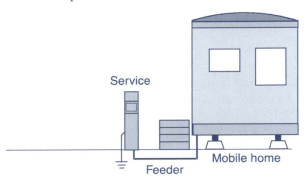

ANSWER _____

PROCEDURES TO ESTABLISH ANSWER
The question is about rating of mobile home service equipment in mobile home parks.

▶ 1. In Index, find "Mobile home parks" under which find "Mobile home service equipment, 550.32."

▶ 2. Scan Section 550.32 and find "550.32(C), Rating," which requires that mobile home service equipment be rated not less than 100 amperes.

▶ 3. The correct answer is C.

QUESTION 8. A single rod electrode is not required to be supplemented by an additional electrode where the resistance to ground of the single rod electrode does not exceed how many ohms resistance to earth?

A. 10
B. 25
C. 50
D. 100

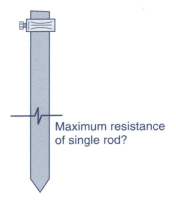

ANSWER _____

PROCEDURES TO ESTABLISH ANSWER
The question is about the resistance to earth of a single rod type electrode.

▶ 1. In Index, find "Rod electrodes" under which find "250.52(A)(5), 250.53, 250.66(A), 250.70."

▶ 2. Section 250.53(A)(2) requires a single rod electrode to be supplemented by an additional electrode.

▶ 3. Under 250.53(A)(2) Exception, if the resistance to earth is 25 ohms or less the additional electrode is not required.

▶ 4. The correct answer is B.

Service Equipment | 1- and 2-Family Study Guide | 63

QUESTION 9. Under which one of the following conditions is an additional lighting outlet not required for illumination of the working spaces about service equipment located in a dwelling unit?

A. The workspace is illuminated by an adjacent light source.
B. The service equipment rating does not exceed 200 amperes.
C. The service equipment is accessible only to authorized persons.
D. The headroom of the workspace is at least 2.0 m (6½ ft) in height.

Service Equipment Illumination

ANSWER _____

PROCEDURES TO ESTABLISH ANSWER
The question is about illumination of the working space about service equipment.

▶ 1. In the Index find "Working space" under which there is a subtitle "About electrical equipment, 110.26."

▶ 2. Section 110.26(D) requires illumination for working spaces about service equipment installed indoors without reference to ampere rating, accessibility, or headroom. However, the lighting may be provided by an adjacent light source.

▶ 3. The correct answer is A.

QUESTION 10. An 450 mm (18 in.) wide 120/240-volt, 200-ampere service disconnect switch mounted on a concrete basement wall opposite a wood paneled wall requires which one of the following working space clearances between the switch and the wall?

A. 762 mm (30 in.) wide and 762 mm (30 in. deep)
B. 914 mm (36 in.) wide and 762 mm (30 in. deep)
C. 762 mm (30 in.) wide and 914 mm (36 in. deep)
D. 610 mm (24 in.) wide and 914 mm (36 in. deep)

ANSWER _____

PROCEDURES TO ESTABLISH ANSWER
The question is about the size of the working space in front of a service disconnect switch.

▶ 1. In Index, find "Working space" under which find "About electrical equipment, 110.26, etc."

▶ 2. Section 110.26(A)(2) requires a minimum of a 762 mm (30 in.) wide workspace. As indicated in 110.26(A)(1) and Table 110.26(A)(1), condition 1 depth of 914 mm (36 in.) for a voltage of 0–150 volts to ground would apply for the depth.

▶ 3. The correct answer is C.

QUESTION 11. A ground rod used to supplement a metal underground water pipe grounding electrode for a dwelling service shall be permitted to be bonded to all of the following EXCEPT:

A. the grounding electrode conductor
B. a grounded flexible metal conduit raceway not over 1.8 m (6 ft) in length
C. the grounded service-entrance conductor
D. the grounded non-flexible service raceway

ANSWER _____

PROCEDURES TO ESTABLISH ANSWER
The question is about supplementing a water pipe grounding electrode.

▶ 1. In Index, find "Water pipe" under which find "As grounding electrode, 250.52(A)(1), 250.53(D)."

▶ 2. Section 250.53(D)(2)," applies to a metal underground water pipe electrode(s). This section requires the supplemental electrode, specifies the permitted bonding locations, and does not include flexible metal conduit as a bonding location.

Note: The exception in this section allows connection of the supplemental electrode to the interior metal water piping system in 250.52(A)(1) is for commercial and industrial building or structures and contains other requirements as well.

▶ 3. The correct answer is B.

QUESTION 12. What is the maximum number of switches or circuit breakers which may be grouped together to serve as the service disconnecting means for each set of service-entrance conductors?

A. 1
B. 2
C. 3
D. 6

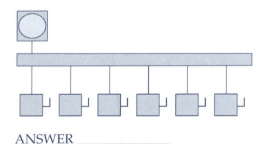

ANSWER _____

PROCEDURES TO ESTABLISH ANSWER
The question is about the number of switches or circuit breakers that can be used to serve as the service disconnecting means.

▶ 1. In Index, find "Service equipment" under which find "Disconnecting means 230–Part VI" under which find "Six switch rule, 230.71."

▶ 2. Section 230.71(A) states the maximum number of switches or circuit breakers is six.

▶ 3. The correct answer is D.

QUESTION 13. The minimum permitted rating of the service disconnecting means for a small lake cottage that does not qualify as a dwelling unit by definition shall not be less than:

A. 30 amperes
B. 60 amperes
C. 70 amperes
D. 100 amperes

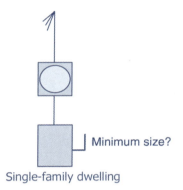

Single-family dwelling

ANSWER _____

PROCEDURES TO ESTABLISH ANSWER
The question is about the minimum rating of the service disconnecting means for services other than dwelling.

▶ 1. In Index, find "Service equipment" under which find "Disconnecting Means" under which find "Rating, 230.79."

▶ 2. Section 230.79(D) establishes 60 amperes as a minimum.

▶ 3. The correct answer is B.

Service Equipment | 1- and 2-Family Study Guide | 65

QUESTION 14. The point of attachment of overhead service conductors above finished grade to a building or other structure shall be not less than:

A. 3.0 m (10 ft)
B. 3.7 m (12 ft)
C. 4.5 m (15 ft)
D. 5.5 m (18 ft)

ANSWER _____

PROCEDURES TO ESTABLISH ANSWER
The question is about attachment of overhead service conductors to a building.

▶ 1. In Index, find "Overhead service conductors" under which find "Point of attachment, 230.26, 230.28."

▶ 2. Section 230.26 requires a minimum of 3.0 m (10 ft.) above finished grade. Section 230.26 refers to 230.24, which also requires a 3.0 m (10 ft.) minimum clearance for the drip loop.

▶ 3. The correct answer is A.

QUESTION 15. What is the minimum permitted vertical clearance for overhead service conductors over a residential driveway?

A. 3.0 m (10 ft)
B. 3.7 m (12 ft)
C. 4.5 m (15 ft)
D. 5.5 m (18 ft)

ANSWER _____

PROCEDURES TO ESTABLISH ANSWER
The question is about service-drop clearances.

▶ 1. In Index, find "Overhead service conductors" under which find "Clearances, 230.24."

▶ 2. Section 230.24(B)(2) requires a minimum of 3.7 m (12 ft).

▶ 3. The correct answer is B.

QUESTION 16. What is the minimum size of Type THW aluminum service-entrance conductors permitted to serve a 3-wire, single-phase 200-ampere residential service?

A. 2/0 AWG
B. 3/0 AWG
C. 4/0 AWG
D. 250 kcmil

ANSWER _____

PROCEDURES TO ESTABLISH ANSWER
The question is about the minimum size of a Type THW aluminum conductor for a 200-ampere 3-wire, single-phase, service.

▶ 1. In Index, find "Service-entrance conductors" under which find "Size, 230.42."

▶ 2. Section 230.42(A) refers to 310.15. Section 310.15(B) refers to the Ampacity Tables 310.15(B)(16) through 310.15(B)(19) and Ampacity Tables 310.15(B)(20) and 31015(B).(21) *as modified* by (B)(1) through (7).

▶ 3. For a service rated 100 through 400 amperes, the service conductors supplying a one-family dwelling shall be permitted to have an ampacity not less than 83% of the service rating per 310.15(B)(7).

▶ 4. The question uses Type THW aluminum conductors. Scan Table 310.15(B)(16), and note that 4/0 AWG Type THW aluminum conductors may be used for a feeder rated at 200 have an allowable amperes rating of 180 amperes at 75°C. It appears the appropriate feeder rating for these conductors would be 200 amperes.

66 | 1- and 2-Family Study Guide | Service Equipment

▶ 5. To verify the 200 ampere feeder rating: 200 x .83 = 166 amperes. The 4/0 aluminum conductors are sufficient for a 200 ampere service to an individual dwelling unit.

▶ 6. The correct answer is C.

QUESTION 17. The smallest size service-entrance conductors permitted to supply two 2-wire branch circuits is:

A. 8 AWG copper
B. 8 AWG aluminum
C. 10 AWG copper
D. 10 AWG aluminum

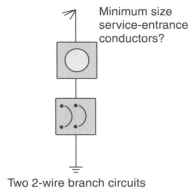

Two 2-wire branch circuits

ANSWER _____

PROCEDURES TO ESTABLISH ANSWER
The question is about the minimum size of service-entrance conductors (assuming a small utility building could be wired utilizing only two 2-wire branch circuits).

▶ 1. In Index, find "Service-entrance conductors, under which find "Size, 230.42."

▶ 2. Section 230.42(B) refers to 230.79.

▶ 3. Section 230.79(B) states that "for installations consisting of not more than two 2-wire branch circuits, the service disconnecting means shall have a rating of not less than 30 amperes."

▶ 4. Refer to Table 310.15(B)(16) for the ampacity of conductors.

▶ 5. Since both 10 AWG copper and 8 AWG aluminum conductors are suitable, select 10 AWG as it is the smallest or minimum physical size as stated in the question.

▶ 6. The correct answer is C.

QUESTION 18. Which one of the following is permitted in the equipment space directly above or below a service panelboard mounted on a basement wall?

A. A metal water pipe supplying a nearby water heater
B. A nonmetallic water pipe supplying an adjacent laundry
C. Electrical metallic tubing protecting Type NM cable fed from the panelboard
D. Heating/cooling duct serving the area where the panelboard is located

ANSWER _____

PROCEDURES TO ESTABLISH ANSWER
The question is about the installation of a panelboard.

▶ 1. In Index, find "Panelboards" under which find "Installation, 110.26(E)."

▶ 2. Section 110.26(E)(1)(a) requires a dedicated space equal to the width and depth of the panelboard and extending from the floor to ceiling, and provides that no piping, ducts, or equipment foreign to the electrical installation may be located in this dedicated space. The EMT protecting the cable is not foreign to the electrical installation.

▶ 3. The correct answer is C.

QUESTION 19. In general, the *Code* requires that a building be supplied by only one service. Under which one of the following conditions may a two-family dwelling have a separate service run to each unit?

A. The overall service capacity is 600 amperes.
B. The two individual occupancies are separated by a firewall.
C. The building has an overall area exceeding 4000 square feet.
D. The services are 120/240-volt, 3-wire

ANSWER _____

PROCEDURES TO ESTABLISH ANSWER
The question is about the number of services allowed to a building.

▶ 1. In Index, find "Services" under which find "Number, 230.2."

▶ 2. Section 230.2(A), (B), (C), and (D) state the different instances where additional services are allowed.

▶ 3. Note that Section 230.2 applies to each building or other structure. In Article 100, Definitions, check the definition of a *building* which includes a structure cut off from adjoining structures by fire walls. With a firewall between the two units, they would be considered separate buildings, and a service may be run to each.

▶ 4. The correct answer is B.

QUESTION 20. Generally, the two to six disconnects for each service are required to be located in a single enclosure or in a group of separate enclosures. Which one of the following disconnects may be located remote from the others?

A. A service disconnect for an outside air conditioning unit
B. A service disconnect used only for a water pump intended for fire protection
C. A service disconnect for a range or dryer
D. A service disconnect for a water heater

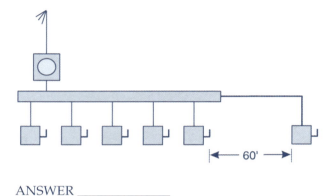

ANSWER _____

PROCEDURES TO ESTABLISH ANSWER
The question is about where the two to six disconnects allowed by the *Code* do not have to be grouped.

▶ 1. In Index, find "Service equipment" under which find "Disconnecting means, 230–Part VI."

▶ 2. Scan Article 230, Part VI, and find "230.72(A), Exception" which permits a water-pump service disconnect where used only for a water pump also intended to provide fire protection to be located remote from the other service disconnect(s).

▶ 3. The correct answer is B.

QUESTION 21. For a single-family dwelling, under which one of the following conditions shall the service disconnecting means have a rating of not less than 100 amperes?

A. Initial load of 8 kVA or more
B. More than 1200 square feet of area
C. 100 amperes is the minimum rating of service disconnect
D. Where the initial installation consists of six of more 2-wire circuits

ANSWER _____

PROCEDURES TO ESTABLISH ANSWER

The question is about when a 100-ampere service is required for a one-family dwelling.

▶ 1. In Index, find "Service equipment" under which find "Disconnecting means" under which find "Rating, 230.79."

▶ 2. Section 230.79(C) indicates that a 100-ampere disconnect is required as a minimum for a single-family dwelling.

▶ 3. The correct answer is C.

QUESTION 22. Service-entrance conductors are permitted to be spliced under all of the following conditions EXCEPT:

A. Where all splices and joints shall be covered with an insulation equivalent to that of the conductors or with an insulating device identified for the purpose.
B. Where service-entrance conductors are tapped to supply two to six disconnecting means grouped at a common location
C. Where terminations are identified for one conductor only
D. Direct-buried conductors or cables shall be permitted to be spliced or tapped, but most employ the use of a listed splice box in all situations.

ANSWER _____

PROCEDURES TO ESTABLISH ANSWER

The question is about splicing of service-entrance conductors.

▶ 1. In Index, find "Service-entrance conductors" under which find "Splices, 230.46."

▶ 2. Section 230.46 states that service-entrance conductors shall be permitted to be spliced or tapped in accordance with 110.14, 300.5(E), 300.13, and 300.15.

▶ 3. Section 110.14(B) requires all splices and joints and the free ends of conductors to be covered with an insulating device identified for the purpose.

▶ 4. Section 300.5(E) states that direct-buried conductors or cables shall be permitted to be spliced or tapped without the use of splice boxes. The splices or taps shall be made in accordance with 110.14(B), which states that conductors shall be spliced or joined with splicing devices identified for the use.

▶ 5. A splice in a conductor involves joining two or more conductors, which eliminates C.

▶ 6. The correct answer is D.

Service Equipment | 1- and 2-Family Study Guide | 69

QUESTION 23. All of the following statements regarding overhead service locations and service heads are true EXCEPT:

A. Other than by exception, service heads shall be located above the point of attachment of the service-drop or overhead service conductors to the building.
B. Service-entrance conductors shall be connected to the service-drop or overhead service conductors below the level of the service head.
C. Where the service head cannot physically be located above the point of attachment of the service-drop or overhead service conductors to the building, the service head may be located up to 900 mm (3 ft) from the point of attachment.
D. A rigid nonmetallic service raceway is required to be equipped with a service head that is listed for wet locations at the point of connection to service-drop or overhead service conductors.

ANSWER _____

PROCEDURES TO ESTABLISH ANSWER
The question is about connections of service-entrance conductors at a service head.

▶ 1. In Index, find "Service-entrance conductors" under which find "Service head, 230.54."

▶ 2. Section 230.54(A), (C), and (F) provides requirements for service heads to be listed for wet locations and location of the service heads.

▶ 3. Note that the exception to 230.54(C) permits the service head to be no farther than 600 mm (24 in.) from the point of attachment where it is impractical to locate the service head above the point of attachment.

▶ 4. The correct answer is C.

QUESTION 24. Where the supplemental electrode for a single rod electrode with a resistance to ground exceeding 25 ohms is a second ground rod, the minimum spacing between the rods shall be:

A. 1.8 m (6 ft)
B. 2.5 m (8 ft)
C. 3.0 m (10 ft)
D. the length of the rods

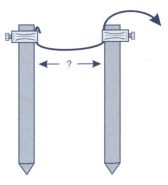

ANSWER _____

PROCEDURES TO ESTABLISH ANSWER
The question is about the installation of a supplemental electrode for a rod electrode (ground rod).

▶ 1. In Index, find "Rod electrodes," under which find "250.52(A)(5), 250.53."

▶ 2. Section 250.52(A)(5) provides construction requirements for rod electrodes and is not applicable here, but 250.53 provides the installation requirements for rod, pipe and plate electrodes.

▶ 3. Section 250.53(A)(3) states that where multiple rods are installed, they shall be not less than 1.8 m (6 ft) apart.

▶ 4. The correct answer is A.

QUESTION 25.
The minimum height of the working space about a 200-ampere panelboard installed in a new dwelling is required to be a minimum of:

A. 1.8 m (6 ft)
B. 3.0 m (10 ft)
C. 2.0 m (6½ ft)
D. 2.44 m (8 ft)

ANSWER _____

PROCEDURES TO ESTABLISH ANSWER
The question is the height of the working space.

▶ 1. There is no direct reference to the "height of the working space" in the Index. However, in the Index, find "Working space" under which find "About electrical equipment, 110.26."

▶ 2. Scanning 110.26, find "110.26(A)(3), Height of the working space."

▶ 3. A review of 110.26(A)(3) reveals that a minimum height of 2.0 m (6 ½ ft) is required, with an exception for existing dwelling units. Our question refers to new dwelling units.

▶ 4. The correct answer is C.

QUESTION 26.
It is permissible to connect the AC system grounding electrode conductor to the grounded service conductor at all of the following locations EXCEPT:

A. on the grounding terminal bus of the service disconnecting means
B. within a subpanel on the load side of the service disconnect
C. in a wireway on the line side of the service disconnecting means
D. at the weatherhead on the load end of the service drop

ANSWER _____

PROCEDURES TO ESTABLISH ANSWER
The question is about the location of the grounding electrode conductor termination.

▶ 1. In Index, find "Grounding" under which find "AC systems, 250.20, 250.24, 250.26."

▶ 2. Section 250.20 explains which AC systems are to be grounded. Section 250.26 states which conductor is to be grounded.

▶ 3. Section 250.24(A)(1) gives the location as any accessible point from the load-end of the service drop or the overhead service conductors to the grounding terminal bus at the service disconnecting means. Section 250.24(A)(5) states that no grounding connections shall be made on the load-side of the service disconnecting means. This eliminates Answer B as a connection point for the service grounding electrode conductor.

▶ 4. The correct answer is B.

QUESTION 27.
Service-entrance cable installed exposed in a location that is subject to physical damage on the side of a dwelling adjacent to a sidewalk shall be considered protected by all of the following EXCEPT:

A. rigid metal conduit
B. intermediate metal conduit
C. flexible metal conduit
D. electrical metallic tubing

ANSWER _____

PROCEDURES TO ESTABLISH ANSWER
The question is about protection of service-entrance cable.

▶ 1. In Index, find "Service-entrance cable (Types SE and USE)" under which none of the subtitles directly apply.

▶ 2. In Index, find "Service-entrance conductors" under which find "Physical damage, 230.50."

► 3. Section 230.50(B)(1) lists the permitted means of protecting service-entrance cables subject to physical damage but does not include flexible metal conduit.

► 4. The correct answer is C.

QUESTION 28.
Whether required or permitted by exception, which of the following is permitted as overcurrent protection for a panelboard used as service equipment supplying a new individual residential occupancy?

A. One circuit breaker or one set of fuses
B. Not more than two main circuit breakers or sets of fuses having a combined rating of not more than the panelboard.
C. Not more than six circuit breakers or sets of fuses
D. All the above

ANSWER _____

PROCEDURES TO ESTABLISH ANSWER
The question is about panelboard overcurrent protection.

► 1. In Index, find "Panelboards," under which find "Overcurrent protection, 408.36."

► 2. The main paragraph of 408.36 requires panelboards to be protected by an overcurrent device having a rating not greater than that of the panelboard. This verifies that answer A is permitted by not more than two main breakers or set of fuses.

► 3. Scan the exceptions to find that Exception No. 2 permits answer B where the panelboard does not contain more than 42 overcurrent devices.

► 4. To verify answer C, two steps are necessary. Exception No. 3 permits multiple disconnecting means in accordance with 230.71 to be the overcurrent protection. Section 230.71 permits up to six switches or circuit breakers to be the service disconnecting means.

► 5. The correct answer is D.

QUESTION 29.
The minimum vertical clearance for overhead service conductors extending horizontally a distance of 3.0 m (10 ft) over a dwelling roof having a slope of 75 mm (3 in.) in 300 mm (12 in.) shall be not less than:

A. 450 mm   (18 in.)
B. 900 mm   (3 ft)
C. 1.8 m   (6 ft)
D. 2.5 m   (8 ft)

ANSWER _____

PROCEDURES TO ESTABLISH ANSWER
The question is about vertical clearances of overhead service conductors over roofs.

► 1. In Index, find "Overhead service conductors," under which find "Clearances, 230.24."

► 2. Section 230.24(A) provides clearances above roofs and requires a minimum vertical clearance of 2.5 m (8 ft) above roofs.

► 3. Scan the exceptions to Section 230.24(A) and find that none applies.

► 4. The correct answer is D.

Note: If the slope had been not less than 100 mm (4 in.) in 300 mm (12 in.), Section 230.24(A), Exception No. 2 would have permitted a reduction to not less than 900 mm (3 ft) vertical clearance.

QUESTION 30. A large single-family dwelling service contains three 4/0 AWG copper conductors per phase. The maximum size copper grounding electrode conductor required to be connected to the concrete-encased electrode where it is the only available electrode is which one of the following?

A. 6 AWG
B. 4 AWG
C. 2 AWG
D. 2/0 AWG

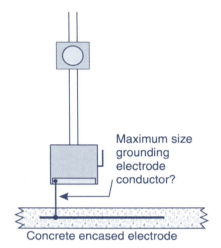

ANSWER _____

PROCEDURES TO ESTABLISH ANSWER
The question is about the method of sizing the grounding electrode conductors.

▶ 1. In Index, find "Grounding electrode conductors" under which find "Sizing, 250.30(A)(6)(a), 250.66, 250.166."

▶ 2. Section 250.30(A) is for separately derived systems and is not applicable to the question. Section 250.66 states the grounding electrode conductor at the service cannot be smaller than Table 250.66 except as permitted in 250.66(A) – (C).

▶ 3. Section 250.66(B) covers connections to concrete-encased electrodes and states the grounding electrode conductor is not required to be larger than 4 AWG where it is the sole connection to the concrete-encased electrode.

▶ 4. Scanning Table 250.66 one recognizes that a 2 AWG copper grounding electrode conductor is required for one 4/0 copper conductor per phase and the question has three per phase. Therefore, in accordance with 250.66(B), Answer B is the correct answer.

▶ 5 To verify step 4 if necessary: Table 250.66 bases the size of the grounding electrode conductor that is required upon the size of the largest ungrounded service-entrance conductor or equivalent area for parallel conductors.

▶ 6. Three size 4/0 conductors do not readily match a size on Table 250.66. Therefore, we return to the Index, and find "Conductors" under which find "Properties of, Chap. 9, Table 8."

▶ 7. Based on Chapter 9, Table 8, Conductor Properties, three 4/0 AWG conductors add up to 3 x 211,600 cm = 634,800 cm or 634.8 kcmil. Referring again to Table 250.66, for ungrounded copper service-entrance conductors sized between 600 through 1100 kcmil, this would require a 2/0 AWG copper grounding electrode conductor.

▶ 8. The correct answer is B.

QUESTION 31. A panelboard used as the service disconnecting means for a dwelling shall be marked with all of the following EXCEPT:

A. a marking to identify it as a service disconnecting means
B. a marking that it is suitable for use as service equipment
C. voltage, current rating and number of phases
D. calculated load of the dwelling

ANSWER _____

PROCEDURES TO ESTABLISH ANSWER
The question is about the marking and suitability of panelboards used for service disconnecting means.

▶ 1. In Index, find "Service equipment" under which find "Disconnecting means" under which find "Marking, 230.70(B)."

Service Equipment | 1- and 2-Family Study Guide | 73

▶ 2. Scanning further in the Index under "Service equipment" find "Marking, 230.66."

▶ 3. Section 230.70(B) requires marking to identify it as a service disconnecting means, verifying answer A.

▶ 4. Section 230.66 requires marking to identify it as being suitable for use as service equipment, verifying answer B.

▶ 5. Since the equipment is a panelboard, in Index, find "Panelboards, Art. 408." under which, find "Marking, 230.58. Section 230.58 requires marking with voltage, current, and number of phases.

▶ 6. Calculated load on the service equipment is not a marking requirement.

▶ 7. The correct answer is D.

QUESTION 32. Which of the following statements about equipment permitted on the supply side of the service disconnecting means is NOT true?

A. Cable limiters are permitted.
B. Meter sockets that are grounded in accordance with Article 250 are permitted.
C. Transfer equipment that is not marked as "suitable for use as service equipment" is permitted on the line side.
D. Taps for stand-by power systems are permitted on the line side of the service.

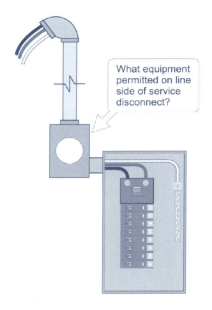

ANSWER _____

PROCEDURE TO ESTABLISH ANSWER
The question is about service-entrance equipment.

▶ 1. In Index, find "Service equipment" under which find "Disconnecting means" under which find "Connections, supply side, 230.82."

▶ 2. Scan through 230.82 and find that (1), (2), and (5) permit cable limiters, grounded meter sockets, and taps on the supply side of the service disconnect as complied with in 230.82. The only equipment that is not permitted on the line side of the service disconnecting means is the transfer equipment.

▶ 3. The correct answer is C.

QUESTION 33. A new 3-wire 400-amp service for a large custom single-family dwelling is installed with two parallel sets of 250-kcmil copper conductors in two separate metallic raceways (one set in each raceway) into the enclosure for the service-disconnect circuit breaker. Where individual supply-side bonding jumpers are installed for each raceway, the minimum size supply-side bonding jumper to the bonding bushing installed on each raceway is:

A. 2 AWG copper
B. 3/0 AWG copper
C. 1/0 AWG copper
D. 1/0 AWG aluminum

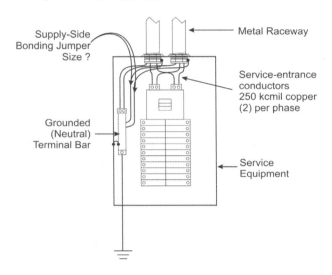

ANSWER _____

PROCEDURE TO ESTABLISH ANSWER
The question is about sizing equipment bonding jumpers for service raceways.

▶ 1 In Index, find "Bonding jumpers" which will refer you to "Jumpers, bonding" under which find "Equipment, 250.102."

▶ 2. Section 250.102(A) states that equipment bonding jumpers shall be copper or other corrosion-resistant material and includes limitations on the use of aluminum conductors.

▶ 3. Section 250.102(C)(1) requires the supply-side bonding jumper(s) to be sized per Table 250.102(C)(1). Table 250.102(C)(1) is new in the 2014 *NEC* and is used for sizing grounded conductors main bonding jumpers, system bonding jumpers and supply-side equipment bonding jumpers, as directed in other sections of the *Code*. Users of the *NEC* were formally directed to Table 250.66 for these sizing requirements.

▶ 4. Section 250.102(C)(2) notes that where two or more raceways are used with parallel conductors, the bonding jumper to each raceway shall be selected from Table 260.102(C)(1) based on the ungrounded conductors in each raceway.

▶ 5. The minimum size copper equipment bonding jumper for each raceway containing ungrounded 250-kcmil copper service conductors is 2 AWG copper.

▶ 6. Per 310.10(H), the smallest size conductor that can be installed in parallel is 1/0 AWG.

▶ 7. The correct answer is C.

Note: If the service conductors were 250 kcmil aluminum, the minimum size equipment bonding jumper for each raceway would be 4 AWG copper.

QUESTION 34. Per question 33, again for the same new 400-amp residential service, find the minimum size copper service grounded (neutral) conductors in parallel. The calculated neutral load is 103 amps.

A. 3/0 AWG copper
B. 2 AWG copper
C. 1/0 AWG aluminum
D. 1/0 AWG copper

ANSWER _____

PROCEDURE TO ESTABLISH ANSWER
The question is about sizing grounded service conductors that are installed in parallel in separate metallic raceways.

▶ 1. In Index, find "Grounded conductor. *see* Conductors, Grounded; Neutral." Under "Conductors," find "Grounded." There is no "Neutral" under "Grounded." However, this is an alternating-current installation, so we will go to "Alternating-current systems, 250.24, 250.26."

▶ 2. In 250.24(C)(1), "Sizing for a Single Raceway," we find that the grounded service conductor shall not be smaller than specified in Table 250.102(C)(1), which would be 1/0 AWG.

▶ 3. Per Table 310.15(B)(16), the maximum ampacity for this conductor is 150 amperes (assuming 75° terminations). However, because this is a 3-wire single-phase dwelling service, 310.15(B)(7) is applicable. Section 310.15(B)(7) permits the service entrance conductors to be sized at 83% of the service rating so the 1/0 copper conductor in this application could be rated at 166 amperes. A point to note here is that no type of insulation was specified in either Question 33 or 34 yet we chose ampacities from the 75°C column in Table 310.15(B)(16). Verification this is the appropriate step can be found in 110.14(C) regarding coordinating the ampacity of conductors with the temperature limitations of terminations, other conductors or devices used. Section 110.14(C)(1)(b) provides that for equipment rated over 100 amperes or sized for conductors greater than 1 AWG the 75°C ampacity can be used.

▶ 4. In step 3, we determined the ampacity of a single 1/0 conductor to be 175 amperes. However, because there are two raceways, in accordance with 250.24(C)(2), a grounded conductor must be installed in each raceway so there are two grounded conductors with a combined ampacity of 350 amperes. This section also requires the grounded conductor to be a minimum of 1/0 when installed in parallel in separate raceways.

In addition to the size determined in steps 2 and 3 which are for ground-fault current, the grounded service conductor(s) must also be sized for the calculated service neutral load, as required by 220.61. In some cases 220.61(B) permits the calculated neutral load to be reduced. In Index, find "Neutral," under which find "Feeder load, 220.61." This section also applies for service load as well. The service neutral load is not over 200 amps, so the demand factor of 70% may not be applied. The two parallel 1/0 conductors are more than adequate to carry the calculated load 103 amperes.

▶ 5. Because the grounded conductors are installed in parallel, we must also find in the Index, "Conductors," under which find "Paralleled, 250.30(A)(3), 250.102(C), 250.122(F), 300.5(I) Ex. 1,300.20, 310.10(H), etc,"

▶ 6. In Section 310.10(H), the minimum size conductor allowed in parallel is 1/0 AWG, "comprising each phase, polarity, neutral, or grounded circuit conductor." The minimum size grounded conductor in each raceway is 1/0 AWG. The question above specifies that copper be used.

▶ 7. The correct answer is D.

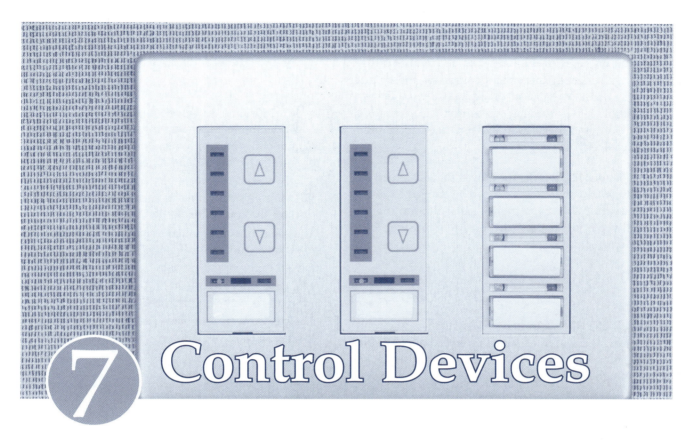

7 Control Devices

QUESTION 1. Thermostatically controlled switching devices for electric baseboard heaters are permitted to serve as both controller and disconnecting means providing all of the following conditions are satisfied EXCEPT:

A. Where provisions for locking the switch or circuit breaker in the open (off) position are required, the locking means must remain in place when the lock is removed.
B. It directly opens all ungrounded conductors when manually placed in the marked "off" position.
C. The circuit may be energized automatically after the device has been placed in the "off" position.
D. The thermostat may be located out-of-sight of the heater if the circuit breaker supplying it can be locked in the open position.

ANSWER _____

PROCEDURE TO ESTABLISH ANSWER
The question is about disconnecting means for fixed electric space-heating equipment.

▶ 1. In Index, find "Fixed electric space-heating equipment" under which find "Control and protection, 424–Part III" under which find "Disconnecting means, 424.19 through 424.21, 424.65." Also under the same heading, find "Controllers, 424.20(A)."

▶ 2. Section 424.20(A) states the type and conditions under which a thermostat may serve as both controller and disconnecting means. Section 424.20(A)(1) states that the thermostatically controlled switching device is provided with a marked "off" position. Section 424.20(A)(2) states that the thermostatically controlled switching device directly opens all ungrounded conductors when in the marked "off" position. Answer (B) is correct.

▶ 3. Section 424.20(A)(4) states that the thermostatically controlled switching device must be located as specified in 424.19. The last sentence of 424.19 requires the locking means to remain in place whether or not the lock in installed. Answer A is correct.

▶ 4. Section 424.19(B)(1) states that the branch circuit switch or circuit breaker must be located within sight of the heater or be capable of being locked in the open position. If the circuit breaker is capable of being locked in open position it is serving the required disconnecting means and thermostat location does not matter. Answer D is correct.

▶ 5. Section 424.20(A)(3) requires the design to be such that the circuit cannot be energized automatically after the thermostat has been manually placed in the "off" position. Answer C is incorrect.

▶ 6 The correct answer is C.

QUESTION 2. In general, switches and circuit breakers used as switches must have the center of their handles, when in the highest position, not higher than:

A. 1.5 m (5 ft)
B. 1.8 m (6 ft)
C. 2.0 m (6 ft 7 in.)
D. 2.1 m (7 ft)

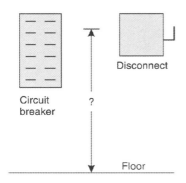

ANSWER _____

PROCEDURE TO ESTABLISH ANSWER
The question is about the height of switch handles.

▶ 1. In Index, find "Switches" under which find "Accessibility and grouping, 404.8."

▶ 2. Section 404.8(A) generally limits the handle height to 2.0 m (6 ft 7 in.) above the floor or working platform.

▶ 3. The correct answer is C.

Note: There are exceptions to the rule, but the question does not mention any conditions of any of the exceptions and applies generally.

QUESTION 3. Which one of the following statements regarding the location of a disconnecting means for the controller for a duct heater installed in a residential heating system is true?

A. The disconnecting means must always be within sight of the controller.
B. The disconnecting means may be located out-of-sight of the controller if it is capable of being locked in the open position.
C. The disconnecting means must be located within 1.0 m (3 ft) of the controller.
D. The disconnecting means and controller must be located within the same enclosure.

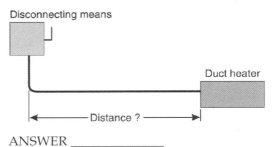

ANSWER _____

PROCEDURE TO ESTABLISH ANSWER
The question is about the disconnecting means for duct heaters in electric space heating equipment.

▶ 1. In Index, find "Fixed electric space heating equipment" under which find "Duct heaters, 424–Part VI" under which find "Disconnecting means, location, 424.65."

▶ 2. Section 424.65 generally requires the disconnecting means at or *within sight from* the controller. Section 424.65 also references 424.19(A)(1), which permits the disconnecting means to be out-of-sight if capable of being locked in the open position.

▶ 3. The correct answer is B.

QUESTION 4. Generally, the *Code* requires that a disconnecting means for a 1/3-horsepower oil burner motor be located:

A. within sight from the appliance
B. at the service equipment
C. out-of-sight from the appliance
D. within 1.8 m (6 ft) of the burner motor

ANSWER _____

PROCEDURE TO ESTABLISH ANSWER
The question is about the location of a disconnecting means for an appliance. Specifically, this appliance has a horsepower rating so it is implied that it is a "motor-driven appliance." There are several ways to approach this through the Index, but the most direct pathway is to look at a motor-driven appliance.

▶ 1. In Index, find "Appliances" under which find "Motor-driven" under which, find "Disconnecting means, 422.31(C)."

As noted there are additional pathways that are not as direct. In the Index you could find "Disconnecting means" under which find "Appliances, 422–Part III" or you can go to "Appliances" under which find "Disconnecting means, 422–Part III." Either way, you have to scan the Part but you end up at 422.31(C).

▶ 2. Section 422.31(C)(1), Motor-Operated Appliances Rated over 1/8 horsepower permits the branch circuit switch or circuit breaker to serve as the disconnecting means where it is located within sight from the appliance. This verifies that Answer A is correct and Answers B, C & D are incorrect.

▶ 3. The correct answer is A.

QUESTION 5. Which one of the following statements concerning connections at three-way switches is NOT true?

A. Three-way switches shall be so wired that all switching is done only in the ungrounded circuit conductor.
B. A switch loop from a luminaire to a three-way switch does not require a grounded conductor.
C. Where a switch loop is contained in a flexible metal conduit, all conductors of the loop shall be run within the same conduit.
D. Three-way switches may be wired so that the switching may be done in both the ungrounded and grounded conductor.

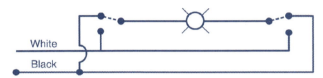

Note: Neutral conductor not shown.

ANSWER _____

PROCEDURE TO ESTABLISH ANSWER
The question is about connecting to three-way switches.

▶ 1. In the Index find "Connections" under which find "Switches, 404.2."

Another pathway through the Index would be to find "Switches, Art. 404"; then scan Article 404 for a section title applicable to the question. Section 404.2 refers to switch connections.

▶ 2. Section 404.2(A) provides that three-way and four-way switches shall only be wired so that all the switching is done in the ungrounded conductor. Where the conductors are installed in metal raceways, they shall comply with 300.20(A) requiring installation in the same raceway. This verifies answers A & C are correct and Answer D is incorrect.

▶ 3. The exception to 404.2(A) provides that switch loops do not require a grounded conductor which verifies Answer B is correct.

▶ 4. The correct answer is D.

QUESTION 6. An electrically operated kitchen waste disposal with a nameplate rating of 6 amperes may be controlled by an AC general-use snap switch rated at a minimum of:

A. 6 amperes
B. 15 amperes
C. 10 amperes
D. 7.5 amperes

ANSWER _____

PROCEDURE TO ESTABLISH ANSWER
The question is about switch ratings.

▶ 1. In Index, find "Switches" under which a find "AC general use snap switch, 404.14(A)."

▶ 2. Section 404.14(A)(3) requires that motor loads shall not exceed 80 percent of the ampere rating of the switch at its rated voltage.

Let's use for an example, a 15-ampere rated AC Snap switch.

15 amperes x .80 (80%) = 12 A
12 amperes x 125% = 15 A

Do you see the reciprocal relationship here?

In the question above, 6 amperes x 125% = 7.5 amperes.

The switch shall be rated at least 7.5 amperes. Since the question is asking for the "minimum" rating, the correct answer is D.

Note the lowest rated standard AC Snap Switch is 15 amperes so that is what will likely be installed in an actual installation; however, the question is asking what is the minimum rating.

▶ 3. The correct answer is D.

QUESTION 7. A 15 or 20 ampere, 125-volt receptacle must be provided with ground fault circuit-interrupter protection when is located within which of the following distances from a bathtub or a shower stall:

A. Where installed within 1.22 m (4 ft) of the outside edge of the bathtub or shower stall
B. Where installed within 1.8 m (6 ft) of the outside edge of the bathtub or shower stall
C. Where installed within 914 mm (3 ft) of the outside edge of the bathtub or shower stall
D. Where installed within 2.5 m (8 ft) of the outside edge of the bathtub or shower stall

ANSWER _____

PROCEDURE TO ESTABLISH ANSWER
The question is about ground-fault circuit-interrupter protection for receptacles near a bathtub or shower stall.

▶ 1. In Index, find "Ground-fault circuit-interrupters" under which find "Receptacles, 210.8."

▶ 2. In 210.8(A) find 210.8(A)(8) which requires that GFCI protection be provided for all 15 or 20 ampere, 125 volt receptacles located within 1.8 m (6 ft) of a bathtub or shower stall.

▶ 3. The correct answer is B.

Note: Traditionally we think of the bathtub or shower stall as being located in a bathroom where GFCI protection would be required by 210.8(A)(1). However, it is not uncommon to have a private bathtub or a shower/steam unit located in the master bedroom of an upscale single family dwelling.

QUESTION 8. Which one of the following statements regarding the Class 2 cable between a thermostat and a forced-air furnace is NOT true?

A. The Class 2 cable is permitted to be secured to the raceway containing the furnace power supply conductors.
B. The Class 2 cable is permitted to be installed within 50 mm (2 in.) of nonmetallic-sheathed cable

containing the furnace power supply conductors.
C. The Class 2 cable may be installed within the same raceway with the furnace power supply conductors.
D. The Class 2 cable may be located within the furnace wiring compartment with the power supply conductors provided there is at least a 6 mm (¼ in.) separation between the conductors.

ANSWER _____

PROCEDURE TO ESTABLISH ANSWER
The question is about the separation of Class 2 cable/circuit conductors from the power supply conductors.

▶ 1. In Index, find "Class 1, 2, and 3 circuits" which refers to "Remote-control, signaling, and power limited circuits."

▶ 2. In Index, find "Remote-control, signaling, and power-limited circuits" under which find "Class 2 and Class 3 circuits, 725–Part III" under which find "Installation, 725.133 through 725.141."

▶ 3. Section 725.133 refers to 725.135 through 725.143 for installation of Class 2 and Class 3 circuits.

▶ 4. 725.136(A) does not permit Class 2 conductors to be placed in raceway with power circuits unless allowed in 725.136 (B) through (I). There is no permission granted for being in the same conduit as the power circuit conductors. Answer C is not true.

▶ 5. Section 725.136(I)(1) requires a minimum spacing of 50 mm (2 in.) unless the power conductors are in a raceway or Type NM cable. Answer B is true.

▶ 6. Section 725.136(D)(1) permits the Class 2 conductors to be located within the furnace wiring compartment with the power supply conductors provided there is at least a 6 mm (¼ in.) separation between the conductors. Answer D is true.

▶ 7. To verify Answer A, we are considering securing of Cables. In the Index find "Cables" under which find "Secured, 300.11, etc."

▶ 8. Section 300.11(B)(2) allows raceways containing power circuits to support Class 2 circuits serving the same equipment. Answer A is true.

▶ 9. The correct answer is C.

QUESTION 9. The purpose of GFCIs installed in dwellings is to:

A. protect persons from shock hazard
B. protect the equipment connected to the GFCI from lightning discharges
C. protect the branch-circuit conductors from overload
D. protect the branch-circuit conductors from a ground fault

ANSWER _____

PROCEDURE TO ESTABLISH ANSWER
The question is about ground-fault circuit interrupters.

▶ 1. In Index, find "Ground-fault circuit interrupters" under which find "Definition, Art. 100–I."

▶ 2. The Article 100 definition confirms that the purpose is intended for the protection of personnel.

▶ 3. The correct answer is A.

QUESTION 10. All of the following 125-volt, single-phase, 15- and 20-ampere receptacles at a dwelling unit are required to have ground-fault circuit-interrupter protection EXCEPT:

A. receptacles in bathrooms
B. receptacles serving both kitchen peninsular and island counters
C. receptacles in an accessory building with a floor at grade
D. receptacles within 8 feet of a laundry sink in a first floor laundry room

ANSWER _____

PROCEDURE TO ESTABLISH ANSWER
The question is about ground-fault circuit-interrupter protection for receptacles.

▶ 1. In Index, find "Ground-fault circuit-interrupters" under which find "Receptacles, 210.8."

▶ 2. Sections 210.8(A)(1), (2), and (6) provide requirements for GFCI protection of receptacles in bathrooms, accessory buildings and kitchen counters.

▶ 3. Section 210.8(7) requires GFCI protection of receptacles within six feet of a laundry sink. Eight feet exceeds the requirement, but it is still important to be aware of the requirement.

▶ 4. The correct answer is D.

QUESTION 11. In a dwelling unit, what is the maximum allowable distance between a laundry receptacle outlet and the appliance it is intended to supply?

A. 600 mm (2 ft)
B. 1.2 m (4 ft)
C. 1.8 m (6 ft)
D. 2.5 m (8 ft)

ANSWER _____

PROCEDURE TO ESTABLISH ANSWER
The question is about the location of a receptacle outlet for an appliance.

▶ 1. In Index, find "Outlets" under which find "Appliance, 210.50(C)."

▶ 2. Section 210.50(C) requires appliance receptacle outlets in a dwelling to be installed within 1.8 m (6 ft) of the intended appliance.

▶ 3. The correct answer is C.

QUESTION 12. Which one of the following configurations of the window, cap or other prominent part will distinguish plug fuses of 15-ampere and lower rating from fuses of higher rating?

A. Round
B. Oval
C. Square
D. Hexagonal

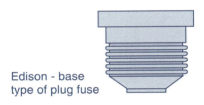

Edison - base type of plug fuse

ANSWER _____

PROCEDURE TO ESTABLISH ANSWER
The question is about the marking or configuration of plug fuses.

▶ 1. In Index, find "Fuses" under which find "Plug, Edison-base type, 240–Part V."

▶ 2. Scan Article 240 Part V and find "240.50(C)," which requires a hexagonal configuration.

▶ 3. The correct answer is D.

QUESTION 13. What is the minimum total number of receptacle outlets required for a dwelling kitchen peninsular counter 2.5 m (8 ft) long by 600 mm (2 ft) wide and an island counter 1.8 m (6 ft) long by 900 mm (3 ft) wide?

A. 2
B. 3
C. 4
D. 5

ANSWER _____

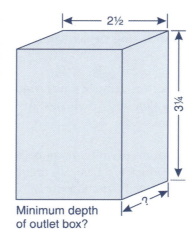
Minimum depth of outlet box?

PROCEDURE TO ESTABLISH ANSWER
Question pertains is about the number of receptacle outlets required for kitchen counter spaces.

▶ 1. In Index, find "Receptacles, etc." under which find "Outlets" under which find "Dwellings, where required, 210.52."

▶ 2. Sections 210.52(C)(2) and (3) require at least one receptacle outlet for each island and peninsular counter space with a long dimension of 600 mm (24 in.) or greater and a short dimension of 300 mm (12 in.) or greater.

▶ 3. The correct answer is A.

ANSWER _____

PROCEDURE TO ESTABLISH ANSWER
The question is about the minimum permitted depth of boxes.

▶ 1. In Index, find "Boxes" under which find "Depth, 314.24."

▶ 2. Section 314.24 requires the depth of an outlet box to be 12.7 mm (1/2 in.) minimum and 23.8 mm (15/16 in.) if the box contains a flush device.

▶ 3. The correct answer is C.

QUESTION 14. The minimum depth of an outlet box that is intended to enclose flush devices is:

A. 13 mm   (1/2 in.)
B. 50 mm   (2 in.)
C. 23.8 mm (15/16 in.)
D. 25 mm   (1 in.)

QUESTION 15. Under which one of the following conditions is it permissible for a switch or circuit breaker to disconnect the grounded conductor (neutral) of a circuit?

A. The switch or circuit breaker is at least 3.0 m (10 ft) away from the device it controls.
B. The switch or circuit breaker simultaneously disconnects all conductors of the circuit.
C. The arrangement is such that the grounded conductor is disconnected before disconnection of the ungrounded conductors.
D. The switch or circuit breaker is mounted within the same enclosure as the device it controls.

ANSWER _____

PROCEDURE TO ESTABLISH ANSWER

Question is about the disconnecting or switching of the grounded conductor.

▶ 1. In Index, find "Conductors" under which find "Grounded" under which find "Switches, disconnection, 404.2(B)."

▶ 2. Section 404.2(B) Exception permits disconnecting the grounded conductor where all circuit conductors are disconnected simultaneously, or where the device is arranged so that the grounded conductor cannot be disconnected until all of the ungrounded conductors of the circuit have been disconnected.

▶ 3. The correct answer is B.

QUESTION 16. In a dwelling unit, a 120/240-volt multiwire branch circuit supplying a split-wired kitchen duplex receptacle with the tab broken off between the ungrounded terminals is permitted if the circuit is supplied by which one of the following?

A. Two single-pole circuit breakers with approved handle ties
B. Two single-pole circuit breakers with no handle ties
C. One single-pole circuit breaker
D. Two plug fuses

ANSWER _____

PROCEDURE TO ESTABLISH ANSWER

The question is about multiwire branch circuits.

▶ 1. In Index, find "Multiwire branch circuit, 210.4."

▶ 2. Section 210.4(B) provides that a multiwire branch circuit have means to simultaneously disconnect all ungrounded conductors at the point where the branch circuit originates. In addition to two single-pole breakers with handle ties, a two-pole common trip circuit breaker also would be acceptable.

▶ 3. The correct answer is A.

QUESTION 17. All of the following are permitted to serve as the disconnecting means for a 1/3-horsepower kitchen sink garbage disposal EXCEPT:

A. a circuit breaker in the service panelboard located in the garage
B. a general-use snap switch on the wall adjacent to the kitchen counter
C. a general-use snap switch located under the sink adjacent to the disposal
D. an attachment plug and receptacle under the sink used to connect the disposal

ANSWER _____

PROCEDURE TO ESTABLISH ANSWER

The question is about disconnecting means for appliances. Specifically, this appliance has a horsepower rating so it is implied that it is a "motor-driven appliance." There are several ways to approach this through the Index, but the most direct pathway is to look at it as a motor-driven appliance.

▶ 1. In Index, find "Appliances" under which find "Motor-driven" under which find "Disconnecting means, 422.31(C)."

As noted there are additional pathways that are not as direct. In the Index you could find "Disconnecting means" under which find "Appliances, 422–Part III" or you can go to "Appliances" under which find "Disconnecting means, 422–Part III. Either way, you have to scan the Part but you end up at 422.31(C).

▶ 2. Section 422.31(C), Motor-Operated Appliances Rated over 1/8 horsepower permits the branch-circuit switch or circuit breaker to serve as the disconnecting means where it is located within sight from the appliance. Answers B & C are permitted. This section, revised for the 2011 *NEC* to clarify the requirements for a motor-driven appliance disconnecting means are more restrictive, does not permit the disconnecting means to be located out of sight of the equipment so Answer A is not permitted.

▶ 3. To verify Answer D locate 422.33, which is located directly below 422.31(C) and titled, Disconnection of Cord-and-Plug-Connected Appliances. This section permits an accessible plug and receptacle for an appliance to serve as the disconnecting means. Answer D is permitted.

▶ 4. The correct answer is A.

QUESTION 18.
Which one of the following is **not** true relative to ground-fault circuit-interrupter (GFCI) protection for 15- or 20-ampere, 125-volt, receptacles located in a dwelling unit garage?

A. A receptacle on the sidewall intended for use only with portable tools requires GFCI protection.
B. A duplex receptacle intended to supply a single freezer occupying dedicated space would require GFCI protection.
C. A locking type (twistlock) receptacle located on the surface of the garage ceiling to supply a garage door opener with a single cord and attachment plug would not require GFCI protection.
D. The ground-fault circuit-interrupter device must be installed in a readily accessible location.

ANSWER _____

PROCEDURE TO ESTABLISH ANSWER
The question is about ground-fault circuit-interrupter protection of receptacles in a dwelling unit garage.

▶ 1. In Index, find "Ground-fault circuit interrupters" under which find "Receptacles, 210.8" under which find "Garages, in dwelling units, 210.8(A)(2)."

▶ 2. The last sentence of the opening paragraph of 210.8 requires the ground-fault circuit interrupter to be located in a readily accessible location. Answer D is true.

▶ 3. Section 210.8(A)(2) requires protection for all 125-volt, single-phase, 15- and 20-ampere receptacles in dwelling unit garages regardless of their accessibility. Therefore, Answers A and B are true.

▶ 4. Section 210.8(A)(2) does not distinguish between locking and nonlocking type receptacles. It only specifies the amperage and voltage rating so 15- and 20-ampere, 125-volt, locking type receptacles are included. Answer C is not true.

▶ 5. The correct answer is C.

QUESTION 19.
Which one of the following statements regarding controlling portable motors of 1/3-horsepower or less connected by an attachment plug and receptacle is true?

A. A switch is required to control the motor.
B. The attachment plug and receptacle are permitted to control the motor.
C. A circuit breaker is required to control the motor.
D. The attachment plug and receptacle are required to be horsepower rated.

ANSWER _____

PROCEDURE TO ESTABLISH ANSWER
The question is about controlling motors so the two likely pathways are going to be "controllers" or "motors." The answers seem to be more related to the "controller" so that is probably going to end up the better choice if you are going to the Index. However, if you go to motors first in the Index, you will be directed to controllers anyway.

▶ 1. In Index, under "Controllers" find "Motor, 430–Part VII."

▶ 2. Scan Article 430 Part VII and find "430.81(B), Portable Motor of 1/3-Horsepower and Less." Knowing that motor controllers are covered in Article 430, another pathway for a more experienced *NEC* user to consider would be to go directly to Figure 430.1 which provides a layout of Article 430. Scanning Figure 430.1 you find "Motor controllers, 430.81 through 430.90, Part VII."

▶ 3. Section 430.81(B) which permits the attachment plug and receptacle to serve as the controller for a portable motor rated 1/3-horsepower or less.

▶ 4. The correct answer is B.

QUESTION 20. Which of the following dwelling unit areas does NOT require arc-fault circuit-interrupter (AFCI) protection for outlets supplied by 120-volt branch circuits?

A. Kitchen
B. Family room
C. Laundry area
D. Garage

PROCEDURE TO ESTABLISH ANSWER

The question is about AFCI protection in dwelling units.

▶ 1. In Index, find "Arc-fault circuit interrupters, Art. 210.12" under which, find "Protection, 210.12(A), 440.65, 550.25." Also find in the Index, find "Dwellings" under which find "Definition, Art. 100–Part I."

▶ 2. Section 210.12(A) states that all 120-volt, single phase, 15- and 20-ampere branch circuits supplying outlets or devices installed in the specified locations shall be protected by any of the means described in 210.12(A)(1) through (6). Scanning the paragraph we find that kitchens, family rooms and laundry areas are included. There is no mention of garages. Answers A, B and C are true. Answer D is not true.

▶ 3. The correct answer is D.

QUESTION 21. A 120/240-volt, 3-wire branch circuit in a dwelling serves a wall heater with a 1000-VA heater element (line-to-line) and a 500-VA fan (line-to-neutral). Which one of the following statements is NOT true?

A. The branch-circuit overcurrent protection may be a 2-pole common-trip circuit breaker.
B. The branch-circuit overcurrent devices may be two single-pole circuit breakers with handle ties.
C. The branch-circuit overcurrent protection may be two single-pole circuit breakers without handle ties.
D. The multiwire branch circuit may supply both the fan and heater.

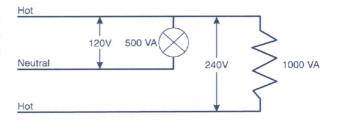

ANSWER _____

PROCEDURE TO ESTABLISH ANSWER

The question is about multiwire branch circuits and circuit breakers used as protection for the circuits.

▶ 1. In Index, find "Multiwire branch circuit, 210.4."

▶ 2. Section 210.4(C), Exception No. 2 permits a multiwire branch circuit to supply line-to-line loads where all ungrounded conductors of the circuit are opened simultaneously by the branch-circuit overcurrent device. Two single-pole circuit breakers without handle ties would not be acceptable.

▶ 3. The *Code* should also be checked for any applicable rules for circuit breakers. Therefore, in the Index, find "Circuit breakers, Art. 240."

▶ 4. Scan Article 240 and find "240.15(B), Circuit Breaker as Overcurrent Device." Section 240.15(B)(2) permits individual single-pole circuit breakers with handle ties for line-to-line connected loads of single-phase circuits. A 2-pole circuit breaker is permitted but not required by this section.

▶ 5. The correct answer is C.

QUESTION 22. Where a stairway from the first to second floor of a dwelling unit has 10 risers (steps), which one of the following arrangements complies with the *Code* for switching the stairway lighting?

A. A wall switch located at each floor level
B. A wall switch located only at the lower level
C. An occupancy sensor that has no manual override located midway up the stairs
D. An occupancy sensor that has no manual override at the first floor and a wall switch at the second floor

ANSWER _____

PROCEDURE TO ESTABLISH ANSWER
The question is about switches controlling lighting outlets at stairways.

▶ 1. In Index, find "Lighting outlets, 210.70, 314.27(A), 410.16(A), 410–Part III."

▶ 2. Section 210.70(A)(2)(c) requires a wall switch at each floor level and landing level that includes an entry way to control the lighting outlet(s) where the difference between floor levels is six risers (steps) or more.

▶ 3. The correct answer is A.

QUESTION 23. If both living units of a two-family dwelling are located at grade level, what is the minimum number of outside receptacle outlets required for the building?

A. 0
B. 1
C. 2
D. 4

ANSWER _____

PROCEDURE TO ESTABLISH ANSWER
The question is about the required number of outdoor receptacle outlets.

▶ 1. In Index, find "Receptacles" under which find "Outdoor. *see* Outdoor receptacles."

▶ 2. In Index, find "Outdoor receptacles, 210.8(A)(3), 210.52(E), 406.9, 680.22(A), 680.32."

▶ 3. Scan Sections 210.8 and 210.52 and find "210.52(E), Outdoor Outlets," which requires each unit of a two-family dwelling that is at grade level to have at least one receptacle outlet installed at the front and back of each dwelling.

▶ 4. The correct answer is D.

QUESTION 24. Which of the following statements about the ratings of control devices such as time clocks or lighting contactors is true?

A. They must be rated for the nominal circuit voltage and current that must be interrupted.
B. They must be rated for the fault current that is available at the line terminals of the equipment.
C. They must be rated for the nominal circuit voltage that the equipment operates on.
D. They must have a minimum rating of 240 volts and 30 amperes.

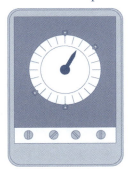

Ratings of control devices like time clocks?

ANSWER _____

PROCEDURE TO ESTABLISH ANSWER
The question is about the interrupter rating of equipment.

▶ 1. In Index, find "Interrupting rating, 110.9, 240.60(C)(3), 240.83(C)."

▶ 2. Section 110.9 requires that the equipment be rated for the nominal circuit voltage and cur-

Control Devices | **1- and 2-Family Study Guide** | 87

rent that must be interrupted and not for the fault current since they are not intended to interrupt fault current.

▶ 3. A review of 240.60(C) shows it does not apply to the question.

▶ 4. A review of 240.83(C) shows it does not apply to the question.

▶ 5. The correct answer is A.

QUESTION 25. Which of the following statements about the temperature rating of terminations is true?

A. Unless marked otherwise, the temperature rating of terminations for conductors sized 14 AWG through 2/0 AWG is 60°C
B. Unless marked otherwise, the temperature rating of terminations for conductors sized 14 AWG through 1/0 AWG is 75°C
C. Unless marked otherwise, the temperature rating of terminations for conductors sized larger than 1 AWG is 75°C
D. Unless marked otherwise, the temperature rating of terminations for conductors sized larger than 1/0 AWG is 90°C

Minimum temperature rating of terminations?

ANSWER _____

PROCEDURE TO ESTABLISH ANSWER
The question is about temperature rating of terminations.

▶ 1. In Index, find "Connections" under which find "Temperature limitations, 110.14(C), 110.40" or look in Index for "Terminals" under which find "Connections to, 110.14, 250.8, 250.68."

▶ 2. Section 110.14(C) applies to the question under consideration.

▶ 3. Section 110.14(C)(1) indicates that unless marked otherwise, terminations for conductors sized 14 AWG through 1 AWG are rated 60°C.

▶ 4. Section 110.14(C)(1)(b) indicates that unless marked otherwise, terminations for conductors larger than 1 AWG are rated 75°C.

▶ 5. The correct answer is C.

QUESTION 26. Dimmer switches are permitted to control all of the following equipment or devices EXCEPT:

A. incandescent luminaires
B. fluorescent luminaires where the dimmer is listed for the purpose
C. track lighting incandescent luminaires
D. single or duplex receptacles

ANSWER _____

PROCEDURE TO ESTABLISH ANSWER
The question is about equipment permitted to be controlled by dimmer switches.

▶ 1. In Index, find "Dimmers" under which find "Switch, 404.9(B), 404.14(E)."

▶ 2. Section 404.9 refers to grounding of snap switches. Next, find Section 404.14(E), which indicates that general use dimmer switches shall be used to control only permanently installed incandescent luminaires unless listed for the control of other loads…"

▶ 3. The correct answer is D.

QUESTION 27. All of the following statements about switches are true EXCEPT:

A. Where no grounding means exists in a snap-switch enclosure or where the wiring method does not include or provide an equipment grounding conductor, a snap switch without a connection to the equipment grounding conductors is permitted for replacement purposes only. Where installed within reach of earth, a concrete floor, or other grounded surface, the faceplate form the switch shall be a nonmetallic, noncombustible material. GFCI protection is not required if a metal faceplate is used.

B. A motor load may not exceed 80 percent of the ampere rating of an AC general-use snap switch at its rated voltage.

C. Snap switches rated 20 amperes or less directly connected to aluminum conductors shall be listed and marked CO/ALR.

D. A circuit breaker is permitted to be used as a switch if it has the required number of poles.

ANSWER _____

PROCEDURE TO ESTABLISH ANSWER
The question is about the use and grounding of switches and switch plates.

▶ 1. In Index, find "Switches, Art. 404" under which find "AC general use snap switch, 404.14(A)." Also in the Index, find "Snap Switches," under which find "Grounding, 404.9(B).

▶ 2. In 404.9(B) Exception, we find that Answer A would be true, except that GFCI protection is required for an ungrounded 2-wire circuit within reach of a grounded surface when a metal faceplate is installed over the snap switch. Note: a snap switch is a standard type light switch used for commercial and residential construction. Answer A is not true.

▶ 3. In 404.14, Rating and Use of snap switches, 404.14(A)(3) confirms that Answer B is true.

▶ 4. In 404.14(C), we find that Answer C is true.

▶ 5. And finally, in 404.11, we find that Answer D is true.

▶ 6. The correct answer is A.

QUESTION 28. Which of the following statements is NOT true about requirements for arc-fault circuit-interrupter (AFCI) protection of 120-volt bedroom branch circuits in dwelling units?

A. Where branch circuits are extended more than 2.5 m (8 ft) AFCI protection shall be provided at the origin of the branch circuit or at the first receptacle outlet in the existing branch circuit.

B. AFCI protection shall not be required where the extension of the existing conductors is not more than 1.8 m (6 ft.) and does not include any additional outlets or devices.

C. The AFCI may be installed at the first outlet in a new installation if the circuit conductors to the AFCI are installed in a metal raceway or a Type MC or steel armor AC cable meeting the requirements of 250.118.

D. A bedroom branch circuit that is AFCI-protected is permitted to supply electrical power to a hallway receptacle outlet.

ANSWER _____

PROCEDURE TO ESTABLISH ANSWER
The question is about AFCI protection in dwelling unit bedrooms.

▶ 1. In Index, find "Arc-fault circuit interrupters, Art. 210.12" under which, find "Protection, 210.12(A), 440.65, 550.25." Also find in the Index, find "Dwellings" under which find "Definition, Art. 100–Part I."

▶ 2. In 210.12(A) and (B), we find that Answer A is false and Answer B is true. The Exception to 210.12(B)(1) & (2), new in the 2014 *NEC*, permits a branch circuit to be extended up to 1.8 m (6 ft) without providing AFCI protection provided there are no additional outlets being installed.

▶ 3 We also find that 210.12(A)(5) permits an MC cable meeting the grounding requirements of 250.118 and metal raceways provided metal junction boxes are used for the portion of the circuit between the branch circuit overcurrent device and the first outlet. Answer C is true.

▶ 4. There is nothing in the *Code* to prohibit a hallway receptacle outlet, for example, from being supplied with electrical power from a bedroom AFCI circuit, providing that the minimum volt-ampere per sq. meter (square foot) requirements in Table 220.12 are not exceeded. Answer D is true.

▶ 5. The correct answer is A.

QUESTION 29. Which of the following is NOT permitted as a means of providing arc-fault circuit-interrupter (AFCI) protection for 120-volt branch circuits where required in dwelling units?

A. A listed combination type arc-fault circuit interrupter, installed to provide protection of the entire branch circuit.
B. A listed outlet branch circuit type arc-fault circuit interrupter installed at the first outlet on the branch circuit in combination with a listed branch circuit overcurrent protective device where all of the specified conditions are met.
C. Listed metal or nonmetallic conduit or tubing or Type MC Cable encased in not less than 50mm (2 in.) of concrete for the portion of the branch circuit between the branch circuit overcurrent device and the first outlet, with a listed outlet branch circuit type AFCI installed at the first outlet to provide protection for the remaining portion of the branch circuit.
D. A listed branch/feeder type AFCI installed at the origin of the branch circuit in combination with a listed outlet branch circuit type arc-fault circuit interrupter installed at any outlet box on the branch circuit.

PROCEDURE TO ESTABLISH ANSWER
The question is about AFCI protection in dwelling units.

▶ 1. In Index, find "Arc-fault circuit interrupters, Art. 210.12" under which, find "Protection, 210.12(A), 440.65, 550.25." Also find in the Index, find "Dwellings" under which find "Definition, Art. 100–Part I."

▶ 2. Section 210.12(A) states that all 120-volt, single phase, 15- and 20-ampere branch circuits supplying outlets or devices installed in the specified locations shall be protected by any of the means described in 210.12(A)(1) through (6).

▶ 3. Section 210.12(A)(1) permits the traditional listed combination type arc-fault circuit interrupter installed at the source. Answer A is true.

▶ 4. Section 210.12(A)(4) permits a listed outlet branch circuit type arc-fault circuit interrupter installed at the first outlet on the branch circuit in combination with a listed branch circuit overcurrent protective device where all of the conditions specified in (a)-(d) are met. This includes being listed and identified as a "System Combination" type AFCI. Answer B is true.

▶ 5. Section 210.12(A)(6) permits listed metal or nonmetallic conduit or tubing or Type MC Cable encased in not less than 50mm (2 in.) of concrete for the portion of the branch circuit between the branch circuit overcurrent device and the first outlet, with a listed outlet branch circuit type AFCI installed at the first outlet. Answer C is true.

▶ 6. Section 210.12(A)(2) permits a listed branch/feeder type AFCI installed at the origin of the branch circuit in combination with a listed outlet branch circuit type arc-fault circuit interrupter installed at the first outlet box on the branch circuit. The first outlet box must be marked as such. Answer D is not true as it states the outlet branch circuit type AFCI may be installed at any outlet on the circuit.

▶ 7. The correct answer is D.

8 Utilization Equipment

QUESTION 1. Which one of the following statements about a built-in dishwasher in a dwelling is NOT true?

A. The flexible cord supplying the dishwasher may be 750 mm (30 in.) long.
B. A flexible cord supplying the dishwasher may be 900 mm (36 in.) long.
C. A flexible cord supplying the dishwasher must be terminated with a grounding-type attachment plug.
D. The receptacle for the dishwasher may be located in the adjacent space where the disposal is located.

ANSWER _____

PROCEDURE TO ESTABLISH ANSWER
The question is about flexible cords used with dishwashers.

▶ 1. In Index, look for "Dishwashers." Not finding this term, look for "Cords" under which find "Flexible, Art. 400, 422.16, 422.23."

▶ 2. Search 422.16, Flexible Cords, and find "422.16(B), Specific Appliances."

▶ 3. Section 422.16(B)(2)(2) provides the requirements for flexible cords for built-in dishwashers. Note that the length of the cord must be 0.9 m to 1.2 m (3 ft to 4 ft). Answer B is correct. Answer A is incorrect.

▶ 4 Section 422.16(B)(2)(1) requires the cord to be terminated with a grounding-type attachment plug. Answer C is correct

▶ 5 Section 422.16(B)(2)(4) states that the receptacle for the dishwasher may be located in the adjacent space where the disposal is located. Answer (D) is true.

▶ 6. The correct answer is A.

Utilization Equipment | 1- and 2-Family Study Guide | 91

QUESTION 2. What is the maximum allowable load on a 240-volt electric resistance element heating branch circuit protected by a 30-ampere circuit breaker?

A. 3000 VA
B. 5760 VA
C. 7200 VA
D. 9000 VA

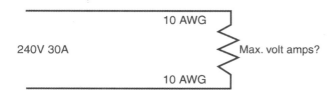

ANSWER _____

PROCEDURE TO ESTABLISH ANSWER
The question is about fixed electric space-heating equipment load on a branch circuit.

▶ 1. In Index, find "Fixed electric space-heating equipment" under which find "Branch circuits for, 424.3."

▶ 2. Section 424.3(B) states that "fixed space-heating equipment shall be considered continuous load." Article 100 defines a *continuous load* as a load where the maximum current is expected to continue for 3 hours or more.

▶ 3. In Index, find "Continuous load" under which find "Applications, 210.19(A), 210.20(A), 215.2(A)." Section 210.19(A)(1) requires the ampacity of the branch-circuit conductors to be not less than 125 percent of the total load. Section 210.20(A) requires the rating of the overcurrent device to be not less than 125 percent of the total load.

▶ 4. Calculate the VA using the following formula:

Circuit VA = 30 amps x 240 volts = 7,200 VA
7,200 VA x .80 = 5760 VA

Double check:
5760 VA /240 volts = 24 amperes
24 amperes x 125% = 30 amperes, the branch circuit rating.

▶ 5. The correct answer is B.

QUESTION 3. Electric water heaters having a capacity of 450 L (120 gal) or less shall have a branch-circuit rating not less than what percentage of the nameplate rating?

A. 80 percent
B. 100 percent
C. 125 percent
D. 150 percent

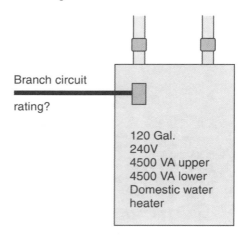

ANSWER _____

PROCEDURE TO ESTABLISH ANSWER
The question is about water heater branch-circuit ratings and protection.

▶ 1. In Index, find "Water heaters, 422.11(E), 422.11(F)(3), 422.13."

▶ 2. Section 422.13 states that a fixed storage-type water heater having a capacity of 450 L (120 gal) or less shall be considered a continuous load.

▶ 3 In Index, find "Continuous load" under which find "Applications, 210.19(A), 210.20(A), 215.2(A)." Section 210.20(A) requires the rating of the overcurrent device to be not less than 125 percent of the total load.

▶ 4. The correct answer is C.

QUESTION 4. Which one of the following statements regarding ceiling-suspended paddle fans is NOT true?

A. A fan weighing less than 32 kg (70 lb) may be supported solely by an outlet box listed and identified for fan support.
B. Outlet boxes designed to support ceiling-suspended fans weighing more than 16 kg (35 lb), the required marking shall include the maximum weight supported.
C. Where separately switched, ungrounded conductors are provided to a ceiling-mounted outlet box, the outlet box must be listed for support of ceiling-suspended fan where the location on the ceiling is acceptable for mounting a fan.
D. A combination fan and luminaire weighing more than 16 kg (35 lb) is not required to be supported independently of a standard outlet box

ANSWER _____

PROCEDURE TO ESTABLISH ANSWER
The question is about support of ceiling fans.

▶ 1. In Index, find "Ceiling fans" under which find "Support of, 314.27(C), 422.18."

▶ 2. Section 314.27(C) prohibits outlet boxes from being used as the sole support for ceiling (paddle) fans unless listed for the application and from supporting ceiling-suspended fans in excess of 70 lbs. Answer A is true.

This section also requires outlet boxes designed to support ceiling fans in excess of 16 kg (35 lb) to include the maximum weight to be supported. Answer B is true.

▶ 3. The last paragraph of 314.27(C) requires the outlet box to be listed of supporting ceiling-suspended fans where spare separately switched conductors are run to the box and the box is mounted in a location that would accept a ceiling-suspended fan. Answer C is true.

▶ 4. Because 314.27(C) requires boxes to be listed in order to be the sole support of ceiling-suspended fan, the fan would have to be supported independently of a standard box. Answer D isn't true.

Note: Section 422.18, Support of Ceiling-Suspended Paddle Fans, requires ceiling-suspended (paddle) fans to be supported independently of an outlet box, unless the box is listed or the support system is identified for the purpose and installed in accordance with 314.27(C).

▶ 5. The correct answer is D.

QUESTION 5. Where calculating a residential load by the standard method, what minimum volt-ampere load is required to be used for the electric clothes dryer where its size is not known?

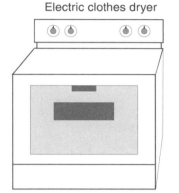

Minimum load for calculations?

A. 1500
B. 3000
C. 4500
D. 5000

ANSWER _____

PROCEDURE TO ESTABLISH ANSWER
The question is about the required load for clothes dryers.

▶ 1. In Index, find "Clothes dryers" under which find "Calculations for, 220.53."

▶ 2. Section 220.54 requires the load for household electric clothes dryers in a dwelling unit to be 5000 watts (volt-amperes) or nameplate rating, whichever is larger.

▶ 3. The correct answer is D.

QUESTION 6. A receptacle outlet for a permanently connected and fastened-in-place dwelling unit kitchen trash compactor with nameplate rating of six amperes may be connected to which one of the following branch circuits?

A. A 20-ampere kitchen lighting circuit supplying a single ceiling-mounted incandescent fixture
B. A 15-ampere circuit supplying a refrigerator
C. A 20-ampere small appliance circuit supplying countertop receptacles
D. A 20-ampere small appliance circuit supplying dining room receptacles

ANSWER _____

PROCEDURE TO ESTABLISH ANSWER
The question is about a trash compactor installed on a kitchen small appliance or lighting branch circuit.

▶ 1. In Index, find "Branch circuits" under which find "Small appliance, 210.11(C)(1)."

▶ 2. Section 210.11(C)(1) requires two or more 20-ampere small-appliance branch circuits for receptacles specified in 210.52(B) for small appliance load.

▶ 3. Section 210.52(B)(1) requires the small appliance branch circuits in the kitchen and dining room to serve only receptacle outlets required by 210.52(A), wall outlets, and 210.52(C), countertop outlets and refrigeration equipment. Answers C & D are incorrect.

▶ 4. Section 210.52(B)(2) provides that the circuits specified in (B)(1) shall have no other outlets; thus the compactor is not permitted on them. This further confirms that Answers C & D are incorrect and it also confirms that Answer B is incorrect. Section 210.52(B)(1) Exception No. 2 permits the refrigerator to be on a 15-ampere individual branch circuit, but 210.52(B)(2) states there shall be no other outlets so the compactor is not allowed to be supplied by the 15-ampere refrigerator circuit. Additionally, this Exception specifically states an "individual" branch circuit which Article 100 defines as supplying only one utilization equipment.

▶ 5. Answer A is regarding permissible loads on a branch circuit; so in the Index find "Loads" under which find Branch circuits. Under branch circuits, find "Permissible, 210.23."

▶ 6. Section 210.23(A) for permissible loads on branch circuits other than the small appliance circuits permits the lighting circuit to supply utilization equipment as long as the total rating of utilization equipment fastened in place does not exceed 50 percent of the branch-circuit rating as indicated in 210.23(A)(2). Under this condition, the trash compactor could be connected to the kitchen lighting branch circuit.

▶ 7. The correct answer is A.

QUESTION 7. The minimum horizontal clearance for a ceiling surface-mounted fluorescent luminaire from the storage area in a clothes closet is:

A. 75 mm   (3 in.)
B. 150 mm   (6 in.)
C. 300 mm   (12 in.)
D. 450 mm   (18 in.)

ANSWER _____

PROCEDURE TO ESTABLISH ANSWER
The question is about clearances of fluorescent luminaires in clothes closets.

▶ 1. In Index, find "Clothes closets" under which find "Luminaires, 410.16."

▶ 2. Section 410.16(C)(2) provides that surface-mounted fluorescent luminaires installed on the ceiling shall be permitted to be installed in a clothes closet, provided there is a minimum clearance of six inches between the luminaire and nearest point of a storage area.

▶ 3. The correct answer is B.

QUESTION 8. A single branch circuit supplies: two 1500-volt-ampere and one 1000-volt-ampere 240-volt electric baseboard heaters. The branch circuit shall have an ampere rating of not less than:

A. 15 amperes
B. 20 amperes
C. 25 amperes
D. 30 amperes

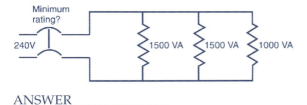

ANSWER _____

PROCEDURE TO ESTABLISH ANSWER
The question is about electric space-heating equipment.

▶ 1. In Index, find "Fixed electric space heating equipment" under which find "Branch circuits for, 424.3."

▶ 2. Section 424.3(B) states that fixed space-heating equipment shall be considered continuous load. Article 100 defines a *continuous load* as a load where the maximum current is expected to continue for 3 hours or more.

▶ 3. In Index, find "Continuous load" under which find "Applications, 210.19(A), 210.20(A), 215.2(A)." Section 210.20(A) requires the rating of the overcurrent device to be not less than 125 percent of the total load.

▶ 4. Calculate the branch circuit ampere rating by using the following formula:
1500 VA + 1500 VA + 1000 VA = 4000 VA/240V = 16.6 amperes
16.6A x 125 percent = 20.75 amperes, so a minimum of a 25-ampere branch circuit is required.

Note: Section 240.4(B) states that conductors must be protected at their ampacities and permits the next standard overcurrent device under the prescribed conditions. One of the conditions is where the conductors are not a standard size. See 240.6 for standard rating of fuses and circuit breakers. As 25 amperes is a standard size, rounding up to 30 amperes is not permitted.

▶ 5. The correct answer is C.

QUESTION 9. Which one of the following methods is NOT acceptable for mounting or securing electrical equipment to masonry or drywall surface on which it is mounted?

A. Anchor bolts
B. Drive pins
C. Wooden plugs
D. Toggle bolts

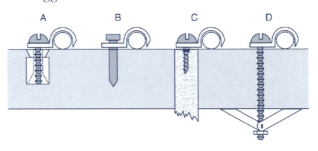

ANSWER _____

PROCEDURE TO ESTABLISH ANSWER
The question is about requirements of installation.

▶ 1. In Index, find "Mounting of equipment, 110.13, 314.23, 404.9(A), 404.10, 410–Part IV."

▶ 2. Section 110.13(A) does not permit the use of wooden plugs.

▶ 3. The correct answer is C.

QUESTION 10. The total computed load for a branch circuit supplying an appliance fastened in place with a five-ampere motor load and a 10-ampere lighting load is:

A. 15 amperes
B. 16.25 amperes
C. 17.50 amperes
D. 20 amperes

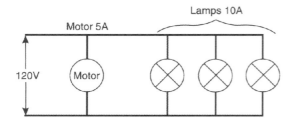

ANSWER _____

PROCEDURE TO ESTABLISH ANSWER
The question is about a branch-circuit combination load.

▶ 1. In Index, find "Branch circuits" under which find "Maximum loads, 220.18."

▶ 2. Section 220.18(A) requires in the last sentence that the total branch circuit computed load shall be based on 125 percent of the largest motor plus the sum of the other loads.

1.25 x 5 amps + 10 amps = 16.25 amperes

Note: Here, we are calculating branch-circuit load only, not sizing the branch circuit at this moment.

▶ 3. The correct answer is B.

QUESTION 11. A main circuit breaker mounted inside of a cabinet shall have the center of the grip of its operating handle in its highest position not more than what distance above the floor?

A. 1.5 m   (5 ft)
B. 1.8 m   (6 ft)
C. 2.0 m   (6 ft 7 in.)
D. 2.5 m   (8 ft)

ANSWER _____

PROCEDURE TO ESTABLISH ANSWER
The question is about the mounting height of circuit breaker handles.

▶ 1. In Index, find "Circuit breakers" under which find "Accessibility and grouping, 404.8" as the only one that appears applicable. Remember that overcurrent devices are generally required to be readily accessible.

▶ 2. Section 404.8(A) provides that the center of the grip in its highest position is not to be more than 2.0 m (6 ft 7 in.) above the floor.

▶ 3. The correct answer is C.

QUESTION 12. The maximum cord- and plug-connected load permitted to be connected to a 15- or 20-ampere circuit, using a 15-ampere rated receptacle is:

A. 7.5 amperes
B. 12 amperes
C. 15 amperes
D. 20 amperes

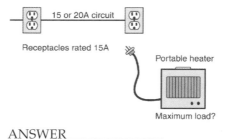

ANSWER _____

96 | 1- and 2-Family Study Guide | Utilization Equipment

PROCEDURE TO ESTABLISH ANSWER

The question is about cord- and plug-connected load on receptacles.

▶ 1. In Index, find "Receptacles, cord connectors, and attachment plugs (caps)" under which find "Maximum cord- and plug-connected load to, 210.21(B)(2), Table 210.21(B)(2), 210.23."

▶ 2. Table 210.21(B)(2) provides that the circuit rating of 15 or 20 amperes utilizing a 15-ampere rated receptacle shall be limited to a maximum of a 12-ampere load.

▶ 3. The correct answer is B.

QUESTION 13. In a new dwelling, metal outlet or junction boxes that are part of the circuit supplying counter-mounted cooking units shall be permitted to be grounded by all of the following EXCEPT:

A. an insulated grounded conductor
B. a metal raceway that is an equipment grounding conductor in accordance with 250.118 and contains the circuit conductors to the unit
C. the bare conductor used for equipment grounding in Type SE cable
D. the bare equipment grounding conductor in Type NM cable

ANSWER _____

PROCEDURE TO ESTABLISH ANSWER

The question is about grounding of ranges, boxes, etc.

▶ 1. In Index, find "Grounding" under which find "Ranges and similar appliances, 250.140."

▶ 2. Section 250.140 requires that outlet or junction boxes that are part of the circuit supplying cook tops, etc., shall be connected to an equipment grounding conductor as specified in 250.134 or 250.138.

Section 250.134(A) requires connection to an equipment grounding conductor, unless connection to the grounded conductor is permitted by 250.140, etc. Connection to the equipment grounding conductor is required for new installations. Equipment grounding by connection to the grounded conductor is only permitted for existing installations where an equipment grounding conductor is not present in the outlet or junction box.

▶ 3. The correct answer is A.

QUESTION 14. Which one of the following statements regarding calculating the feeder load for fixed appliances in dwelling units is true?

A. A 70 percent demand factor may be used where there are three appliances.
B. A 75 percent demand factor may be used where there are more than three appliances.
C. An 80 percent demand factor is required to be used where there are four or more appliances.
D. A 100 percent demand factor is required regardless of the number of appliances.

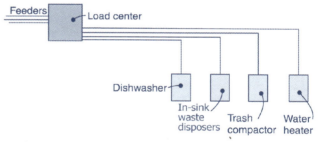

ANSWER _____

PROCEDURE TO ESTABLISH ANSWER

The question is about calculating feeder loads for several fixed appliances in dwellings..

▶ 1. In Index, find "Loads" under which find "Feeders, calculation of, 215.2(A), Article 220 Annex D."

▶ 2. Section 215.2(A) requires feeders to have sufficient ampacity to supply the load calculated in accordance with Parts III, IV, and V of Article 220.

▶ 3. Scan Article 220, Part II, and find "220.53, Appliance Load — Dwelling Unit(s)," permitting a demand factor of 75 percent to the nameplate rating of four or more appliances fastened in place except ranges, clothes dryers, space-heating and air-conditioning equipment.

▶ 4. The correct answer is B.

QUESTION 15.
Which one of the following types of luminaires is NOT permitted in clothes closets?

A. Open tube fluorescent
B. Open lamp incandescent
C. Recessed fluorescent
D. Surface-mounted incandescent with enclosed lamp

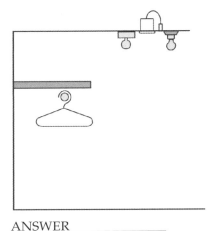

ANSWER _____

PROCEDURE TO ESTABLISH ANSWER
The question pertains to type of luminaires permitted in clothes closets.

▶ 1. In Index, find "Clothes closets" under which find "Luminaires, 410.16."

▶ 2. Section 410.16(B) lists luminaires not permitted.

▶ 3. Section 410.16(B) does not permit open or partially enclosed incandescent luminaires.

▶ 4. The correct answer is B.

QUESTION 16.
All of the following are permitted for a recessed luminaire not identified as suitable for direct contact with insulation EXCEPT:

A. Recessed portions of the luminaire (fixture) enclosure other than support points shall be spaced at least 13 mm (½ in.) from combustible material.
B. Thermal insulation shall not be installed within 75 mm (3 in.) of the luminaire (fixture) enclosure.
C. Recessed portions of a fluorescent luminaire (fixture) enclosure may be in contact with combustible materials such as ceiling joists.
D. Thermal insulation shall not be installed within 75mm (3 in.) of an LED driver or power supply.

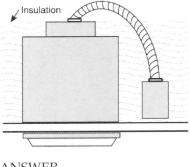

ANSWER _____

PROCEDURE TO ESTABLISH ANSWER
The question is about recessed lighting fixtures.

▶ 1. In Index, find "Recessed luminaires, 410–X, 410– XI" under which find "Clearances, installation, 410.116."

▶ 2. Section 410.116(A)(1) requires recessed portions of fixture enclosures, regardless of type of fixture, to be at least 13 mm (½ in.) from combustible material. Answer A is permitted, Answer B is not permitted.

▶ 3. Section 410.116(B) requires that thermal insulation not be installed above a luminaire or within 75 mm (3 in.) of the luminaire unless listed Type IC, enclosure, LED driver, etc. Answers B & D are permitted.

▶ 4. The correct answer is C.

QUESTION 17. All of the following statements regarding flexible cord for a kitchen in-sink waste disposer are true EXCEPT:

A. The cord length shall be 0.9 m to 1.2 m (3 ft to 4 ft).
B. The cord shall be terminated with a grounding-type attachment plug.
C. The receptacle for the cord attachment shall be located to avoid physical damage to the cord.
D. The receptacle for the disposer shall be accessible.

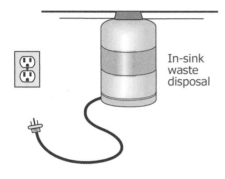

ANSWER _____

PROCEDURE TO ESTABLISH ANSWER
The question is about a flexible cord for a specific appliance.

▶ 1. In Index, find "Appliances" under which find "Installation, 422–Part II."

▶ 2. Scan Article 422, Part II, and find "422.16(B)(1), Electrically Operated Kitchen In-Sink Waste Disposers."

▶ 3. Section 422.16(B)(1)(1) requires the flexible cord to be terminated with a grounding type attachment plug. Answer B is true.

▶ 4. Section 422.16(B)(1)(2) provides that the cord length shall be not less than 450 mm (18 in.) and not over 900 mm (36 in.). Answer A is not true.

▶ 5. Section 422.16(B)(1)(4) specifies the receptacle must be accessible. Answer D is true.

▶ 6. The correct answer is A.

QUESTION 18. A built-in dishwasher in the kitchen of a single-family dwelling receives its power from a 15-ampere circuit breaker in a service panel in the basement. The disconnecting means for the dishwasher is permitted to be all of the following EXCEPT:

A. a built-in unit switch with a marked "off" position that disconnects all ungrounded conductors
B. a 1.2 m (4 ft) long cord plugged into an accessible receptacle
C. a general-use snap switch mounted on the wall within sight of the dishwasher
D. a built-in unit switch that operates a control circuit and does not directly disconnect the ungrounded conductors

ANSWER _____

PROCEDURE TO ESTABLISH ANSWER
This question is about the disconnecting means for an appliance.

▶ 1. In Index, find "Appliances" under which find "Motor driven" under which find "Disconnecting means, 422.31(C)"

▶ 2. Section 422.31(C) permits the circuit switch or circuit breaker to be the disconnecting means provided it is within sight of the appliance. Answer C is permitted.

▶ 3. To verify Answer A find 422.34, Unit Switches as Disconnecting Means." Section 422.34 permits a built-in unit switch with a marked "off" position and which opens all ungrounded conductors to serve as the disconnecting means provided any necessary occupancy requirements in 422.34 (A)–(D) are met. Answer A is permitted.

▶ 4. Also scan Article 422, Part III, and find "422.33, Disconnection of Cord- and Plug-Connected Appliances," which recognizes, in accordance with 422.33(A), an attachment plug and receptacle for the disconnecting means.

▶ 5. To confirm if the 1.2 m (4 ft) cord length is acceptable, scan Article 422, Part II, and "422.16, Flexible Cords," under which 422.16(B)(2)(2) permits the length of the cord to be 0.9 m to 1.2 m (3 ft to 4 ft). Answer B is true.

▶ 6. The correct answer is D.

QUESTION 19. All of the following items are prohibited within a zone measured 900 mm (3 ft) horizontally and 2.5 m (8 ft) vertically from the top of a bathtub rim EXCEPT:

A. a ceiling-suspended (paddle) fan
B. a surface-mounted incandescent luminaire
C. lighting track
D. a hanging luminaire

ANSWER _____

PROCEDURE TO ESTABLISH ANSWER
The question is about luminaires and other equipment above bathtubs.

▶ 1. In Index, find "Bathtubs" under which find, "Luminaires (lighting fixtures), 410.10(D), 550.14(D), 551.53(B)."

▶ 2. Section 410.10(D) prohibits hanging luminaires, lighting track and ceiling-suspended (paddle) fans in the zone described in the question. Surface-mounted incandescent luminaires are not prohibited, though it should be noted that they shall be listed for damp or wet locations, depending upon the direction of the shower spray.

▶ 3. The correct answer is B.

QUESTION 20. All of the following statements regarding cord- and plug-connected wall-mounted ovens and counter-mounted cooking units are true EXCEPT:

A. Cord- and plug-connection is permitted for ease in servicing.
B. An accessible plug and receptacle combination is permitted as the appliance disconnecting means.
C. Plug and receptacle must be approved for the temperature of the space in which they are located.
D. Cord length shall be between 0.9 and 1.2m (3 ft and 4 ft).

ANSWER _____

PROCEDURE TO ESTABLISH ANSWER
The question is about wall-mounted ovens.

▶ 1. In Index, find "Ovens, wall-mounted" under which find "Connections, 422.16(B)(3), 422.31(B)."

▶ 2. The opening paragraph of 422.16(B)(3) permits cord-and-plug-connection for the ease of servicing or installation. Answer A is true.

▶ 3. The second paragraph of 422.16(B)(3) requires the separable connector of plug and receptacle to be approved for the temperature of the space where it is located. Answer C is true.

▶ 4. To verify Answer B, find 422.33(A) which permits an accessible plug and receptacle for an appliance to be the disconnecting means. Answer B is true.

▶ 5. Section 422.16(B) permits cord- and plug-connections but does not specify a cord length. Answer D is false.

▶ 6. The correct answer is D.

QUESTION 21. A branch circuit supplying a single non-motor-operated appliance rated, but not marked, at 16.7 amperes shall be protected by an overcurrent device rated at not more than which one of the following percentages of the appliance rating?

A. 100 percent
B. 125 percent
C. 150 percent
D. 175 percent

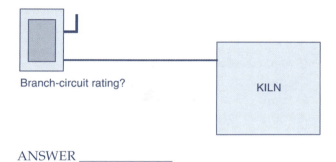

Branch-circuit rating?   KILN

ANSWER _____

PROCEDURE TO ESTABLISH ANSWER
The question is about appliance overcurrent protection.

▶ 1. In Index, find "Appliances" under which find "Overcurrent protection, Single, 422.11, 210.20, 422.11(E)."

▶ 2. Section 422.11(E)(3) provides that a single non-motor-operated appliance rated over 13.3 A and has no marked overcurrent protection rating on the nameplate shall not be protected at more than 150 percent of its rating.

▶ 3. The correct answer is C.

QUESTION 22. Resistance-type electrical space heating units shall have the heating elements subdivided when the unit rated load exceeds:

A. 30 amperes
B. 40 amperes
C. 48 amperes
D. 55 amperes

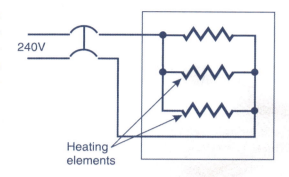

Heating elements

ANSWER _____

PROCEDURE TO ESTABLISH ANSWER
The question is about fixed electrical space heating.

▶ 1. In Index, find "Fixed electric space-heating equipment" under which find "Overcurrent protection for, 424.22, etc."

▶ 2. Section 424.22(B) provides that equipment rated more than 48 amperes, and employing resistance-type heating elements, shall have the heating elements subdivided.

▶ 3. The correct answer is C.

QUESTION 23. Types SJ and SJO flexible cords shall be marked with type, designation, size and number of conductors and the operating temperature at intervals not to exceed:

A. 300 mm   (12 in.)
B. 400 mm   (16 in.)
C. 500 mm   (20 in.)
D. 610 mm   (24 in.)

ANSWER _____

Utilization Equipment | 1- and 2-Family Study Guide | 101

PROCEDURE TO ESTABLISH ANSWER

The question is about flexible cords.

▶ 1. In Index, find "Cords" under which find "Marking, 400.6."

▶ 2. Section 400.6 requires Types SJ and SJO flexible cords to be durably marked on the surface at intervals not exceeding 610 mm (24 in.).

▶ 3. The correct answer is D.

QUESTION 24. A luminaire mounted on a pole in the front yard of a single-family dwelling shall be marked with which one of the following markings?

A. Suitable for wet locations
B. Suitable for damp locations
C. Sunlight-resistant
D. Suitable for pole mounting

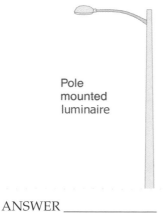

ANSWER _____

PROCEDURE TO ESTABLISH ANSWER

The question is about outdoor luminaires.

▶ 1. In Index, find "Luminaires" under which find "Damp, wet or corrosive locations, 410.10(A), 410.10(B), etc." or find "Wet, 410.4(A).

▶ 2. Section 410.10(A) provides that luminaires shall be installed so water cannot enter or accumulate in wiring compartments, lampholders or other electrical parts and that luminaires installed in wet locations be marked, "Suitable for Wet Locations."

To verify this is a wet location find "Wet locations" in the Index under which find "Definition 100-I" (Article 100-Part I). Under Locations, Wet, we will find that an unprotected location exposed to weather is included.

▶ 3. The correct answer is A.

QUESTION 25. An incandescent luminaire with a completely enclosed lamp is mounted on the ceiling of a clothes closet. What is the minimum clearance required between the luminaire and nearest point of the storage area?

A. 75 mm   (3 in.)
B. 150 mm   (6 in.)
C. 300 mm   (12 in.)
D. 450 mm   (18 in.)

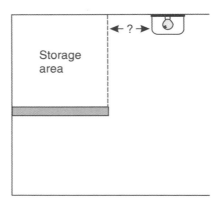

ANSWER _____

PROCEDURE TO ESTABLISH ANSWER

The question is about the location of luminaires in clothes closets.

▶ 1. In Index, find "Clothes closets" under which find "Luminaires, 410.16."

▶ 2. Section 410.16(C)(1) requires a minimum clearance of 300 mm (12 in.) for a surface-mounted incandescent luminaire that is totally enclosed.

▶ 3. The correct answer is C.

QUESTION 26. Generally, a luminaire shall be supported independently of the outlet box when it weighs more than how many pounds?

A. 3 kg   (6 lb)
B. 11.5 kg   (25 lb)
C. 6 kg   (12 lb)
D. 23 kg   (50 lb)

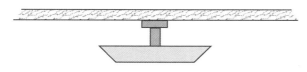

ANSWER _____

PROCEDURE TO ESTABLISH ANSWER
The question is about luminaires supported by the outlet box.

▶ 1. In Index, find "Luminaires" under which find "Supports, 314.23(F) 410–IV."

You can also scan Article 410, IV, and find "410.36, Means of Support," under which (A) refers to 314.23, 314.27(A)(1) and (2) for outlet boxes. Section 314.23 deals more with the support for the box itself and not the luminaire.

▶ 2. Next, find 314.27(A)(2), requires a luminaire weighing more than 23 kg (50 lb) to be supported independently of the box unless the outlet box is listed and marked on the interior of the outlet box for the maximum weight to be supported.

▶ 3. The correct answer is D.

QUESTION 27. Unless marked suitable for direct contact within thermal insulation, LED drivers or power supplies for a recessed luminaire must be spaced from thermal insulation a minimum distance of:

A. 75 mm   (3 in.)
B. 150 mm   (6 in.)
C. 300 mm   (12 in).
D. 450 mm   (18 in.)

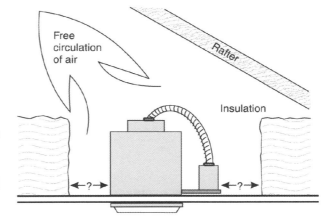

ANSWER _____

PROCEDURE TO ESTABLISH ANSWER
This question is about the installation of recessed incandescent luminaires.

▶ 1. In Index, find "Recessed luminaires (lighting fixtures), 410– X, 410– XI" under which find "Clearances, installation, 410.116."

▶ 2. Section 410.116(B) requires minimum 75 mm (3 in.) spacing from the thermal insulation, unless the luminaire is identified as suitable for the insulation to be in direct contact with the luminaire enclosure, LED driver or power supply, etc., (Type IC).

▶ 3. The correct answer is A.

QUESTION 28. Where supplying two or more outlets for fixed electric space heating equipment in residential occupancies, all of the following branch circuit ratings are acceptable EXCEPT:

A. 15-ampere
B. 20-ampere
C. 30-ampere
D. 40-ampere

ANSWER _____

PROCEDURE TO ESTABLISH ANSWER
The question is about branch circuits for fixed electric space-heating equipment.

▶ 1. In Index, find "Fixed electric space-heating equipment" under which find "Branch circuits for, 424.3."

▶ 2. Section 424.3(A) provides that branch circuits supplying two or more outlets for fixed electric space-heating equipment be rated 15, 20, or 30 amperes.

▶ 3. The correct answer is D.

QUESTION 29. A wall-switch-controlled lighting outlet shall be provided at all of the following locations of a dwelling EXCEPT:

A. outside a door from a master bedroom to a patio
B. outside a vehicle door for an attached garage
C. in a stairway from first floor to basement
D. in a 3.0 m (10 ft) long hallway

ANSWER _____

PROCEDURE TO ESTABLISH ANSWER
The question is about lighting outlets in dwellings.

▶ 1. In Index, find "Lighting outlets, 210.70, 314.27(A), 410.36(A), 410– III."

▶ 2. Section 210.70(A) specifies locations where lighting outlets are required and 210.70(A)(2)(b) requires lighting outlets at the exterior side of an outdoor entrance or exit. Answer A is true.

▶ 3. The last sentence of 210.70(A)(2)(b) notes that a vehicle door in a garage is not considered to be an outdoor entrance or exit. Answer B is false.

▶ 4. Section 210.70(A)(a) requires at least one wall switch-controlled lighting outlet in hallways, stairways, etc. Answers C & D are true.

▶ 5. The correct answer is B.

QUESTION 30. 240-volt electric baseboard heaters are installed in a residence protected with Edison-base plug fuses and controlled by wall-mounted double-pole thermostats that have a marked "off" position and open both ungrounded conductors. Which one of the following statements about this arrangement is NOT true?

A. A disconnecting means is required to disconnect the heaters from all ungrounded conductors.
B. The thermostat may serve as the disconnecting means if the circuit can't be automatically energized after placing the thermostat in the "off" position.
C. The thermostat may serve both as controller and disconnecting means if the circuit can't be automatically energized after manually placing the thermostat in the "off" position.
D. The thermostat is not required to be within sight of all of the heaters that it controls.

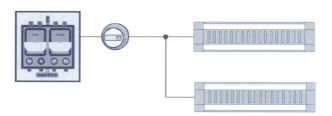

ANSWER _____

PROCEDURE TO ESTABLISH ANSWER
The question is about disconnects for fixed electric space-heating equipment.

▶ 1. In Index, find "Fixed electric space-heating equipment" under which find "Control and protection, 424– Part III" under which find "Controllers, 424.20(A)", "Disconnecting means, 424.19 through 424.21, 424.65," and "Indicating, 424.21."

104 | 1- and 2-Family Study Guide | Utilization Equipment

▶ 2. Section 424.19(A)(1), Disconnecting Means, requires a means to disconnect the ungrounded conductors from the heaters. Answer A is true.

▶ 3. Section 424.20, Thermostatically Controlled Switching Devices, in subsection (3) permits the thermostat described in the question to serve as both controller and disconnecting means if it is designed so the circuit cannot be energized automatically. Answers B & C are true.

▶ 4. Section 424.20(A)(4) requires the thermostat to be located as specified in 424.19.

▶ 5. Sections 424.19(A)(1)(1) & (2) require the heater disconnecting means to be within sight of the heater or capable of being locked in the open position respectively. Because the branch circuit is supplied from plug fuses and not a switch or circuit breaker, and the thermostat which is serving as the disconnect cannot be locked open, it must be within sight of all of the heaters that it controls.

▶ 6. The correct answer is D.

QUESTION 31.
The term *identified* as it relates to electrical equipment means that the equipment:

A. is recognized as suitable for the purpose for which it is intended
B. is acceptable to the authority having jurisdiction
C. is included in a list published by a testing organization
D. has a label attached stating that it is an "identified" product

ANSWER _____

PROCEDURE TO ESTABLISH ANSWER
The question is about the definition of the term *identified*.

▶ 1. In Index, find "Identified" under which find "Definition, Art. 100–Part I."

▶ 2. In Article 100, find the definition of *Identified* as it applies to equipment, which is "Recognizable as suitable for the specific purpose, function, use, environment, and so forth…"

▶ 3. The correct answer is A.

QUESTION 32.
In a plaster ceiling, adjacent runs of heating cable not exceeding 9 watts/m (2 3/4 watts/ft) shall be installed not less than what distance on centers?

A. 25 mm (1 in.)
B. 38 mm (1½ in.)
C. 50 mm (2 in.)
D. 75 mm (3 in.)

ANSWER _____

PROCEDURE TO ESTABLISH ANSWER
The question is about the installation of heating cables which are considered as fixed electric space heating.

▶ 1. In Index, find "Heating cables, Art. 424" or find "Fixed electric space heating" under find "Cables, Art. 424-V."

▶ 2. Scan Article 424 Part V, under which find "424.41, Installation of Heating Cables on Dry Board, in Plaster, and on Concrete Ceilings," in which (B) provides an installation spacing of not less than 38 mm (1½ in.) on center.

▶ 3. The correct answer is B.

QUESTION 33. Which of the following statements about connecting luminaires to equipment grounding conductors is NOT true?

A. Exposed metal parts of luminaires (lighting fixtures) must be grounded or be insulated from ground or be accessible to qualified persons only.
B. Lamp tie wires, mounting screws, clips and decorative bands on glass spaced at least 38 mm (1½ in.) from lamp terminals are not required to be grounded.
C. Luminaires that are installed at outlets where there is no equipment grounding conductor are not required to be grounded and must be installed at least 2.5 m (8 ft) above the floor.
D. Luminaires that are installed at outlets where there is an equipment grounding conductor are required to be grounded.

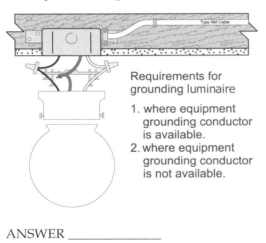

ANSWER _____

PROCEDURE TO ESTABLISH ANSWER
The question is about grounding luminaires (lighting fixtures).

▶ 1. In Index, find "Grounding" under which find "Fixtures, lampholders, etc., 410.155(B), 410–V." Or, find "Luminaires" under which find "Grounding, 410–Part V." There are two ways to direct you to the same answer, in this case.

▶ 2. Scan Article 410, Part V, and find "410.42, Luminaires with Exposed Conductive Parts."

▶ 3. Read through 410.42 and find that choices A, B and D are true.

▶ 4. Section 410.44 is located directly below 410.42 and it requires mechanical connection to the equipment grounding conductor. Exception No. 1 recognizes luminaires made of insulating materials with no exposed conductive parts that are supplied by wiring methods without an equipment grounding conductor as not requiring grounding. Answer C is not true as there is no height specified in 410.44.

Note: Section 250.110 requires equipment fastened in place or connected by permanent wiring methods to be connected to an equipment grounding conductor.

▶ 5. Selection D is a true statement based on requirements of 410.42 & 44, and 250.110.

▶ 6. The correct answer is C.

QUESTION 34. Which of the following is *not* true of heating equipment?

A. Fixed electric space-heating equipment is considered a continuous load for branch circuit sizing.
B. Fixed electric space-heating equipment shall be installed to provide the required spacing between the equipment and adjacent combustible material, unless listed to be installed in direct contact with combustible material.
C. Fixed electric space-heating equipment requiring conductors with over 60°C insulation shall be clearly and permanently marked.
D. Permanently connected air-conditioning equipment is not permitted to be connected to the same branch circuit as central heating equipment.

ANSWER _____

PROCEDURE TO ESTABLISH ANSWER
The question is about fixed electric space heating and air conditioning equipment.

▶ 1. In Index, find "Heating Equipment" under which find, "Central, 422.12" and "Fixed. *see* Fixed electric heating equipment for pipelines and vessels, Fixed electric space heating equipment, etc."

▶ 2. In Index, find "Fixed electric space-heating equipment, Art. 424" under which find, "Branch circuits for, 424.3," and "Installation, 424–Part II" under which find, "Spacing, combustible materials, 424.13" and "Supply conductors, 424.11."

▶ 3. Section 424.3(B) states that fixed electric space-heating equipment shall be considered a continuous load. Answer A is true.

▶ 4. In 424.13, we find that Answer B is true.

▶ 5. In 424.11, we find that Answer C is true.

▶ 6. In 422.12, for central heating equipment, we find that permanently connected air-conditioning equipment is permitted to be connected to the same branch circuit as central heating equipment. Answer D is not true.

▶ 7. The correct answer is D.

Note: A circuit that powers the electric controls and blower motor for an oil or natural gas fueled central heating furnace in a dwelling unit is an example of the type of circuit that may have permanently connected, for example, hard-wired air-conditioning load connected to it. An electric furnace is not.

QUESTION 35.
All of the following statements about range hoods that are cord-and-plug connected with a flexible cord identified as *suitable for the use* are true EXCEPT?

A. The flexible cord is connected with a grounding-type attachment plug. A listed range hood that is double insulated is not required to be terminated in a grounding-type attachment plug.
B. The receptacle must be accessible.
C. The receptacle must be located to avoid physical damage to the cord.
D. The receptacle is not required to be supplied by an individual branch circuit.

ANSWER _____

PROCEDURE TO ESTABLISH ANSWER
The question is about heating equipment.

▶ 1. In Index, find "Ranges" under which find "Hoods, cord- and plug-connected, 422.16(B)(4)."

▶ 2. In 422.16(B)(4)(1)-(5), we find that Answers A, B, and C are true. Answer D is false as the range hood is required to be on an individual branch circuit. Mainly this is because new range hoods often include microwave ovens or existing range hoods are replaced with ones that include a microwave oven.

▶ 3. The correct answer is D.

9. Cabinets

QUESTION 1. Insulated ungrounded conductors entering a cabinet from a raceway are required to be protected by an identified insulating fitting (bushing) or identified insulating material where they are what size?

A. 8 AWG or larger
B. 6 AWG or larger
C. 4 AWG or larger
D. 2 AWG or larger

ANSWER _____

PROCEDURE TO ESTABLISH ANSWER
The question is about insulation at bushings for conductors entering cabinets.

▶ 1. In Index, find "Conductors" under which find "Insulation" under which find "At bushings, 4 AWG and larger, 300.4(G), 312.6(C)."

▶ 2. Section 300.4(G) requires an identified insulating fitting or identified insulating material that provides protection for conductors where raceways containing insulated ungrounded conductors 4 AWG or larger enter a cabinet.

▶ 3. The correct answer is C.

QUESTION 2. Which of the following statements related to enclosures for panelboards is false?

A. The enclosure is required to be marked with an enclosure-type mark.
B. The enclosures are intended to protect against conditions of condensation, icing or corrosion that occur within the enclosure.
C. Enclosures located in environments subject to rain, sleet and snow can be marked with "3R" designation.
D. The enclosure is not intended to protect against contamination that enters through a conduit or unused openings.

108 | 1- and 2-Family Study Guide | Cabinets

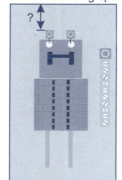

ANSWER _____

PROCEDURE TO ESTABLISH ANSWER
The question is about the types of enclosures for panelboards.

▶ 1. In Index, find "Enclosures" under which find "Types, 110.28."

▶ 2. Section 110.28 requires enclosures for panelboards to be marked with an enclosure-type mark in accordance with Table 110.28. Answer A is true.

▶ 3. Section 110.28 also states the enclosure is not intended to protect against conditions of condensation, corrosion, ice or contamination that may occur within the enclosure or enter through a conduit or unsealed opening. This verifies Answer B is false and Answer D is true.

▶ 4. Section 110.28 points to Table 110.28 with regard to the enclosure marking, so scan Table 110.28 and find the first column in the "For Outdoor Use" portion of the table. This column specifies the environmental conditions so find "Rain, snow and sleet." Follow the row across and find that Type "3" enclosures are suitable for environments subject to rain, sleet and snow. Answer C is true.

▶ 5. The correct answer is B.

QUESTION 3. Which one of the following statements regarding the position of the front edge of cabinets installed in walls is NOT true?

A. It may be set back up to 6 mm (1/4 in.) if in a concrete wall.
B. It may be flush with a concrete wall.
C. It may be set back up to 6 mm (1/4 in.) if it is in a wall constructed of combustible material.
D. It must be flush with or project therefrom a wall constructed of combustible material.

ANSWER _____

PROCEDURE TO ESTABLISH ANSWER
The question is about the location of cabinets in walls.

▶ 1. In Index, find "Cabinets, cutout boxes, and meter socket enclosures, Art. 312" under which find "Position in walls, 312.3."

▶ 2. Section 312.3 gives the position in walls and requires cabinets in walls constructed of combustible material to be flush with the finished surface or project therefrom.

▶ 3. The correct answer is C.

QUESTION 4. Which of the following statements regarding cabinets or cutout boxes installed in a wet location is NOT true?

A. Watertight cabinets are permitted.
B. Weatherproof cabinets are permitted.
C. Watertight cutout boxes are permitted.
D. Weatherproof cutout boxes are not permitted.

ANSWER _____

PROCEDURE TO ESTABLISH ANSWER
The question is about cabinets and cutout boxes in wet locations.

▶ 1. In Index, find "Cabinets, cutout boxes, and meter socket enclosures" under which find "Damp and wet locations, 312.2."

▶ 2. Section 312.2 provides that cabinets or cutout boxes installed in wet locations shall be weatherproof.

▶ 3. See Article 100 definition of *Weatherproof*, and the Informational Note which states that watertight equipment can fulfill the requirements for weatherproof where conditions such as snow, ice, dust, or temperature extremes are not a factor. Since the question only addresses wet locations, watertight equipment can be considered weatherproof. Answer D is not true.

▶ 4. The correct answer is D.

QUESTION 5. A dwelling service is supplied by 4/0 AWG aluminum conductors which enter the top of the enclosure for the 225 ampere rated panelboard directly opposite the line side terminals for the 200 ampere main breaker. The minimum distance from the enclosure wall to the terminals must not be less than_____.

A. 102 mm (4 in.)
B. 114 mm (4 1/2 in.)
C. 165 mm (6 1/2 in.)
D. 178 mm (7 in.)

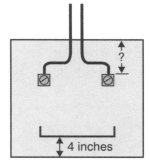

Service panel gutter space

ANSWER _____

PROCEDURE TO ESTABLISH ANSWER
The question is about the wire-bending space (gutter width) in panelboard enclosures.

▶ 1. In Index, find "Panelboards" under which find "Wire bending space, 408.55."

▶ 2. Section 408.55 requires an enclosure containing a panelboard to have top and bottom wire-bending space according to Table 312.6(B). Section 408.55, Exception No. 1, permits either top or bottom to have wire-bending space according to Table 312.6(A) when the panelboard is rated 225 amperes or less. Table 312.6(A) permits a smaller bending space than Table 312.6(B).

▶ 3. Table 312.6(A) provides for a 102 mm (4 in.) bending space for 4/0 AWG conductors, which is shown for the bottom gutter space.

▶ 4. Since the bottom space where there are no direct connections normally would be sized based on the smaller dimensions of Table 312.6(A), the top gutter width must be based on Table 312.6(B) which is 178 mm (7 in.), per 408.55, Exception No. 1.

▶ 5. The correct answer is D.

QUESTION 6. In damp or wet locations, metal cabinets and cutout boxes of the surface type shall be mounted so there is a minimum air space between the enclosure and wall or other supporting surface of how many inches?

A. 6 mm   (1/4 in.)
B. 10 mm (3/8 in.)
C. 13 mm (1/2 in.)
D. 25 mm (1 in.)

ANSWER _____

PROCEDURE TO ESTABLISH ANSWER
The question is about cabinets and cutout boxes installed in damp or wet locations.

▶ 1. In Index, find "Cabinets, cutout boxes, and meter socket enclosures" under which find "Damp, wet, or hazardous (classified) locations, 312.2."

▶ 2. Section 312.2 requires cabinets or cutout boxes located in wet or damp locations to be mounted so there is at least 6 mm (1/4 in.) air space between the enclosure and the wall or supporting surface.

▶ 3. The correct answer is A.

QUESTION 7. An enclosure designed either for surface or flush mounting and provided with a frame or trim in which a swinging door is, or can be, hung is a:

A. Cabinet
B. Cutout box
C. Panelboard
D. Switchboard

ANSWER _____

PROCEDURE TO ESTABLISH ANSWER
The question is describing a type of enclosure so in the end we will likely be considering definitions. Looking at the choices you can identify that answers A and B are the only two that are actually "enclosures" but all the choices are defined terms.

▶ 1. In Index, find "Definitions, Art. 100."

▶ 2. In Article 100, find the definition of *Cabinet*, which agrees with the information given in the question. Answer A is correct.

▶ 3. In Article 100, a review of the definitions of *Cutout Boxes*, *Panelboards*, and *Switchboard* verifies that Answers C and D are not "enclosures" and Answer B is not the enclosure described in the question.

▶ 4. The correct answer is A.

QUESTION 8. Which one of the following statements about identification or the marking of branch circuits at panelboards is NOT true?

A. They are required to be legibly identified to indicate their purpose.
B. Circuit modifications are required to be marked on the directory.
C. Modifications to existing circuits are not required to be further identified or re-identified
D. The marking is required to be on a circuit directory on the face of or on the inside of the panel door.

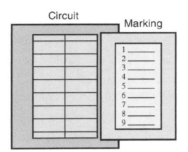

ANSWER _____

PROCEDURE TO ESTABLISH ANSWER
The question is about the marking or identification of the circuits in panelboards.

▶ 1. In Index, find "Panelboards, Art. 408" under which find "Circuit directory, 408.4."

▶ 2. Also, since the question refers to identification of branch circuits, in Index, find "Identification" under which find "Disconnecting means, 110.22, 230.70(B), 620.51(D)."

▶ 3. Section 408.4 requires panelboard circuits and circuit modifications to be identified as to purpose or use on a circuit directory located on the face or inside the panel doors. Answer C is not true.

▶ 4. Section 110.22 generally requires branch circuit identification at the point where they originate; they shall be legibly marked to indicate their purpose unless its location makes its purpose readily evident.

▶ 5. The correct answer is C.

QUESTION 9. Which of the following statements regarding several nonmetallic-sheathed cables entering a surface-mounted cabinet through a raceway are NOT true:

A. The raceway must enter the top of the enclosure.
B. Cables entering the cabinet through a non-flexible metric designator 53 (2 in.) raceway must be secured within 300 mm (12 in.) of where they enter the raceway.
C. Non-flexible raceways are permitted.
D. The cable sheath must be continuous through the raceway and extend into the enclosure beyond the fitting not less than 6mm (1/4 in.).

ANSWER _____

PROCEDURE TO ESTABLISH ANSWER
The question is about conductors and cables entering a cabinet.

▶ 1. In the Index find "Cabinets, cutout boxes and meter socket enclosures" under which find "Installation, 312-I. Scan Part I and find "312.5, Cabinets, Cutout Boxes and Meter Socket Enclosures."
In the Index you can also find "Conductors" under which find "Cabinets and cutout boxes, 312.5 through 312.7."

▶ 2. Section 312.5(C) requires each cable to be secured to the cabinet or cutout box. The exception permits several cables to enter the top of a surface-mounted enclosure through a raceway where all the conditions in (a) – (g) are met. This opening paragraph specifies the raceway must enter the top of the enclosure. Answer A is true.

▶ 3. Subdivision (a) requires the cable to be secured within 12" of the raceway and the opening paragraph of 312.5(C) requires a nonflexible raceway. Answer B is true. Answer C is not true.

▶ 4. Subdivision (e) requires the cable sheath to extend into the enclosure at least 6 mm (1/4 in.) beyond the fitting. Answer D is true.

▶ 5. The correct answer is C.

QUESTION 10. A single-family dwelling is provided with a 100-ampere, 3-wire, single-phase service with all equipment terminations rated at least 75°C. Type THW copper service-entrance conductors enter a service disconnect switch at the top and connect to the top lugs of the service disconnecting switch. What is the minimum required space between the top lugs and the top of the enclosure?

A. 50.8 mm (2 in.)
B. 63.5 mm (2 1/2 in.)
C. 76.2 mm (3 in.)
D. 102 mm (4 in.)

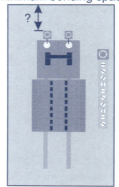

Minimum bending space

ANSWER _____

PROCEDURE TO ESTABLISH ANSWER
The question is about wire bending space in a switch enclosure, which is a cutout box.

▶ 1. In Index, find "Cutout boxes" which advises to see "Cabinets, cutout boxes, and meter socket enclosures."

▶ 2. In Index, find "Cabinets, cutout boxes, and meter socket enclosures" under which find "Wire bending space at terminals, 312.6(B)."

▶ 3. Section 312.6(B)(2) specifies that Table 312.6(B) shall apply where conductors enter or leave the enclosure through the wall opposite its terminal.

▶ 4. Since the conductor size is not given in the question and is required to determine the bending space in panel, in Index, find "Ampacities" under which find "Conductors, 310.15, Tables 310.15(B)(16) through 310.15(B)(21)…"

▶ 5. Scan Section 310.15 and find "310.15(B)(7)," which, assuming 75°C terminations, permits 4 AWG Type THW copper conductors for a 100-ampere service. Section 310.15(B)(7) permits service conductors supplying all the load of a one-family dwelling to be sized not smaller than 83% of the service rating (83 amperes in our question). A 4 AWG, Type THW, copper conductor with all equipment terminations rated 75°C has an ampacity of 85 amperes.

▶ 6. Referring to Table 312.6(B), a 4 AWG conductor requires a minimum of 76.2 mm (3 in.) of bending space.

▶ 7. The correct answer is C.

QUESTION 11.
Which one of the following statements regarding conduit bushings that are constructed wholly of insulating material is true?

A. They shall not be used to secure a raceway to a box or other enclosure.
B. They shall be installed on all raceways.
C. They shall be used only with nonmetallic raceways.
D. They are only permitted on raceways smaller than metric designator 53 (2 in.) in diameter.

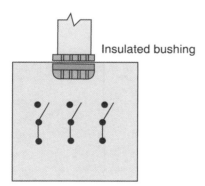

ANSWER _____

PROCEDURE TO ESTABLISH ANSWER
The question is about insulated bushings.

▶ 1. In Index, find "Bushings," under which find "Insulated, 300.4(G), 312.6(C)."

▶ 2. Section 300.4(G) provides that conduit bushings constructed wholly of insulating material shall not be used to secure a raceway.

▶ 3. Reviewing 300.4(G) further confirms that the other statements in the question are not true.

▶ 4. The correct answer is A.

QUESTION 12.
All of the following statements about cutout boxes are true EXCEPT:

A. The box is designed for surface mounting.
B. The box may be flush mounted if not over 2.0 m (6-1/2 ft) from the floor.
C. The box has swinging doors or covers.
D. The box doors or covers may be telescoping with the walls of the box.

ANSWER _____

PROCEDURE TO ESTABLISH ANSWER
The question is about cutout boxes. A quick review of the answers reveals the choices are describing the enclosure which indicates a definition. Because the term *cutout box* is used in more than one article, the definition will likely be in Article 100.

▶ 1. In Index, find "Cutout boxes" under which find "Definition, Art. 100–Part I."

▶ 2. In Article 100, find definition of *Cutout Box*, which does not recognize flush mounting under any condition. Answer B is not true.

▶ 3. The remaining choices are part of the definition. Answers A, C & D are true.

▶ 4. The correct answer is B.

QUESTION 13.
Which one of the following statements about panelboard enclosures (cabinets) is NOT true?

A. The panelboard shall have sufficient space to accommodate all conductors installed in them without crowding.
B. Panelboards containing switches or overcurrent devices may be used as junction boxes where adequate space is provided.
C. Conductors may fill panelboard gutters up to 40 percent of the cross-sectional area of the gutter.
D. Taps may fill the panelboard gutter to a maximum of 60 percent of the gutter area.

ANSWER _____

PROCEDURE TO ESTABLISH ANSWER
The question is about space in enclosures.

▶ 1. In Index, find "Enclosures" under which find "Cabinets and cutout boxes, 312.7 through 312.9, 312.11(D)."

In the Index you can also go to "Cabinets, cutout boxes and meter socket enclosures and find "Installation, 312-I."

▶ 2. A review of 312.7 confirms that Answer A is true.

▶ 3. Section 312.8 provides that enclosures containing switches or overcurrent devices may be used for conductors feeding through, spliced, etc., if the conductors do not fill the wiring space (gutters) to more than 40 percent of the area. Answers B and C are true.

▶ 4. Section 312.8 provides that taps may fill the wiring space (gutters) to 75 percent of the area, which makes selection D an incorrect statement.

▶ 5. The correct answer is D.

QUESTION 14.
A large dwelling service consists of a single 400-ampere disconnect switch, which feeds to a metallic wireway with a removable cover where taps are made to two 200-ampere panelboards. The splices or taps shall not fill the cross-sectional area of the wireway more than:

A. 30 percent
B. 45 percent
C. 60 percent
D. 75 percent

ANSWER _____

PROCEDURE TO ESTABLISH ANSWER
The question is about splices or taps in wireways.

▶ 1. In Index, find "Wireways, metal" under which find "Splices, and taps, 376.56."

▶ 2. Section 376.56(A) permits the conductors, including splices and taps, to fill the wireway to not more than 75 percent of its area.

▶ 3. The correct answer is D.

QUESTION 15.
A branch-circuit panelboard in a dwelling is located in a utility room on a wall opposite a water heater. What is the minimum permitted depth and width of the working space required between front of the panelboard and the water heater?

A. 600 mm wide x 900 mm deep
   (24 in. wide x 36 in. deep)
B. 750 mm wide x 750 mm deep
   (30 in. wide x 30 in. deep)
C. 750 mm wide x 900 mm deep
   (30 in. wide x 36 in. deep)
D. 900 mm wide x 900 mm deep
   (36 in. wide x 36 in. deep)

ANSWER _____

PROCEDURE TO ESTABLISH ANSWER

The question is about the minimum working space required in front of panelboards.

▶ 1. In Index, find "Working space" under which find "About electrical equipment, 110.26, 110.32 through 110.34, 110.72, 110.73."

▶ 2. Section 110.26(A)(1) requires the working space to comply with Table 110.26(A)(1), unless the requirements of 110.26(A)(1)(a), (A)(1)(b), or (A)(1)(c) are met. Since the voltage to ground would be in the 0–150 range, the minimum clear distance is 900 mm (3 ft) regardless of what is opposite the panelboard.

▶ 3. Section 110.26(A)(2) also requires the working space to be not less than 750 mm (30 in.) wide in front of the panelboard.

▶ 4. The correct answer is C.

QUESTION 16. Which one of the following statements about the maximum number of current-carrying conductors in a sheet metal auxiliary gutter is true?

A. Under no condition may the gutter contain more than 30 conductors.
B. The gutter may contain more than 30 conductors if the ampacity of the conductors is adjusted (derated) for the number of current-carrying conductors and limited to not more than 20 percent fill at any interior cross-section of the gutter.
C. The gutter may be filled to 40 percent of its area if the conductor ampacities are derated due to conductor fill.
D. A gutter containing 30 conductors requires an ampacity adjustment due to conductor fill.

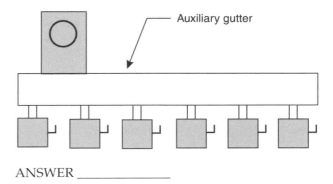

ANSWER _____

PROCEDURE TO ESTABLISH ANSWER

The question is about conductor fill for auxiliary gutters.

▶ 1. In Index, find "Auxiliary gutters" under which find "Conductors" under which find "Number of, 366.22."

▶ 2. Section 366.22(A) requires the conductors to be adjusted (derated) according to 310.15(B)(3)(a) where there are more than 30 conductors in the auxiliary gutter but does not limit the number of conductors to 30. Answers A and D are incorrect.

▶ 3. The opening sentence of 366.22 limits the number of the conductors to 20 percent fill at any interior cross-sectional area of the auxiliary gutter. Answer C is incorrect.

▶ 4. Reviewing the information learned in Steps 2 and 3, we can verify that Answer B is true.

▶ 5. The correct answer is B.

QUESTION 17. Which of the following statements regarding spacing in cabinets is false?

A. They must have adequate room for conductor and cable distribution and for separation of metal parts and devices mounted in them.
B. Other than at the points of support a 1.59 mm (0.0625 in.) of airspace must be maintained between the device base and a metal cabinet wall.
C. There shall be at least 2.54 mm (1.00 in.) between any live metal part and the door.
D. Cabinets shall be deep enough to allow closing of the doors when branch-circuit panelboard switches rated not more than 20-amperes are in any position.

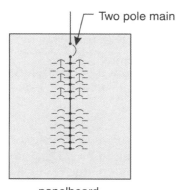

ANSWER _____

PROCEDURE TO ESTABLISH ANSWER
The question is about spacing in a cabinet.

▶ 1. In the Index find "Spaces" under which find "Cabinets and cutout boxes, 312.7, 312.9, 312.11."

▶ 2. Scanning 312.7 and 312.9 you find they are not relevant to the answers provided.

▶ 3. Section 312.11(A) provides that there be ample room for distribution of conductors and cables as well as space for separation of metal parts of devices. Answer A is true.

▶ 4. Section 312.11(A)(1) requires at least 1.59 mm (0.0625 in.) between the base of a device and any metal wall of a cabinet.

▶ 5. Section 312.11(A)(2) requires at least 2.54 mm (1.00 in,) between any live metal part and the door. Answer C is true.

▶ 6. Section 312.11(B) provides that the enclosure must be deep enough to permit closing of the door when 30-ampere branch-circuit panelboard switches are in any position. Answer D is false as it specifies "not more than 20-ampere" branch-circuit panelboard switches.

▶ 7. Answer D is correct answer.

QUESTION 18. A dwelling service is upgraded and an additional panelboard is added adjacent to the original one such that it would be necessary to pass conductors from one panelboard enclosure through the other panelboard enclosure. Which one of the following statements regarding conductors that pass through a cabinet that contains overcurrent devices is true?

A. Conductors are never permitted to feed through one panelboard to supply another panelboard.
B. They may fill up to 75 percent of the cross-sectional area of the gutter space.
C. They may fill up to 40 percent of the cross-sectional area of the gutter space.
D. A warning label identifying the location of the disconnect for the conductors feeding through is not required.

ANSWER _____

PROCEDURE TO ESTABLISH ANSWER
The question is about conductors passing through wiring spaces (gutters) of panelboard enclosures.

▶ 1. In Index, find "Panelboards" under which find "Use as enclosure, 312.8." Or,

▶ 2. In Index, find "Cabinets, cutout boxes, and meter socket enclosures" under which find "Switch enclosures, splices, taps, 312.8." Either reference in Step 1 or Step 2 will get you to Section 312.8.

► 3. Section 312.8 permits conductors to feed through enclosures for overcurrent devices where the conditions of subdivisions (1)–(3) are met. Answer A is false.

► 4. Section 312.8(1) limits the total number of conductors to 40 percent of the space. Answer C is true.

► 5. Section 312.8(2) limits the total area of conductors, splices and taps to not more than 75 percent of the area of any space. Answer B is false. At first glance it may appear that Answer B is true so this type of answer/question relationship is one to look at closely before choosing your answer. The question as asking which of the choices about "conductors" is true. Therefore, Answer B is saying that "conductors" can fill the space to 75% when the *Code* requirement considers the total area of conductors, splices and taps.

► 6. Section 312.8(3) requires a warning label to be placed on the enclosure that identifies the closest disconnecting means for the conductors passing through. Answer D is false.

► 7. The correct answer is C.

QUESTION 19. A large single family dwelling had been provided with a 400-ampere service supplied by two sets of 3/0 copper THWN conductors. The conductors **do not** enter the enclosure through the wall opposite the terminals of the 400-ampere main breaker. Which of the following is the correct minimum width of the gutter space where the conductors enter the enclosure?

A. 152 mm (6 in.)
B. 127 mm (4 in.)
C. 165 mm (6-1/2 in.)
D. 203 mm (8 in.)

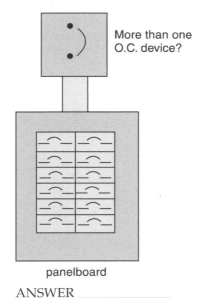

ANSWER _____

PROCEDURE TO ESTABLISH ANSWER
The question is about the gutter space within a panelboard enclosure.

► 1. In Index, find "Panelboards" under which find "Wire bending space, 408.55."

► 2. Section 408.55 provides that Table 312.6(A) shall be used for side wire-bending space. Because the question does not specify the conductors are terminating in the side wire-bending space, we are looking for the general requirements wiring gutter spaces.

► 3 Section 312.6(A) requires that conductors shall not be deflected within a cabinet or cutout box unless a gutter having a width in accordance with Table 312.6(A) is provided.

► 4 Find that the "3/0–4/0" Row and the "2 Wires Per Terminal" Column (2 sets of 3/0 conductors) in Table 312.6(A) requires 152 mm (6 in.) minimum gutter width.

► 5. The correct answer is A.

QUESTION 20. Overcurrent protection for panelboards equipped with snap switches rated 30 amperes or less shall not exceed:

A. 60 amperes
B. 100 amperes
C. 150 amperes
D. 200 amperes

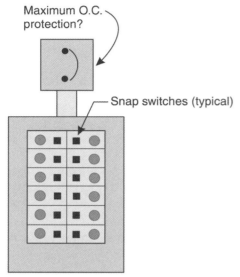

ANSWER _____

PROCEDURE TO ESTABLISH ANSWER
The question relates to overcurrent protection of panelboards.

▶ 1. In Index, find "Panelboards" under which find "Overcurrent protection, 408.52, 408.36, etc."

▶ 2. Section 408.36(A) does not permit overcurrent protection in excess of 200 amperes for a panelboard containing snap switches rated 30 amperes or less.

▶ 3. The correct answer is D.

QUESTION 21. Which of the following statements about the use of a raceway through which cables enter a panelboard cabinet is NOT true?

A. The raceway is permitted be a flexible type.
B. The raceway is not permitted to penetrate a structural ceiling.
C. The raceway must be sealed at the outer end in an approved manner.
D. The raceway must be secured at the outer end and at other points in accordance with the applicable article.

ANSWER _____

PROCEDURE TO ESTABLISH ANSWER
The question is about rules under which it is not required to secure cables to panelboard cabinets.

▶ 1. In Index, find "Cabinets, cutout boxes, and meter socket enclosures" under which find "Installation, 312–Part I."

▶ 2. Scan Article 312 and find "312.5(C), Cables," and review all of the conditions in the exception.

▶ 3. The opening paragraph of the exception requires the use of nonflexible raceways. Answer A is not true.

▶ 4. Condition (b) of the Exception does not permit the raceway to penetrate a structural ceiling. Answer B is true.

▶ 5. Condition (d) of the Exception requires the outer end to be sealed in an approved manner. Answer C is true.

▶ 6. Condition (f) of the Exception requires the raceway to be fastened.

▶ 7. The correct answer is A. The raceway is not permitted to be a flexible type.

QUESTION 22. A 200-ampere dwelling panelboard is supplied by 4/0 AWG compact stranded aluminum conductors entering the side of the enclosure and terminating in main lugs on the top of the panelboard. The minimum distance from the enclosure wall to the terminal must not be less than _____.

A. 102 mm (6 in.)
B. 114 mm (4-1/2 in.)
C. 152 mm (4 in.)
D. 178 mm (7 in.)

ANSWER _____

PROCEDURE TO ESTABLISH ANSWER
The question is about the minimum wire bending space in panelboards.

▶ 1. In Index, find "Panelboards" under which find "Wire bending space, 408.55"

▶ 2. Section 408.55 requires panelboards to have top and bottom wire-bending space according to Table 312.6(B). Section 408.55, Exception No. 1, permits either top or bottom to have wire bending space according to Table 312.6(A) when rated 225A or less. Table 312.6(A) permits a smaller bending space than Table 312.6(B).

▶ 3. Table 312.6(A) provides for a 102 mm (4 in.) bending space for 4/0 AWG conductors.

▶ 4. Since Table 312.6(A) applies where the conductors do not enter or leave the wall opposite the terminal, the minimum space required must be based on Table 312.6(A) and must be at least 102 mm (4 in.) for 4/0 compact stranded aluminum conductors.

▶ 5. The correct answer is C.

QUESTION 23. All of the following statements regarding cabinets that are installed in wet locations are true EXCEPT:

A. Surface-type enclosures installed in wet locations shall be mounted so there is at least 6 mm (1/4 inch) airspace between the wall or other supporting material.
B. Enclosures installed in wet locations shall be weatherproof.
C. Raceways or cables entering above the level of uninsulated live parts must use fittings that are listed for wet locations.
D. Raceways or cables entering above the level of uninsulated live parts must use wet location fittings.

ANSWER _____

PROCEDURE TO ESTABLISH ANSWER
The question is about cabinets that are installed in wet locations.

▶ 1. In Index, find "Cabinets, cutout boxes, and meter socket enclosures" under which find "Damp and wet locations, 312.2."

▶ 2. In 312.2(A), surface-type enclosures installed in wet locations shall be mounted so there is at least 6 mm (1/4 inch) airspace between the enclosure and the wall or other supporting material, and enclosures installed in wet locations shall be weatherproof. Answers A and B are true.

▶ 3. Section 312.2(A) also requires that raceways or cables entering above the level of uninsulated live parts must use fittings *listed* for wet locations. Answer C is true, and Answer D is not as there is no indication the fittings are listed.

▶ 4. The correct answer is D.

QUESTION 24. Which of the following statements regarding meter disconnect switches is true?

A. Meter disconnect switches are not permitted to be installed on the supply side of the service under any condition.
B. Meter disconnect switches rated 1000 volts or less that have a short circuit current rating equal to or greater than the available short circuit current are permitted to be installed on the supply side of the service if all metal housings and service enclosures are grounded and bonded.
C. Meter disconnect switches rated 1000 volts or less and installed on the supply side of the service are not required to be marked to indicate they are a meter disconnect.
D. Meter disconnect switches rated over 1000 volts nominal are permitted to be installed on the supply side of the service.

ANSWER _____

PROCEDURE TO ESTABLISH ANSWER
The question is about the locations permitted and required ratings of meter socket disconnects.

▶ 1. In Index, find "Meters" under which find "Connection and location at services, 230.82, 230.94 Ex. 5."

▶ 2. Section 230.82(3), Equipment Connected to the Supply Side of Service Disconnect, permits meter socket disconnects rated 1000 volts or less that have a short-circuit current rating equal to or greater than the available short circuit current to be installed on the supply side of the service if all metal housings and service enclosures are grounded in accordance with Part VII and Bonded in accordance with Part V of Article 250 and the meter disconnect is marked "METER DISCONNECT NOT SERVICE EQUIPMENT." Answers A and C are not true. Answer B is true.

▶ 3. Scan 230.82(3) and 230.94, and you will find that meter socket enclosures are not permitted in excess of 1000 volts. There is also no mention of meter sockets in Article 490, Equipment Over 1000 volts, nominal. Answer D is not true.

▶ 4. Answer B is correct.

10 Calculations

QUESTION 1. What is the approximate percent of voltage drop in the circuit shown in the diagram? [Assume an ambient temperature of 75°C (167°F).]

A. 3 percent
B. 3.4 percent
C. 4 percent
D. 4.3 percent

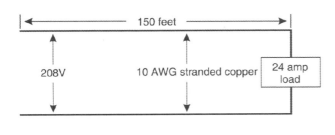

ANSWER _____

PROCEDURE TO ESTABLISH ANSWER
The question is about calculating the voltage drop of an electrical circuit.

▶ 1. Use Ohms Law
   E (voltage) = I (current) x R (resistance)

▶ 2. R = 1.24 ohms per 1000 feet (*NEC* Chapter 9, Table 8)

▶ 3. VD = I x R = 24 amps x (1.24 ohms/1000 ft) x 300 ft
   VD = 8.93 volts

▶ 4. Percent drop = 8.93/208
                   = .0429 x 100
                   = 4.3% voltage drop

▶ 5. The correct answer is D.

Note: Section 210.19(A) Informational Note No. 4 recommends a 3 percent maximum voltage drop for branch circuits.

QUESTION 2. What is the minimum number of 15-ampere lighting circuits required for a 2600 square foot residence?

A. 4
B. 5
C. 6
D. 8

ANSWER _____

PROCEDURE TO ESTABLISH ANSWER
The question is about the number of lighting branch circuits required for a dwelling.

▶ 1. In Index, find "Branch circuits." Scanning this item does not indicate a subtitle regarding number of branch circuits but does include "Calculation of loads, 220–Part II."

▶ 2. Scan Article 220, Part I, and find "220.12, Lighting Load for Listed Occupancies," which refers to Table 220.12 for minimum lighting load.

▶ 3. Table 220.12 requires a 3 VA per square foot minimum lighting load for dwelling units.

Note: Although there is no specific reference in the Index, Section 210.11(A) and (B) state that the number of branch circuits shall be determined from the total computed load and size or rating of the circuit.

▶ 4. Proceed with the calculations.
Multiply 2600 square feet by 3 VA per square foot.
= 2600 x 3
= 7800 VA

Next divide by 120 volts.
= 7800 VA / 120V
= 65A
= 65A / 15A
= 4.33 or 5 circuits, minimum

▶ 5. The correct answer is B.

QUESTION 3. What is the maximum demand load required for a household electric range rated 12 kW?

A. 80 percent of the nameplate rating
B. 8 kW
C. 11 kW
D. 12 kW

ANSWER _____

PROCEDURE TO ESTABLISH ANSWER
The question is about demand loads for electric ranges.

▶ 1. In Index, find "Ranges" under which find "Loads, demand factors, and Table 220.55."

▶ 2. Table 220.55 requires column C to be used in all cases, except as otherwise permitted by Note 3.

▶ 3. The correct answer is B.

QUESTION 4. What is the load demand for a household electric range rated 20 kVA at 240 volts?

A. 33.3 amperes
B. 46.7 amperes
C. 50.0 amperes
D. 83.3 amperes

ANSWER _____

PROCEDURE TO ESTABLISH ANSWER
The question is about load calculations for ranges.

▶ 1. In Index, find "Ranges" under which find "Branch circuits" under which find "Calculation of load, 220.55, Table 220.55."

▶ 2. Refer to Table 220.55. Since 20 kVA range is not directly covered by the table headings, refer to the notes to the table. Note 1 applies to a range rated at 20 kVA.

▶ 3. Note 1 states, "For ranges individually rated more than 12 kW but not more than 27 kW, the maximum demand in Column C shall be increased 5 percent for each additional kilowatt of rating or major fraction thereof by which the rating of individual ranges exceeds 12 kW."

▶ 4. Proceed with the calculations.
= 20 kVA – 12
= 8 kVA
(Additional kVA rating over 12 kVA)
= 8 x 5%
= 40%
= 40% x 8000
= 3200
= 3200 + 8,000
= 11,200 VA
11,200 VA / 240 V = 46.7 amperes

▶ 5. The correct answer is B.

QUESTION 5. A 16 kVA range is installed in a mansion-type dwelling unit. What is the minimum size Type THW copper conductors required to serve this range?

A. 10 AWG
B. 8 AWG
C. 6 AWG
D. 4 AWG

ANSWER _____

PROCEDURE TO ESTABLISH ANSWER

▶ 1. Calculate minimum ampacity
VA/Volts = 16,000 VA /240V
VA = 66.7 amperes

▶ 2. Since the temperature ratings of the terminations are not known, assume a 60°C rating based on Section 110.14(C)(1)(a)(1).

▶ 3. Referring to Table 310.15(B)(16), a 4 AWG conductor with a 70-ampere capacity would be required.

▶ 4. The correct answer is D.

Note: If the terminations on both ends of the circuit were rated 75°C, Table 310.15(B)(16) would still require a 4 AWG copper conductor for a load of 66.7 amperes.

QUESTION 6. What is the minimum demand load permitted for a 4500 VA household electric dryer?

A. 3000 watts
B. 4500 watts
C. 5000 watts
D. 8000 watts

ANSWER _____

PROCEDURE TO ESTABLISH ANSWER
The question is about calculations for clothes dryers.

▶ 1. In Index, find "Clothes dryers" under which find "Calculations for, 220.54."

▶ 2. Section 220.54 requires the load for a household dryer to be 5000 watts (volt-amperes) or the nameplate rating, whichever is larger. Note: When calculating for more than one dryer, refer to Table 220.54.

▶ 3. The correct answer is C.

QUESTION 7. What is the minimum branch-circuit rating permitted for two 1500-VA, 240-volt, and one 500-VA, 240-volt baseboard electric heaters all installed on one circuit?

A. 15 amperes
B. 20 amperes
C. 30 amperes
D. 40 amperes

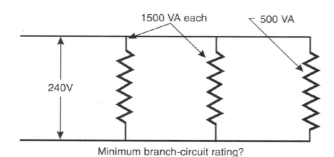

ANSWER _____

PROCEDURE TO ESTABLISH ANSWER
The question is about branch circuits for electric space-heating equipment.

▶ 1. In Index, find "Fixed electric space-heating equipment" under which find "Branch circuits for, 424.3."

▶ 2. Section 424.3(B), Branch-Circuit Sizing, states, "Fixed electric space heating equipment and motors shall be considered continuous load."

▶ 3. In Index, find "Continuous Load" under which find "Definition, Art. 100–Part I." In Article 100, *Continuous load* is defined as "a load where the maximum current is expected to continue for 3 hours or more."

▶ 4. The question relates to branch-circuit overcurrent protective device ratings. In Index, find "Branch circuits" under which find "Overcurrent Protection, 210.20, 240.3." Find 210.20, and look for 210.20(A), which requires the branch-circuit to be rated at 125 percent of the continuous load(s) on the circuit.

▶ 5. Proceed with the calculations.
1500 VA + 1500 VA + 500 VA
   = 3500 VA
   = 3500 VA / 240 volts
   = 14.6 amperes
   = 14.6 A x 1.25
   = 18.25 amperes

▶ 6. A minimum of a 20-ampere circuit is required.

▶ 7. The correct answer is B.

QUESTION 8. Which one of the following Type THW conductors is the minimum size permitted for a 230-volt, AC single-phase, 1-1/2-horsepower pump motor?

A. 14 AWG copper
B. 14 AWG aluminum
C. 12 AWG copper
D. 12 AWG aluminum

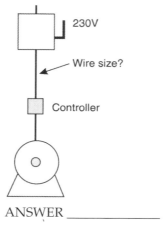

ANSWER _____

PROCEDURE TO ESTABLISH ANSWER
The question is about the size of a motor branch circuit.

▶ 1. In Index, find "Motors" under which find "Branch circuits" under which find "Single motor, 430.22."

▶ 2. Section 430.22 requires the conductor ampacity to be sized 125 percent of motor full-load current rating.

▶ 3. In Index, find "Full-load current motors" under which find "Alternating current" under which find "Single-phase, Table 430.248."

▶ 4. In Table 430.248, find 1-1/2 horsepower. Read across to the 230 volts column and find 10 amperes.

▶ 5. 125 percent x 10 amperes = 12.5 amperes.

▶ 6. Refer to Table 310.15(B)(16) for allowable ampacities. 14 AWG copper is the minimum size.

▶ 7. The correct answer is A.

QUESTION 9. The voltmeter reading across the 10-ohm resistance (R1) is how many volts?

A. 24 volts
B. 48 volts
C. 120 volts
D. 192 volts

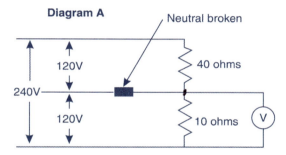

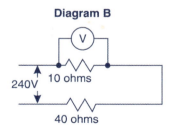

ANSWER _____

PROCEDURE TO ESTABLISH ANSWER
The problem can be solved by using Ohms law: *E (voltage) = I (current) x R (resistance)*. This formula is good to know because you can figure the voltage drop on a 240-volt circuit if the neutral were broken.

▶ 1. $R_T = R_1 + R_2$ $R_T = 10 + 40$ $R_T = 50$ ohms

▶ 2. $I = E/R$ $I = 240$ volts/50 ohms $I = 4.8$ amperes

▶ 3. Voltage across the 10-ohm resistance
   $E = I \times R$
   $E = 4.8$ amperes x 10 ohms
   $E = 48$ volts

▶ 4. Voltage across the 40-ohm resistance
   $E = I \times R$
   $E = 4.8$ amperes x 40 ohms
   $E = 192$ volts

▶ 5. The correct answer is B.

QUESTION 10. A dwelling unit has three 3-wire multiwire branch circuits in 3/4-inch electrical metal tubing. All conductors are 12 AWG Type THW conductors. What is the maximum allowable ampacity for each conductor?

A. 16 amperes
B. 17.5 amperes
C. 20 amperes
D. 25 amperes

ANSWER _____

PROCEDURE TO ESTABLISH ANSWER
The question is about allowable ampacity of conductors.

▶ 1. In Index, find "Conductors" under which find "Ampacities of, 310.15, etc."

▶ 2. Section 310.15(B) requires ampacities to be as specified in the Allowable Ampacity Tables 310.15(B)(16) through 310.15(B)(19), and Ampacity Tables 310.15(B)(20) and Table 310.15(B)(21) as modified by (B)(1) through (B)(7).

▶ 3. In Table 310.15(B)(16), 12 AWG THW = 20 amperes. See 310.15(B)(5) regarding neutral conductors, and 310.15(B)(2) regarding adjustment factors.

▶ 4. Based on 310.15(B)(5), the neutrals are not counted so there would be six current-carrying conductors. (There are nine conductors total in the raceway, but the neutral conductors that carry the unbalanced current are not counted.)

▶ 5. Because there are six current-carrying conductors in the raceway, 310.15(B)(3)(a) requires an 80 percent adjustment factor (derating) to be applied.

▶ 6. 80% x 20 amperes = 16 amperes.

▶ 7. The correct answer is A.

QUESTION 11.
What is the maximum overcurrent protection permitted for a 4500-VA, 240-volt, 60-gallon water heater?

A. 20 amperes
B. 25 amperes
C. 30 amperes
D. 35 amperes

ANSWER _____

PROCEDURE TO ESTABLISH ANSWER
The question is about overcurrent protection for water heaters.

▶ 1. In Index, find "Water heaters" under which find "Protection, 422.11(E). 422.11 (F)(3) and 422.13."

▶ 2. Section 422.13, Storage-Type Water Heaters, requires fixed storage type water heaters that have a capacity of 450 L (120 gallons) or less to be considered a continuous load. In Index, find "Continuous Load" under which find "Definitions, Art. 100–Part I." In Article 100, *Continuous load* is defined as "a load where the maximum current is expected to continue for 3 hours or more."

▶ 3. The question relates to branch-circuit overcurrent protective device ratings. In Index, find "Branch circuits" under which find "Overcurrent Protection, 210.20, 240.3." Find 210.20, under which subsection (A) requires the branch-circuit to be rated at 125 percent of the continuous load(s) on the circuit. Therefore, 422.13 requires the minimum branch-circuit rating to be 125 percent of the nameplate rating of storage water heaters.

▶ 4. 4500 VA / 240 = 18.75 A
= 18.75 A x 125% = 23.4 amperes.
The question, however, asks for maximum overcurrent protection.

▶ 5. Section 422.11(E) permits the overcurrent protection for a single non-motor-operated appliance to be not greater than 150 percent of the rating of the appliance. 422.11(E)(3) allows the next higher standard rating overcurrent protective device to be used.

▶ 6. 150% x 18.75 amperes = 28.1 amperes. The next higher standard rating overcurrent protective device (found in Section 240.6) is 30 amperes.

▶ 7. The correct answer is C.

QUESTION 12.
One counter-mounted cooking unit rated at 3000 volt-amperes and two wall-mounted ovens rated at 3500 volt-amperes each are installed in a kitchen of a dwelling unit and are supplied by a single branch circuit. What is permitted as the minimum calculated demand load for this branch circuit?

A. 5500 VA
B. 7000 VA
C. 8000 VA
D. 10,000 VA

ANSWER _____

PROCEDURE TO ESTABLISH ANSWER
The question is about counter-mounted cooking units and built-in ovens, which are synonymous with ranges so there are actually three different approaches to the answer. No matter which way you go, you will end up in the same location.

▶ 1. In the Index find "Cooking unit, counter-mounted," *also see* Ovens, wall mounted; Ranges" or in the Index find "Ovens, wall-mounted," *also see* Cooking unit, counter-mounted; Ranges." The common denominator is "Ranges."

In Index, find "Ranges" under which find "Loads, demand factors and, Table 220.55"

▶ 2. Section 220.55 refers you to Table 220.55. In Table 220.55, Note 4 provides that the load shall be computed by adding the nameplate rating of the individual appliances and treating this total as equivalent to one range.

▶ 3. 3000 VA + 3500 VA + 3500 VA = 10,000 VA or 10 kVA

Referring to Table 220.55 Column C, 8000 VA is the demand load.

▶ 4. The correct answer is C.

QUESTION 13. The net computed load for a single-family dwelling that has a floor area of 2,000 square feet plus a 12 kVA electric range is:

A. 13,100 VA
B. 14, 000 VA
C. 18,000 VA
D. 11,000 VA

ANSWER _____

PROCEDURE TO ESTABLISH ANSWER
The question is about computing the load in a single-family dwelling.

▶ 1. Assume that the only load is based on the question, namely, 2000 square feet, a 12 kVA range, and the minimum number of small appliance circuits normally provided in a dwelling — (2 @ 1,500 VA each for the kitchen — per section 210.11(C). Also assume that there are no laundry facilities for the dwelling (for example, no clothes washer or dryer). Note that laundry facilities are not required to be installed in or at a dwelling, though they usually are for the convenience of the occupants.

▶ 2. Proceed with the calculations.
Lighting load [Table 220.12)]
= 2000 x 3 VA
= 6000 VA

Small appliance load [Sections 210.11(C) (1) and 220.16(A)]
= 1500 x 2
= 3000 VA
Total lighting and small appliance load
= 6000 VA + 3000 VA
= 9,000 VA

▶ 3. Section 220.52(A) permits the small appliance load to be included with the general lighting load and subject to the demand factors permitted in Table 220.42.

▶ 4. Per Table 220.42 first
= 3000 VA x 100%
= 3000
Balance at 35%
= 9,000 – 3000
= 6000
= 6000 x 35%
= 2100 VA

= 3000 VA + 2100 VA
= 5100 VA
Range load from Table 220.55
= 8000 VA
Total computed load
= 5100 VA + 8000 VA
= 13,100 VA

▶ 5. The correct answer is A.

QUESTION 14. A two-story, single-family dwelling measures 28-feet x 50-feet. It has an attached garage with two ceiling lights and three duplex receptacles, plus three weatherproof duplex receptacles and two weatherproof lighting fixtures on the exterior of the dwelling. Using the standard calculation method, what is the computed total general lighting and appliance loads for a 120/240-volt, single-phase service?

A. 17 amperes
B. 27 amperes
C. 35 amperes
D. 54 amperes

ANSWER _____

PROCEDURE TO ESTABLISH ANSWER
The question is about lighting and appliance loads for a dwelling.

▶ 1. In Index, find "Dwellings" under which find "Lighting loads for, Table 220.12."

Note: Section 220.14(J), Dwelling Occupancies, requires receptacle and lighting outlets specified in (J)(1), (J)(2), and (J)(3) to be included in load calculations for dwelling units.

Section 220.12 states that for lighting loads for dwellings, the floor area shall not include garages.

▶ 2. Scan Article 220 in addition to Table 220.12, and find Table 220.42, which provides lighting load demand factors and Section 220.52(A) and (B), which permit the small appliance and laundry load to be included with the lighting load and subject to the demand factors of Table 220.42.

▶ 3. Proceed with the calculations.
General lighting load
(Table 220.12) – 28′ x 50′
= 1400 sq ft x 2 floors
= 2800 sq ft
= 2800 sq ft x 3 VA
= 8400 VA
Small appliance load
(220.52(A))
= 1500 VA x 2
= 3000 VA
Laundry load
(220.52(B))
= 1500 VA x 1
= 1500 VA

Total Load
= 8400 VA + 3000 VA + 1500 VA
= 12,900 VA

Applying demand factors of Table 220.42
First 3000 VA @ 100%
= 3000 VA
= Balance of 12,900 – 3000
= 9900 VA x 35%
= 3465 VA
Total
= 3000 VA + 3465 VA
= 6,465 VA
Computed general lighting and appliance loads
= 6,465 VA / 240V
= 27 amperes

▶ 4. The correct answer is B.

QUESTION 15. When using the optional calculation method for a service for a new dwelling unit, the first 10 kVA of all loads other than heating and cooling loads shall be included at:

A. 40 percent
B. 65 percent
C. 80 percent
D. 100 percent

ANSWER _____

PROCEDURE TO ESTABLISH ANSWER
The question is about load calculations for dwellings.

▶ 1. In Index, find "Dwellings" under which find "Feeder load, calculations for, 220.14(J), 220.82 through 220.85, Annex D."

▶ 2. Section 220.82 applies to optional calculations, and 220.82(B) requires 100 percent of first 10 kVA of other loads to be included.

▶ 3. The correct answer is D.

QUESTION 16. Using the optional calculation method, what is the minimum ampacity required for the current-carrying conductors of a 3-wire, 120/240-volt service for a 2000 square foot single-family dwelling with the following electrical equipment?

Range — rated at 12.5 kVA
Central A/C — rated at 10 kVA
Water heater — rated at 4.5 kVA
Dishwasher — rated at 1.2 kVA
Clothes dryer — rated at 5.0 kVA

A. 81 amperes
B. 100 amperes
C. 123 amperes
D. 140 amperes

ANSWER _____

PROCEDURE TO ESTABLISH ANSWER
The question is about sizing of service-entrance conductors.

▶ 1. In Index, find "Service-entrance conductors" under which find "Size, 230.42."

▶ 2. Section 230.42 requires the service-entrance conductors to be of sufficient size to carry the load computed in Article 220.

▶ 3. Scan Article 220 and find "220.80" and "220.82," which provide an optional calculation method for service load.

▶ 4. Proceed with the calculations, per 220.82. Calculate the "General Loads (B)"
General lighting
= 3 VA x 2,000 sq ft
= 6,000 VA or 6.0 kVA
Range   = 12.5 kVA
Water heater = 4.5 kVA
Dishwasher   = 1.2 kVA
Clothes Dryer = 5.0 kVA
Small appliance circuits
= 1500 VA x 2
= 3000 or 3.0 kVA
Laundry circuit
= 1500 VA x 1
= 1500 or 1.5 kVA

Other loads
= 33.7 kVA
= 1st 10 kVA @ 100%
= 10.0 kVA
= 33.7 kVA – 10 kVA
= 23.7 kVA
= 23.7 kVA x .4 (40%)
= 9.5 kVA
= 10 kVA + 9.5 kVA
= 19.5 kVA Total Load per Part B

Plus 100% of the air conditioning load (assumed larger than heating load)
= 10.0 kVA
= 19.5 kVA + 10 kVA
Air Conditioner Load
= 29.5 kVA

▶ 5. Required ampacity = 29,500 VA / 240V = 123 amperes

▶ 6. The correct answer is C.

QUESTION 17. Using the standard calculation method, what is the minimum ampacity required for the 120/240-volt service-entrance conductors to a 4,000 square foot single-family residence with the following load:

1. 4,000 square feet
2. Built-in oven, 8 kVA, 120/240 volt
3. Counter-mounted cooktop, 4 kVA, 120/240 volt
4. Dishwasher, 9 amp, 120 volt
5. Disposer, 6 amp, 120 volt
6. Four vent fans, each 300 VA, 120 volt
7. Water heater, 4.5 kVA, 240 volt
8. Dryer, 4,500 VA, 120/240 volt
9. Sprinkler system, 300 VA, 120 volt
10. A/C, 35 amp, 240 volt
11. Heat, (10 separately controlled units), 20 kVA, 240 volt

A. 194 amperes
B. 200 amperes
C. 202 amperes
D. 231 amperes

ANSWER _____

PROCEDURE TO ESTABLISH ANSWER

The question is about the sizing of service-entrance conductors.

▶ 1. In Index find "Service-entrance conductors," under which find "Size, 230.42."

▶ 2. Section 230.42 requires the service-entrance conductors to be of sufficient size to carry the load computed in Article 220.

▶ 3. Proceed with the calculations.

General lighting per (Table 220.12)
= 4000 sq ft x 3 VA
= 12,000 VA

Kitchen small appliance [210.11(C)(1) & 220.52(A)],
= 1500 x 2
= 3,000 VA

Laundry circuit (210.11(C) (2) & 220.52(B))
= 1500 x 1
= 1,500 VA

Total General lighting and small appliance load

= 12,000 VA + 3000 VA + 1500 VA
= 16,500 VA

Table 220.42,
1st 3,000 VA @ 100%
= 3000 VA
Balance of 13,500 VA @ 35%
= 4725 VA

Net General Lighting and small appliance load
= 3000 VA + 4725 VA
= 7725 VA

Oven and Countertop Unit (Table 220.55, Note 4),
= 8 kVA + 4 kVA
= 12 kVA (Treat as one range)
Demand factor = 8000 VA or 8kVA per Table 220.55

Other Appliance Loads (220.53)
Dishwasher
= 9A x 120V
= 1080 VA
Disposer
= 6A x 120V
= 720 VA
Vent fans
= 4 x 300 VA
= 1200 VA
Water heater
= 4500 VA
Sprinkler
= 300 VA
Total Appliance Load (220.53)
= 7800 VA x .75
= 5850 VA

Dryer (220.54) 5000 VA or nameplate, whichever is larger
= 5000 VA

A/C or Heating Load (220.60) only required to include:
Largest noncoincident load, which is heating load.
Heating (220.51) 20 kVA @ 100%
= 20,000 VA
25% of largest motor [430.24].

Since largest motor would be the A/C motor load and the A/C load is not included, do not include 25%.

Total calculated load
= 46,575 VA

▶ 4. Required ampacity
= VA / volts
= 46, 575 / 240
= 194 amperes

▶ 5. The correct answer is A.

QUESTION 18. Using the optional method of calculation, what is the minimum ampacity for the same dwelling and load as stated in Question 17?

A. 107 amperes
B. 129 amperes
C. 148 amperes
D. 215 amperes

ANSWER _____

PROCEDURE TO ESTABLISH ANSWER

The question is about the sizing of service-entrance conductors.

▶ 1. In Index, find "Service-entrance conductors" under which find "Size, 230.42."

▶ 2. Section 230.42 requires the service-entrance conductors to be of sufficient size to carry the load computed in Article 220.

▶ 3. Scan Article 220 and find Sections 220.80 and 220.82, which provide an optional calculation method for service load.

▶ 4. Proceed with the calculations.

First calculate the "general loads."
General lighting
= 3 kVA x 4000 sq ft
= 12,000 or 12.0 kVA
Small appliance circuits
= 1500 VA x 2
= 3000 or 3.0 kVA
Laundry circuit
= 1500 VA x 2
= 1500 or 1.5 kVA
Built-in oven
= 8.0 kVA
Counter-mounted cooking unit
= 4.0 kVA
Dishwasher
= 9 A x 120 V
= 1080 or 1.08 kVA
Disposer
= 6 A x 120 V
= 720 or 0.72 kVA
Vent fans
= 4 x 300 VA
= 1,200 or 1.2 kVA
Water heater
= 4.5 kVA
Dryer
= 5.0 kVA (5,000 is larger per 220.54)
Sprinkler system
= 300VA or 0.3 kVA
The sum of all general loads
= 41.3 kVA

1st 10 kVA @ 100% = 10.0 kVA
(41.3 - 10.00 = 31.3)
Plus remainder @ 40%
= 31.3 kVA x 40% or 0.4
= 12.52 kVA
(1st 10 kVA + remainder @ 40%)
10 kVA + 12.52 kVA = 22.52 kVA

General loads (amperes)
= 22,520 VA / 240 volts
= 93.83 amperes

Per Section 220.82 (C),
A/C load
= 100% x 35 amps
= 35 amperes
Heating load
= 40% x 20,000 VA
= 8,000 VA / 240V
= 33.3 amperes
(40% based on 4 or more separately controlled unit)
Use larger A/C load of 35 amps, per 220.82(C)

▶ 5. Calculated minimum ampacity
= 35 amperes + 93.83 amps
= 128.83 amperes.
Round up to 129 amperes.

▶ 6. The correct answer is B.

QUESTION 19. Where the residential lighting load is computed on the three volt-amperes per square foot basis, the Code requires one 15-amp, 120-volt branch circuit for each:

A. 350 square foot
B. 500 square foot
C. 575 square foot
D. 600 square foot

ANSWER _____

PROCEDURE TO ESTABLISH ANSWER
The question is about dwelling lighting load.

▶ 1. In Index, find "Branch circuits" under which find "Calculation of loads, 220–Part II, Annex D."

▶ 2. Section 220.12 and Table 220.12 require 3 VA per square foot for dwelling units.

▶ 3. Proceed with the calculations.
= 15 amps x 120 volts
= 1800 VA
= 1800 VA / 3 VA per sq. ft.
= 600 square feet.

▶ 4. The correct answer is D.

Note: Section Table 220.12 and 220.14(J), as well as the examples in Annex D, affirm the answer.

QUESTION 20. Three Type NM 2-wire with ground cables (two 12 AWG and one 14 AWG) enter a single-gang nonmetallic outlet box with standard internal cable clamps. The 12 AWG conductors are spliced together within the box and the 14 AWG conductors connect to a switch within the box. What is the minimum size outlet box required?

A. 295 cm^3 (18.0 cubic in.)
B. 344 cm^3 (21.0 cubic in.)
C. 353 cm^3 (21.5 cubic in.)
D. 395 cm^3 (24.0 cubic in.)

ANSWER _____

PROCEDURE TO ESTABLISH ANSWER
The question is about box fill.

▶ 1. In Index, find "Boxes (outlet, device, pull, and junction)" under which find "Fill calculations, 314.16(B)."

▶ 2. Section 314.16(B) requires adding together conductor volumes in paragraphs (1) through (5).

▶ 3. Proceed with the calculations.
(1) The 12 AWG conductors count as four (4) 12 AWG.
(2) The 14 AWG conductors count as two (2) 14 AWG.
(3) The internal cable clamps count as one (1) 12 AWG.
(4) The device (switch) counts as two (2) 14 AWG.
(5) The equipment grounding conductors count as one (1) 12 AWG.

▶ 4. From the above calculations, the conductor fill totals six (6) 12 AWGs and four (4) 14 AWGs
= Six (6) 12 AWG @ 36.9 cm^3 (2.25 cu. in.)
= 13.5 cu. in.
= Four (4) 14 AWG @ 32.8 cm^3 (2.0 cu. in.)
= 8.0 cu. in.

Minimum size box
= 21.5 cubic in

▶ 5. The correct answer is C.

Note: For a nonmetallic box, or a box whose size is not found in Table 314.16, it is necessary to check the cubic inch capacity marked on the box to verify that it has a capacity of at least 21.5 cubic inches.

QUESTION 21. The minimum permitted ampacity of a 240-volt electrical distribution system feeder to six mobile home sites is:

A. 116 amperes
B. 232 amperes
C. 400 amperes
D. 600 amperes

ANSWER _____

PROCEDURE TO ESTABLISH ANSWER
The question is about size of feeders in mobile home parks.

▶ 1. In Index, find "Mobile home parks" under which find "Electrical wiring system" under which find "Feeder and service demand factors, 550.18, 550–Part III, Table 550.31."

▶ 2. Section 550.31 provides for demand factors for more than one mobile home site.

▶ 3. Table 550.31 permits a demand factor of 29 percent (for six sites) of that permitted for a single site (16,000 VA) per Section 550.31, Item (1).

▶ 4. Proceed with the calculations.
= 16, 000 VA per home x 6 (for six M.H. sites)
= 96,000 VA

= 96,000 VA x .29 (29% demand factor for six sites)
= 27,840 VA
Total load of 27,840 VA / 240 V
= 116 amperes

▶ 5. The feeder ampacity shall be a minimum of 116 amperes.

▶ 6. The correct answer is A.

QUESTION 22. A two-family dwelling in which each unit is over 1000 square feet without laundry facilities has a final calculated load of 23,000 volt-amperes. The plans are changed to provide laundry facilities in each unit. The clothes dryers will be natural gas type. The revised final calculated load would be:

A. 23,150 VA
B. 24,050 VA
C. 24,500 VA
D. 26,000 VA

ANSWER _____

PROCEDURE TO ESTABLISH ANSWER
The question is about the calculation of laundry load.

▶ 1. In Index, find "Laundry" under which find "Circuit load, 220.52(B)."

▶ 2. Section 220.52(B) requires a laundry load of 1500 VA for each laundry circuit. This load is permitted to be included with the general lighting load and subject to the demand factors in Section 220.42.

▶ 3. The final calculated load in question already included the demand factors of Table 220.42. Since the original calculation included the first 3000 VA at 100 percent, only 35 percent would be applied to the two additional laundry circuits.

▶ 4. Two laundry circuits x 1,500 VA
    = 3000 VA x 35%
        = 1050 VA.

▶ 5. The final revised calculated load is:
    = 23,000 VA + 1050 VA
    = 24,050 VA.

▶ 6. The correct answer is B.

QUESTION 23. A nonmetallic junction box that contains two 12 AWG and four 14 AWG Type NM cables with ground copper conductors shall have a minimum capacity of how many cubic inches?

A. 353 cm^3 (21.5 cu in)
B. 395 cm^3 (24.0 cu in)
C. 409 cm^3 (27.25 cu in)
D. 418 cm^3 (25.5 cu in)

ANSWER _____

PROCEDURE TO ESTABLISH ANSWER
The question is about box fill.

▶ 1. In Index, find "Boxes (outlet, device, pull, and junction)" under which find "Fill calculations, 314.16(B)."

▶ 2. Section 314.16(B)(1), Conductor Fill, requires the conductor to be computed using Table 314.16(B).

▶ 3. Section 314.16(B)(5) requires that where one or more equipment grounding conductors enter a box, a single volume allowance in accordance with Table 314.16(B) shall be made based on the largest equipment grounding conductor present in the box.

   4— 12 AWG @ 36.9 cm^3 (2.25 cu. in.)
    = 9.00 cu. in.
   8 — 14 AWG @ 32.8 cm^3 (2.00 cu. in.)
    = 16.00 cu. in.
   1 — 12 AWG @ 36.9 cm^3 (2.25 cu. in.)
    = 2.25 cu. in.
   Total minimum capacity
    = 9.00 cu. in. + 16.00 cu. in. + 2.25 cu. in.
    = 27.25 cu. in.

▶ 4. The correct answer is C.

Calculations | 1- and 2-Family Study Guide | 133

QUESTION 24. What is the minimum size metal device box required for four 12 AWG Type THWN copper conductors, two 12 AWG bare equipment grounding conductors and one duplex receptacle?

A. 75 mm x 50 mm x 90 mm
 (3 in. x 2 in. x 3½ in.)
B. 75 mm x 50 mm x 70 mm
 (3 in. x 2 in. x 2¾ in.)
C. 75 mm x 50 mm x 65 mm
 (3 in. x 2 in. x 2½ in.)
D. 75 mm x 50 mm x 57 mm
 (3 in. x 2 in. x 2¼ in.)

ANSWER _____

PROCEDURE TO ESTABLISH ANSWER
The question is about box fill.

▶ 1. In Index, find "Boxes (outlet, device, pull, and junction)" under which find "Fill calculations, 314.16(B)."

▶ 2. Section 314.16(B) requires adding together conductor volumes in paragraphs (1) through (5).
(1) Conductor fill, four (4) 12 AWG conductors count as 4 conductors.
(2) Using a metal box, internal cable clamps would be required to be counted as 1 conductor.
(4) Device fill, one receptacle counts as 2 conductors.
(5) Equipment grounding conductor fill, two grounds count as 1 conductor.

Total number of conductors is = 8 conductors

▶ 3. Since all of the conductors are 12 AWG, the fill is based on that size.

▶ 4. [From Table 314.16(B)]
 = 8 conductor volumes x 2.25 cu. in.
  = 18 cu. in.

▶ 5. Scanning down the "Minimum Volume" column of Table 314.16(A) indicates that a 75 mm x 50 mm x 57 mm (3 in. x 2 in. x 3 1/2 in.) device box is required.

▶ 6. Since all of the conductors are the same size, the answer can be confirmed by scanning down the "12 AWG" column under "Maximum Number of Conductors*" of Table 314.16(A), which confirms that Answer A is true. There are two other sizes of boxes in the table that would allow 18 maximum, 12-AWG conductors to be installed. However the question asks for the size of a "device" box and Answer A is the only one of the three that is specified as a "device" box in Table 310.16(A) with a size that is included in the choice of answers.

▶ 7. The correct answer is A.

QUESTION 25. The following information is stated on the nameplate of a central air conditioning unit: "COMPRESSOR RLA – 19.0 AMPS; FAN MOTOR – 1.4 AMPS; MAX FUSE OR C/B SIZE – 40 AMPS." What is the minimum size THW conductor permitted to supply this A/C unit?

A. 12 AWG
B. 10 AWG
C. 8 AWG
D. 6 AWG

ANSWER _____

PROCEDURE TO ESTABLISH ANSWER
The question is about branch-circuit conductors for an air conditioning unit.

▶ 1. In Index, find "Air conditioning and refrigerating equipment" under which find "Branch circuit" under which find "Conductors, 440–Part IV."

▶ 2. Scan Article 440, Part IV, and find "440.33," which applies to motor-compressors with additional motor loads. This section requires conductors to have an ampacity not less than the rated-load rating (RLA) of motor-compressors plus full-load currents of other motors plus 25 percent of the highest motor rating.

▶ 3. Proceed with the calculations.

134 | 1- and 2-Family Study Guide | Calculations

Compressor RLA
= 19.0 amps
Fan motor compressor RLA
= 1.4 amps
Plus 25% compressor RLA (19.0 A x .25)
= 4.75 amps
Minimum conductor ampacity
= 19.0 amps + 1.4 amps + 4.75 amps
= 25.15 amps

▶ 4. Reviewing Ampacity Table 310.15(B)(16) confirms that a 10 AWG is the minimum size permitted. Conductor terminations per 110.14 (C)(1)(a) are not specified, so the ampacity of the conductor is taken from the 60°C column of Table 310.15(B)(16).

▶ 5. The correct answer is B.

Note: Section 110.5 provides that where conductor material is not specified, the sizes shall apply to copper conductors.

Note: Although the nameplate information given in the question does not include it, typical A/C nameplates will also include a term "MINIMUM CIRCUIT AMPACITY" or "MIN CKT AMPS." If this term is provided, the figure given for it already includes the calculations and it is only necessary to use a conductor with an ampacity based on this stated circuit ampacity.

QUESTION 26. The minimum neutral ampacity for a branch circuit supplying a range where its maximum demand was computed according to Column C of Table 220.55 shall be not less than what percent of the branch-circuit rating?

A. 70 percent
B. 75 percent
C. 80 percent
D. 100 percent

ANSWER _____

PROCEDURE TO ESTABLISH ANSWER
The question is about branch-circuit conductors for ranges.

▶ 1. In Index, find "Ranges" under which find "Branch circuits, 210.19(A)(3)" under which find "Conductors, 210.19."

▶ 2. Section 210.19(A)(3), Exception No. 2, requires the neutral ampacity to be at least 70 percent of the branch-circuit rating.

▶ 3. The correct answer is A.

Note: Section 220.61(B) contains the same 70 percent rule with regard to feeders or services.

QUESTION 27. The load of a single-family residence has been computed at 138 amperes with a 120/240-volt, single-phase service. The service consists of three 2/0 AWG THW copper conductors terminating in a main 200-ampere fusible disconnect. What is the maximum ampere rating permitted for the fuses in the main disconnect?

A. 125 amperes
B. 150 amperes
C. 175 amperes
D. 200 amperes

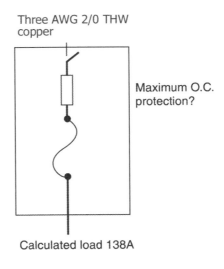

ANSWER _____

PROCEDURE TO ESTABLISH ANSWER
The question is about the size and overcurrent protection for service-entrance conductors.

▶ 1. In Index, find "Conductors" under which find "Ampacities of, 310.15, etc."

▶ 2. Section 310.15(B) provides that the ampacities of conductors rated 0 to 2000 volts are to be as shown in Tables 310.15(B)(16) through 310.15(B)(19) as modified by 310.15(B)(1) through (7).

▶ 3. Section 310.15(B)(7) permits the services conductors supplying all the load to a 200-ampere dwelling service to be sized at 83% the rating of the service. In this case; 200 ampere rating x .83 = 166 amperes.

In Table 310.15(B)(16) the specified 2/0 AWG THW copper conductor has an allowable ampacity of 175 amperes which exceeds the minimum required by 310.15(B)(7).

▶ 4. In Index, find "Service-entrance conductors" under which find "Overcurrent protection, 230.90, 230.91, 230.92, 230.208."

▶ 5. Section 230.90(A) requires each ungrounded service-entrance conductor to have overcurrent protection not higher than the allowable ampacity of the conductor. Although the actual ampacity of 2/0 AWG Type THW copper is 175 amperes based on Table 310.15(B)(16), Exception No. 5 to Section 230.90(A) allows the overcurrent protection to be based on service sizes permitted by 310.15(B)(7).

▶ 6. Therefore, a 175-ampere overcurrent device is allowed.

▶ 7. The correct answer is C.

QUESTION 28. The maximum watts per square foot of heated area for heating panels installed in concrete or masonry floors shall not exceed:

A. 3
B. 15
C. 33
D. 120

ANSWER _____

PROCEDURE TO ESTABLISH ANSWER
The question is about the installation of heating panels.

▶ 1. In Index, find "Heating panels and heating panel sets, radiant. see Fixed electric space-heating equipment." Next, in Index, find "Fixed electric space-heating equipment" under which find Radiant heating panels and heating panel sets, 424–Part IX, 427.23(B)" under which find "Installation of, 424.93, 424.98 and 424.99."

▶ 2. Section 424.98(A), Maximum Heated Area, requires heating panels or heating panel sets to not exceed 33 watts per square foot of heated area.

▶ 3. The correct answer is C.

QUESTION 29. What is the minimum size electrical metallic tubing required to enclose all of the following conductors?

Six – 10 AWG Type THHN
Three – 4 AWG Type THW
Two – 12 AWG Type THWN

A. Metric designator 27
   (Trade size 1 in.)
B. Metric designator 35
   (Trade size 1¼ in.)
C. Metric designator 41
   (Trade size 1½ in.)
D. Metric designator 53
   (Trade size 2 in.)

ANSWER _____

PROCEDURE TO ESTABLISH ANSWER
The question is about conductor fill in electrical metallic tubing.

▶ 1. In Index, find "Conductor fill" under which find "Electrical metallic tubing, 358.22."

▶ 2. Section 358.22 refers to Table 1, Chapter 9, which permits a 40 percent raceway fill.

▶ 3. Note 6 to Table 1 provides that for combinations of conductors of different size, use Tables 5 and 5A in Chapter 9 for dimensions of conductors and Table 4 for applicable conduit or tubing dimensions.

▶ 4. Referring to Table 5 for conductor area,
10 AWG Type THHN area of
= .0211 x 6 conductors
= 0.1266
4 AWG Type THW area of
= .0973 x 3 conductors
= 0.2919
12 AWG Type THWN area of
= .0133 x 2 conductors
= 0.0266
Total
= 0.1266 + 0.2919 + 0.0266
= 0.4451 sq. in.

▶ 5. Per Table 4 for "Electrical Metallic Tubing," under the "Over 2 Wires 40%" column, a metric designator 27 (1 in.) EMT conduit has an area of 0.346 sq. in. A metric designator 35 (1-1/4 in.) EMT conduit has an area of 0.598 square inches.

▶ 6. Therefore, a metric designator 35 (1 ¼ in.) EMT is required.

▶ 7. The correct answer is B.

QUESTION 30. Which of the following statements about the minimum size of a raceway that is 1.2 m (48 in.) long, through which 6 cables enter a panelboard cabinet is true?

A. The actual dimensions of the cables are permitted to be used to determine the minimum size of raceway.
B. For cables that have elliptical cross sections, the cross-sectional calculation must be based on the major diameter of the ellipse as a circle diameter, and the maximum % fill is 40 percent.
C. The raceway is permitted to be filled to 60 percent.
D. The raceway is permitted to be filled to 53 percent.

ANSWER _____

PROCEDURE TO ESTABLISH ANSWER
The question is about rules for installing cables in a raceway to enter a panelboard cabinet.

▶ 1. In Index, find "Cabinets, cutout boxes, and meter socket enclosures, Art. 312."

▶ 2. Scan Article 312 and find "312.5(C), Cables."

▶ 3. Subdivision (g) of the exception requires that the raceway, where installed as conduit or tubing, must comply with Table 1 of Chapter 9 and all applicable notes thereto. Answer A is not true.

▶ 4. Note 9 to Table 1 of Chapter 9 indicates that cables having elliptical cross sections, the cross-sectional area calculation shall be based on using the major diameter of the ellipse as a circle diameter. Answer B is true.

▶ 5. Since the raceway is longer than 600 mm (24 in.), it is not permitted to be filled to 60 percent per Note 4 to Table 1 of Chapter 9. Answer C is not true.

▶ 6. Since the raceway has more than one cable, it is not permitted to be filled to 53 percent per Table 1. Answer D is not true.

▶ 7. The correct answer is B.

QUESTION 31. When using the optional calculation, loads added to an existing dwelling unit are permitted to be calculated per Section:

A. 220.83
B. 220.43
C. 220.44
D. 220.14(F)

ANSWER _____

PROCEDURE TO ESTABLISH ANSWER
The question is about calculations for existing dwelling unit loads.

▶ 1. In Index, find "Calculations, Annex D. *see also* Loads." In "Loads," there is no mention of existing dwelling units. Next, go to the "Table of Contents" in the front of the book. Under Article 220, we find "Part IV–Optional Service and Feeder Load Calculations."

▶ 2. Scanning Article 220, Part IV, we find "220.83, Existing Dwelling Unit." Sections 220.43,

220.44, and 220.14(F) are all used for non-dwelling unit calculations.

▶ 3. The correct answer is A.

QUESTION 32.
The calculated feeder load for 23 dryers rated at 4500 VA each connected to a multi-family dwelling service is:

A. 103,500 VA
B. 115,000 VA
C. 40,250 VA
D. 36,225 VA

ANSWER _____

PROCEDURE TO ESTABLISH ANSWER
The question is about calculations for dwelling unit dryer loads.

▶ 1. In Index, find "Clothes dryers" under which find "Calculations, for, 220.54."

▶ 2. In 220.54, unless stated at a larger load, the minimum load for one individual dryer is 5000 watts (volt-amperes). Use of the demand factors in Table 220.54 is permitted.

▶ 3. = 23 dryers x 5,000 VA per dryer
= 115,000 VA x 35% (.35)
= 40,250 VA

▶ 4. The correct answer is C.

QUESTION 33.
A dwelling unit has three 2-wire multiwire branch circuits in 3/4-inch electrical metal tubing. All conductors are 12 AWG Type THW conductors. What is the maximum allowable ampacity for each conductor?

A. 16 amperes
B. 17.5 amperes
C. 20 amperes
D. 25 amperes

ANSWER _____

PROCEDURE TO ESTABLISH ANSWER
The question is about allowable ampacity of conductors.

▶ 1. In Index, find "Conductors" under which find "Ampacities of, 310.15, etc."

▶ 2. Section 310.15(B) requires ampacities to be as specified in the Allowable Ampacity Tables 310.15(B)(16) through 310.15(B)(19), and Ampacity Tables 310.15(B)(20) and 310.15(B)(21) as modified by (B)(1) through (B)(7).

▶ 3. In Table 310.15(B)(16), 12 AWG THW = 20 amperes. See 310.15(B)(4)(a) regarding "Neutral Conductors" and 310.15(B)(3) regarding "Adjustment Factors."

▶ 4. Section 310.15(B)(5)(a) applies in this installation, and the neutrals are not required to be counted as current-carrying conductors, so there would therefore be six current-carrying conductors.

Three circuits x 2 wires per circuit = 6 wires total.

▶ 5. Because there are six current-carrying conductors in the raceway, 310.15(B)(3)(a) requires an 80 percent derating factor to be applied.

▶ 6. = 80% x 20 amperes
= 16 amperes.

▶ 7. The correct answer is A.

11 Swimming Pools

QUESTION 1. Which one of the following statements concerning swimming pool wiring is NOT true?

A. A standard duplex 125-volt receptacle for a pool water pump motor must be located at least 1.83 m (6 ft) from the inside wall of a permanently installed pool.
B. All 125-volt receptacles installed within 6.0 m (20 ft) of the inside wall of a pool must be GFCI-protected.
C. Utility-owned service drop wires may not be run over swimming pools under any condition.
D. Underground wiring is permitted to be installed within 2.5 m (8 ft) of permanently installed swimming pool.

ANSWER _____

PROCEDURE TO ESTABLISH ANSWER
The question is about receptacles, overhead and underground wiring near swimming pools.

▶ 1. In Index, find "Swimming pools, fountains, and similar installations" under which find "Receptacles, location and protection, 680.22(A), 680.32, 680.34, 680.43(A), 680.62(E)."

▶ 2. Section 680.22(A)(2) states receptacles that do not meet conditions (1) through (3) must be at least 3.0 m (10 ft) from pool. Answer A is true.

▶ 3. Section 680.22(A)(4) confirms Answer B as true.

▶ 4. In Index, find "Swimming pools, fountains and similar installations" under which find "Overhead conductor clearances, 680.8." Section 680.8(A) permits service drops over pools in accordance with the minimum clearances given in Table 680.8. Answer C is not true.

▶ 5. In Index, find "Underground wiring" under which find "Swimming pools, 680.10." Section 680.10 allows underground wiring near a pool under the stated conditions. Answer D is true.

▶ 6. The correct answer is C.

Swimming Pools | 1- and 2-Family Study Guide | 139

QUESTION 2. A receptacle provided for a swimming pool water pump shall comply with which one of the following?

A. May be located between 3.0 m and 6.0 m (10 ft and 20 ft) from the pool with no GFCI protection
B. May be located between 1.83 m and 3.0 m (6 ft and 10 ft) from the pool if it is of the single, locking and grounded type with GFCI protection.
C. Shall be located more than 6.0 m (20 ft) from the pool
D. Shall be located at least 1.5 m (5 ft) above the pool deck level

ANSWER _____

PROCEDURE TO ESTABLISH ANSWER
The question is about receptacles at swimming pools.

▶ 1. In Index, find "Swimming pools, fountains and similar installations" under which find "Receptacles, location and protection, 680.22(A), 680.32, etc."

▶ 2. Section 680.22(A) provides the requirements for receptacles at pools. Section 680.22(A)(2) permits a receptacle that provides power for a water pump for the circulation or sanitation system to be between 1.83 m and 3.0 m (6 ft and 10 ft) from the pool if of the single, locking, and grounding type with GFCI protection. Answer B is true and Answers A and C are not true. There is no height requirement specified in 680.22(A)(2) so Answer D is also not true.

▶ 3. The correct answer is B.

QUESTION 3. Which one of the following statements about bonding all metal parts of permanently installed swimming pools is true?

A. A solid 8 AWG copper conductor is required to be installed as a complete loop around all swimming pools.
B. A separate ground rod must be driven near each metal part of the pool.
C. The earth contact with the metal parts of the pool is sufficient bonding.
D. Where bonded together by a conductor, all metal parts of the pool required to be bonded together by a solid 8 AWG copper wire that can be insulated, covered or bare.

ANSWER _____

PROCEDURE TO ESTABLISH ANSWER
The question is about bonding at swimming pools.

▶ 1. In Index, find "Swimming pools, fountains and similar installations" under which find, "Bonding, 680.26…"

▶ 2. Section 680.26(B) requires all parts specified in 680.26(B)(1)-(7) to be bonded together by a solid conductor not smaller than 8 AWG that can be insulated covered or bare or with rigid metal conduit of brass or other identified corrosion-resistant metal. Answer D is true. Answer C is not true.

▶ 3. The last sentence of 680.26(B) notes a solid copper bonding conductor provided to reduce voltage gradients in the pool area shall not be required to be extended or attached to remote panelboards, service equipment, or electrodes. Answer B is not true.

▶ 4. The correct answer is D.

QUESTION 4. On a new residence, a luminaire or lighting outlet within 1.2 m (4 ft) of the inside wall of an outdoor pool shall have a height of not less than what distance above maximum water level?

A. 1.5 m (5 ft)
B. 2.5 m (8 ft)
C. 3.7 m (12 ft)
D. 4.5 m (15 ft)

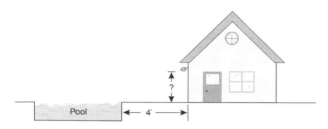

ANSWER _____

PROCEDURE TO ESTABLISH ANSWER
The question is about lighting fixtures at swimming pools.

▶ 1. In Index, find "Swimming pools, fountains and similar installations" under which find "Lighting, 680.22(B), 680.23, 680.26(B)(2), 680.33, etc."

▶ 2. Section 680.22(B)(1) requires luminaires and lighting outlets installed within 1.5 m (5 ft) horizontally from the inside walls of a swimming pool to be located at least 3.7 m (12 ft) above water level.

▶ 3. Since the luminaire or lighting outlet is less than 1.5 m (5 ft) horizontally from the pool it must have a height of not less than 3.7 m (12 ft).

▶ 4. The correct answer is C.

QUESTION 5. Existing luminaires rigidly attached to the existing structure and located less than 1.5 m (5 ft) measured horizontally from the inside walls of a pool shall be at least _____ above the surface of the maximum water level and GFCI-protected?

A. 1.2 m (4 ft)
B. 1.5 m (5 ft)
C. 3.0 m (10 ft)
D. 4.5 m (15 ft)

ANSWER _____

PROCEDURE TO ESTABLISH ANSWER
The question is about lighting fixtures at swimming pools.

▶ 1. In Index, find "Swimming pools, fountains and similar installations" under which find "Lighting, 680.22(B), 680.23, 680.26(B)(2), 680.33, etc"

▶ 2. Section 680.22(B)(3) requires that existing luminaires and outlets located less than 1.5 m (5 ft) horizontally from the pool be at least 1.5 m (5 ft) above the maximum water level.

▶ 3. The correct answer is B.

QUESTION 6. Overhead communications conductors other than utility owned are required to be maintained at least _____ above a swimming pool?

A. 3.0 m (10 ft)
B. 3.7 m (12 ft)
C. 4.5 m (15 ft)
D. 4.9 m (16 ft)

ANSWER _____

Swimming Pools | 1- and 2-Family Study Guide | 141

PROCEDURE TO ESTABLISH ANSWER
The question is about overhead conductor clearances near pools.

▶ 1. In Index, find "Swimming pools, fountains and similar installations" under which find "Overhead conductor clearances, 680.8."

▶ 2. Section 680.8(B) is relevant to communications systems conductors and requires a minimum of 3.0 m (10 ft) above a swimming pool for overhead communication conductors.

▶ 3. The correct answer is A.

QUESTION 7. Utility service-drop conductors not over 750-volts to ground passing over a diving platform shall have a minimum clearance of _____ in any direction to the diving platform?

A. 3.0 m (10 ft)
B. 3.7 m (12 ft)
C. 4.4 m (14.5 ft)
D. 5.5 m (18 ft)

ANSWER _____

PROCEDURE TO ESTABLISH ANSWER
The question is about overhead clearances near swimming pools.

▶ 1. In Index, find "Swimming pools, fountains and similar installations" under which find "Overhead conductor clearances, 680.8."

▶ 2. Section 680.8(A) refers to Table 680.8 for service drops and overhead conductors. Find the "0-750 Volts to Ground" column and intersect with "Row B" which requires a minimum of 4.4 m (14.5 ft) clearance in any direction to a diving platform.

▶ 3. The correct answer is C.

QUESTION 8. Which one of the following statements regarding a flexible cord used to supply the pump for a permanently installed pool is NOT true?

A. The flexible cord shall have a copper equipment grounding conductor not smaller than 12 AWG.
B. The flexible cord shall be equipped with a grounding-type attachment plug.
C. The cord shall not exceed 900 mm (3 ft) in length.
D. The cord is permitted to be 6.0 m (20 ft) in length if protected by a GFCI.

ANSWER _____

PROCEDURE TO ESTABLISH ANSWER
The question is about cord- and plug-connections for permanently installed swimming pools.

▶ 1. In Index, find "Swimming pools, fountains and similar installations" under which find "Cord-and-plug-connected equipment, 680.7, 680.21(5), 680.22(B)(5), 680.31, 680.42(A)(2), 680.56."

▶ 2. Section 680.7(A) requires for pools, other than storable pools, that the flexible cord not exceed 900 mm (3 ft) in length. Answer C is true. Answer D is not true.

▶ 3. Section 680.7(B) requires the cord to have a copper equipment grounding conductor not smaller than 12 AWG with a grounding-type attachment plug. Answers A and B are true.

▶ 4. The correct answer is D.

QUESTION 9. Which one of the following wiring methods is permitted to supply a permanently installed swimming pool filter pump motor that is located in the attached garage of a dwelling unit?

A. Type NM cable with bare equipment grounding conductor
B. Rigid polyvinyl chloride conduit (PVC) with an insulated equipment grounding conductor
C. Liquidtight flexible metal or nonmetallic conduit with an insulated equipment grounding conductor
D. All of the above

ANSWER _____

PROCEDURE TO ESTABLISH ANSWER
The question is about wiring methods and grounding at a swimming pool.

▶ 1. In Index, find "Swimming pools, fountains and similar installations" under which find "Permanently installed, 680–Part II" and "Grounding, 680.6, 680.7(B), 680.23(B)(3) & (4), and (F)(2), 680.24(D) and (F), 680.25(B), 680.43(F), 680.54, 680.55."

▶ 2. Scan 680, Part II, and find "680.21, Motors."

▶ 3. Section 680.21(A)(1) requires the branch circuit to be installed in rigid metal or intermediate conduit, polyvinyl chloride conduit (PVC) or reinforced thermal resin conduit (RTRC) or MC cable listed for the location. The last sentence specifies that any wiring method employed must have an insulated copper equipment grounding conductor sized in accordance with Table 250.122 but not smaller than 12 AWG. Answer B is a permitted wiring method.

▶ 4. Section 680.21(A)(3) covers flexible connections at or adjacent to motors and permits liquidtight flexible metal or nonmetallic conduit to be used. Answer C is a permitted wiring method.

▶ 5. Section 680.21(A)(4) is specific to one-family dwellings and permits cable assemblies that contain a bare equipment grounding conductor where it is covered by the outer sheath of the cable and installed in interior installations of one-family dwellings or accessory buildings associated with the one-family dwelling. Answer A is a permitted wiring method.

▶ 6. The correct answer is D.

QUESTION 10. Where a wet-niche underwater luminaire is installed in a permanently installed swimming pool, all of the following wiring methods between the forming shell and the suitable junction box located at least 1.2 m (4 ft) from the inside wall of the pool are acceptable EXCEPT:

A. steel intermediate metal conduit
B. rigid nonmetallic conduit
C. liquidtight flexible nonmetallic conduit
D. brass rigid metal conduit

ANSWER _____

PROCEDURE TO ESTABLISH ANSWER
The question relates to wet-niche luminaires for swimming pools.

▶ 1. In Index, find "Swimming pools, fountains and similar installations" under which find "Underwater luminaires, 680.23, 680.26(B)(2), 680.33, 680.43(B)(2)."

▶ 2. Under 680.23(B), Wet-Niche Luminaires, find 680.23(B)(2)(a) which recognizes metal conduit of brass or other approved corrosion-resistant metal. Steel intermediate metal conduit and rigid metal conduit are not considered a corrosion-resistant metal. Answer D is true.

▶ 3. Section 680.23(B)(2) recognizes liquidtight flexible nonmetallic conduit, or rigid nonmetallic conduit. Answers B and C are true.

▶ 4. The correct answer is A.

QUESTION 11. A wet-niche underwater luminaire is installed in a permanently installed swimming pool. The junction box serving this fixture is provided with three threaded conduit hubs. How many grounding terminals are required in this box?

A. 1
B. 2
C. 3
D. 4

ANSWER _____

PROCEDURE TO ESTABLISH ANSWER
The question is about junction boxes at swimming pools.

▶ 1. In Index, find "Swimming pools, fountains and similar installations" under which find "Junction boxes and enclosures, 680.23(C)(2), 680.24."

▶ 2. Section 680.24(D), Grounding Terminals, requires that the junction box which is connected to the forming shell by a conduit shall be provided with one more grounding terminal than the number of conduit entries.

▶ 3. The correct answer is D.

QUESTION 12. Which one of the following statements about installing receptacles at permanently installed swimming pools is NOT true?

A. Receptacles other than the required 15 or 20 ampere, 125-volt, receptacle and the receptacle for a water pump motor for the circulation system are not permitted closer than 1.83 m (6 ft) from inside wall of the pool.
B. The required 15 or 20 ampere, 125-volt, receptacle installed between 1.83 m (6 ft) and 6.0 m (20 ft) from inside walls of the pool shall be protected by a GFCI.
C. A receptacle that provides power for a water-pump for a permanently installed pool may be located within 1.83 m (6 ft) of the inside walls of the pool provided it is single and of the locking and grounding type and is GFCI-protected.
D. Where a permanently installed pool is installed, at least one 15 or 20 ampere, 125-volt, receptacle shall be located between 1.83 m (6 ft) and 6.0 m (20 ft) from the inside walls of the pool.

ANSWER _____

PROCEDURE TO ESTABLISH ANSWER
The question is about receptacles at swimming pools.

▶ 1. In Index, find "Swimming pools, fountains and similar installations" under which find "Receptacles, location and protection, 680.22(A), 680.32, 680.34, 680.43(A), 680.62(E)."

▶ 2. Section 680.22(A)(3) requires receptacles other than the required 15 or 20 ampere, 125 volt receptacle and a receptacle for a pool pump motor in accordance with 680.22(A)(2) to be located at least 1.83 m (6 ft) from the inside walls of the pool. Answer A is true.

▶ 3. Section 680.22(A)(1) requires at least one 125-volt receptacle shall be located between 1.8 m (6 ft) and 6.0 m (20 ft) from the inside walls of the pool. Answer D is true.

▶ 4. Section 680.22(A)(2) permits a receptacle for a pump motor to be located between 1.83 m (6 ft) and 3.0 m (10 ft) from the pool, but not within 1.83 m (6 ft). Answer C is not true.

▶ 5. Section 680.22(A)(4) requires GFCI protection for all 125-volt receptacles located within 6.0 m (20 ft) of the inside wall of the pool. Answer B is true.

▶ 6. The correct answer is C.

QUESTION 13. Which one of the following statements about luminaires in storable pools is true?

A. Luminaires in the walls of storable pools are permitted if they fulfill the same requirements as those for permanently installed pools.

B. Luminaires shall be part of a cord- and plug-connected lighting assembly specifically listed for the purpose.
C. Luminaires are not allowed in the walls of storable pools.
D. Luminaires in the wall of a storable pool shall have lamps operating at no more than 250-volts to ground.

ANSWER _____

PROCEDURE TO ESTABLISH ANSWER
The question relates to luminaires at storable pools.

▶ 1. In Index, find "Swimming pools, fountains and similar installations" under which find "Storable, 680–Part III."

▶ 2. Scan Article 680, Part III, and find "680.33, Luminaires."

▶ 3. Section 680.33(A) requires that a luminaire within the low voltage contact limit installed in or on the wall of a storable pool shall be part of a listed cord- and plug-connected lighting assembly and installed to meet the conditions of 680.33(A)(1) through (4). Answer A is not true.

▶ 4. The requirements for luminaires installed in the walls of a storable pool differ from those for a permanently installed pool. The first sentence in 680.33 confirms that Answer C is not true.

▶ 5. Section 680.33(B) provides that lighting assembly without a transformer or power supply is permitted to be cord- and plug-connected when the lamps are operating at not more than 150 volts. Answer D is not true.

▶ 6. Section 680.33(B) for luminaires over the low voltage contact limit permits a cord-and plug-connection where the assembly is listed for the purpose and complies with 680.23(A)(5) and includes the construction features specified in 680.33(B)(1) through (5). Answer B is true.

▶ 7. The correct answer is B.

QUESTION 14. Which one of the following statements about underwater luminaires located in the wall of a permanently installed swimming pool is NOT true?

A. A suitable luminaire is permitted if the top of the fixture lens is at least 450 mm (18 in.) below the normal water level unless listed for lesser depth, but not less than 100 mm (4 in.).
B. Luminaires are not permitted to be installed for operation on supply circuits operating at over 150 volts between conductors.
C. A luminaire is permitted to be installed at a depth of not less than 75 mm (3 in.) below normal water level if it is identified for such use.
D. A GFCI is required in the branch circuit supplying fixtures operating at more than 15 volts.

ANSWER _____

PROCEDURE TO ESTABLISH ANSWER
The question is about lighting fixtures at swimming pools.

▶ 1. In Index, find "Swimming pool, fountains and similar installations" under which find "Underwater luminaires, 680.23, 680.26(B)(2), 680.33, 680.43(B)(2)."

▶ 2. Section 680.23(A)(5) requires that luminaires in the walls of the pool shall be installed with the top of the lens at least 450 mm (18 in.) below the normal water level of the pool. Answer A is true. Section 680.23(A)(4) limits the voltage for a underwater luminaire to 150 volts between conductors. Answer B is true. Section 680.23(A)(3) requires GFCI protection for any underwater luminaire operating at more than 15 volts. Answer D is true.

▶ 3. Section 680.23(A)(5), however, permits a minimum of 100 mm (4 in.) below water level where the luminaire is listed and identified for the use and identified for use at a depth of less than 450 mm (18 in.) and installed not less than 100 mm (4 in.) below the normal water level of the pool. Answer C is not true.

▶ 4. The correct answer is C.

Swimming Pools | 1- and 2-Family Study Guide | 145

QUESTION 15. Receptacles for general use installed adjacent to a swimming pool are generally required to be located a minimum of what distance from the inside walls of the pool?

A. 1.5 m (5 ft)
B. 1.83 m (6 ft)
C. 3.0 m (10 ft)
D. 4.5 m (15 ft)

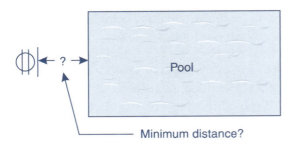

ANSWER _____

PROCEDURE TO ESTABLISH ANSWER
The question is about receptacles at swimming pools.

▶ 1. In Index, find "Swimming pools, fountains and similar installations" under which find "Receptacles, location and protection, 680.22(A), 680.32, 680.34, 680.43(A), 680.62(E)."

▶ 2. Section 680.22(A)(1), (2) and (3) generally require receptacles to be located at least 1.83 m (6 ft) from the inside walls of the pool.

▶ 3. The correct answer is B.

QUESTION 16. Which one of the following swimming pools can be considered to be a storable pool?

A. One constructed partially in the ground but which can be readily disassembled for storage
B. One that is 1.2 m (4 ft) deep and 4.5 m (15 ft) in diameter
C. One constructed partially in the ground that is only 600 mm (24 in.) deep
D. One that is above ground, 900 mm (3 ft) deep and 5.5 m (18 ft) across

ANSWER _____

PROCEDURE TO ESTABLISH ANSWER
The question is about the definition of a storable pool.

▶ 1. In Index, find "Swimming pools, fountains and similar installations" under which find "Storable, 680–Part III" under which find "Definition, 680.2."

▶ 2. Section 680.2's definition of a *Storable Swimming, Wading* or *Immersion Pool or Storable/Portable Spas and Hot Tubs* is one constructed on or above ground and is capable of holding water to a maximum depth of 1.0 m (42 in.). No other dimension such as diameter is mentioned.. Answer B is not correct because it can hold water to a depth of more than 1.0 meters (42 in.) and Answers A and C are not correct as they are not "on or above ground."

▶ 3. Because there is no minimum width specified in the definition, Answer D is correct.

▶ 4. Also refer to the definition of *Permanently Installed Swimming, Wading, Immersion and Therapeutic Pools*, which confirms that this group includes pools constructed partially in the ground and all others holding water in a depth greater than 1.0 m (42 in.)

▶ 5. The correct answer is D.

QUESTION 17. Totally-enclosed luminaires protected by a GFCI and located above an indoor swimming pool shall be installed at a minimum height above maximum water level of:

A. 2.3 m (7½ ft)
B. 3.0 m (10 ft)
C. 3.7 m (12 ft)
D. 4.9 m (16 ft)

146 | 1- and 2-Family Study Guide | Swimming Pools

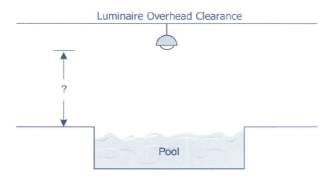

ANSWER _____

PROCEDURE TO ESTABLISH ANSWER
The question is about luminaires above swimming pools.

▶ 1. In Index, find "Swimming pools, fountains and similar installations" under which find "Lighting, 411.4(B), 680.22(B), 680.23, 680.26(B)(4), 680.33, 680.43(B), 680.51, 680.62(F), 680.72."

▶ 2. Section 680.22(B)(1) requires luminaires in outdoor pool areas to be located not less than 3.7 m (12 ft) above the pool maximum water level.

▶ 3. Section 680.22(B)(2) permits a 2.3 m (7 ft 6 in.) distance for indoor installations of totally enclosed luminaires that are GFCI-protected.

▶ 4. The correct answer is A.

QUESTION 18. Underground wiring for electrical equipment not related to a permanently installed swimming pool is generally required to be installed a minimum of _____ horizontally from the inside walls of the pool.

A. 3.0 m   (10 ft)
B. 6.0 m   (20 ft)
C. 1.5 m   (5 ft)
D. 450 mm   (18 in.)

ANSWER _____

PROCEDURE TO ESTABLISH ANSWER
The question is about underground wiring at permanently installed swimming pools.

▶ 1. In Index, find "Swimming pools, fountains, and similar installations" under which find "Permanently installed, 680–Part II."

▶ 2. Scan to Part II of Article 680 and find 680.20, which requires electrical installations at permanently installed swimming pools to comply with the provisions of Parts I and II of Article 680.

▶ 3. Scan Part I of Article 680 and find 680.10, which does not permit wiring within the area extending 1.5 m (5 ft) horizontally from the inside walls of the pool unless the wiring is necessary to supply pool equipment permitted by Article 680.

▶ 4. The correct answer is C.

QUESTION 19. A maintenance disconnecting means for a swimming pool, outdoor spa or hot tub shall be accessible, located within sight from the pool, spa, or hot tub equipment, and shall be located at least _____ horizontally from the inside walls of the pool, spa or hot tub?

A. 1.5 m (5 ft)
B. 3.0 m (10 ft)
C. 6.0 m (20 ft)
D. 15 m (50 ft)

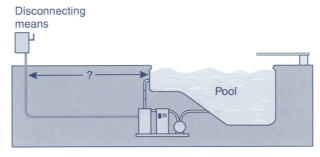

ANSWER _____

PROCEDURE TO ESTABLISH ANSWER
The question is about maintenance disconnecting means for a pool, or outdoor spa or hot tub.

▶ 1. In Index, find "Swimming pools, fountains, and similar installations" under which find "Switches and switching devices, 680.22(C), 680.41"

Swimming Pools | 1- and 2-Family Study Guide | 147

▶ 2. Section 680.22(C) requires switching devices (the disconnecting means) to be at least 1.5 m (5 ft) horizontally from the inside walls of the equipment.

Note: Also, since the disconnecting means requirement probably would be a general requirement, scan the sections in Article 680 Part I, General, and find "680.12, Maintenance Disconnecting Means," which requires the disconnecting means to be readily accessible and within sight from its equipment. Please refer to Article 100 for definitions of these two terms.

▶ 3. The correct answer is A.

QUESTION 20. Electric pool water heaters shall have the heating elements subdivided into loads not exceeding 48 amperes and protected at not more than:

A. 50 amperes
B. 60 amperes
C. 70 amperes
D. 100 amperes

ANSWER _____

PROCEDURE TO ESTABLISH ANSWER
The question is about electric pool heaters for swimming pools.

▶ 1. In Index, find "Swimming pools, fountains and similar installations" under which find "Heaters and heating equipment" under which find "Pool water heaters, 680.9."

▶ 2. Section 680.9, Electric Pool Water Heaters, requires heating elements to be subdivided into loads not exceeding 48 amperes and protected at not more than 60 amperes. Answer B is correct.

This section also requires the ampacity of the branch-circuit conductors and the rating or setting of the overcurrent protective devices cannot be less than 125% of the nameplate rating.

= 48 amperes x 1.25 (125%
= 60 amperes).

▶ 3. The correct answer is B.

QUESTION 21. What is the maximum supply circuit voltage for luminaires installed beneath a swimming pool water surface?

A. Not more than 15 volts between conductors
B. Not more than 50 volts to ground
C. Not more than 150 volts to ground
D. Not more than 150 volts between conductors

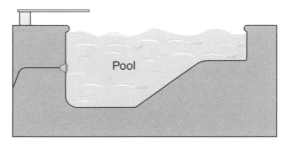

ANSWER _____

PROCEDURE TO ESTABLISH ANSWER
The question is about underwater luminaires at pools.

▶ 1. In Index, find "Swimming pools, fountains and similar installations" under which find "Underwater luminaires, 680.23, 680.26(B)(2), 680.33, 680.43(B)(2)."

▶ 2. Section 680.23(A)(4) does not permit a luminaire to be installed for operation on supply circuits of over 150 volts between conductors.

▶ 3. The correct answer is D.

QUESTION 22. Which one of the following statements about protecting underwater swimming pool luminaires that depend upon submersion for safe operation is true?

A. A float switch which disconnects the luminaire when water level drops below the top of the luminaire is required.
B. The luminaire is required to have inherent protection against overheating when not submerged.
C. They may operate at no more than 250 volts between conductors.
D. This type of luminaire only requires GFCI protection if operating at more than 150 volts between conductors.

ANSWER _____

PROCEDURE TO ESTABLISH ANSWER
The question is about underwater luminaires at swimming pools.

▶ 1. In Index, find "Swimming pools, fountains and similar installations" under which find "Underwater luminaires, 680.23, 680.26(B)(4), 680.33, 680.43(B)(2)."

▶ 2. Section 680.23(A)(7) requires luminaires that depend on submersion for safe operation are to be inherently protected against hazards of overheating when not submerged. Answer B is true.

▶ 3. Section 680.23(A)(4) does not permit a luminaire to be installed for operation on supply circuits of over 150 volts between conductors. Answer C is not true.

▶ 4. Section 680.23(A)(3) requires luminaires operating at over the low voltage contact limit to be provided with ground fault circuit-interrupter (GFCI) protection. Article 100 defines the low voltage contact limit and GFCI protection is required at levels well below 150 volts between conductors. Answer D is not true.

▶ 3. The correct answer is B.

QUESTION 23. Flush deck boxes are permitted for underwater luminaires at swimming pools where the lighting system operating voltage is which of the following?

A. At or below the low voltage contact limit
B. 15 volts
C. At or above the low voltage contact limit
D. 150 volts

ANSWER _____

PROCEDURE TO ESTABLISH ANSWER
The question is about junction boxes for swimming pool lighting that are installed flush, and in the pool deck.

▶ 1. In Index, find "Swimming pools, fountains and similar installations" under which find "Junction boxes and enclosures, 680.23(C)(2), 680.24."

▶ 2. Section 680.24(A)(2)(c) permits a flush deck box for lighting system operating at or below the low voltage contact limit, if an approved potting compound is used to fill the box to prevent the entrance of moisture, and the flush deck box is located not less than 1.2 m (4 ft) from the inside wall of the pool.

▶ 3. The correct answer is A.

Swimming Pools | 1- and 2-Family Study Guide

QUESTION 24. The parts that are required to be connected to the equipotential bonding grid of a swimming pool shall be connected with a solid 8 AWG copper conductor by means of a:

A. reinforced steel tie wire
B. insulated compound
C. listed pressure connectors
D. Sheet metal screw

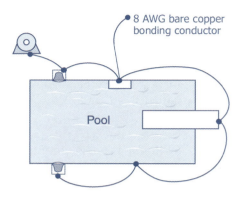

ANSWER _____

PROCEDURE TO ESTABLISH ANSWER
The question is about bonding at swimming pools.

▶ 1. In Index, find "Swimming pools, fountains and similar installations" under which find "Bonding, 680.26, 680.42(B), 680.43(D) and (E), etc."

▶ 2. Section 680.26(B) covers the common bonding grid and requires connection to bonded parts to be made in accordance with 250.8.

▶ 3. In Article 250, find 250.8 which provides a list of means to connect equipment grounding conductors, grounding electrode conductors and bonding jumpers. List Item No. 1 recognizes "listed pressure connectors." Answer C is correct.

▶ 4. The correct answer is C.

QUESTION 25. Which one of the following statements about a hydromassage bathtub located in a bathroom is true?

A. A wall-mounted light switch may be installed 900 mm (3 ft) horizontally from the bathtub.
B. A hanging luminaire is permitted directly above the bathtub with a vertical distance of 2.3 m (7 ft 6 in.) from the maximum water level to the lowest part of the fixture.
C. A ceiling-suspended paddle fan is permitted directly above the bathtub with a vertical distance of 2.3 m (7 ft 6 in.) from the maximum water level to the fan blades.
D. A receptacle outlet used to supply the hydromassage bathtub equipment does not require GFCI protection if located behind an access door rendering it inaccessible when the door is closed.

ANSWER _____

PROCEDURE TO ESTABLISH ANSWER
The question is about equipment at a hydromassage bathtub.

▶ 1. In Index, find "Hydromassage bathtubs, 680–Part VII."

▶ 2. Scan Article 680, Part VII, and find "680.71, Protection," which requires the electric equipment associated with the bathtub to be GFCI-protected. Answer D is not true.

▶ 3. Section 680.72 requires electric equipment in the same room and not directly associated with a hydromassage bathtub to be installed according to Chapters 1 through 4 covering the installation of that equipment in bathrooms. Section 680.70 does not require hydromassage bathtubs to comply with other parts of Article 680, for example, 680.22(C).

▶ 4. In Index, find "Bathtubs" under which find "Luminaires, 410.10(D), 550.14(D), 551.53(B)."

▶ 5. Section 410.10(D) prohibits hanging luminaires and ceiling-suspended (paddle) fans within 2.5 m (8 ft) vertically from the top of the bathtub rim. Answers B and C are not true. However, there is no requirement limiting the distance from a light switch to the tub.

▶ 6. The correct answer is A.

QUESTION 26. Which one of the following statements about an equipment grounding conductor installed within rigid nonmetallic conduit to a metal forming shell for underwater audio equipment (speakers) in swimming pools is true?

A. An 8 AWG insulated solid or stranded copper bonding jumper is required.
B. An 8 AWG bare solid copper conductor is permitted.
C. An 8 AWG bare stranded copper conductor is permitted.
D. The 8 AWG grounding conductor may be spliced in the forming shell with a direct burial type connector.

ANSWER _____

PROCEDURE TO ESTABLISH ANSWER
The question is about the equipment grounding conductor in rigid polyvinyl chloride conduit (PVC) for underwriter audio equipment.

▶ 1. In Index, find "Swimming pools, fountains and similar installations" under which find "Underwater audio equipment, 680.23."

Note: Unfortunately, there is an error in the Index of the softbound *NEC*-2014. The Index states that the reference is 680.23, which is incorrect. The correct reference is 680.27.

▶ 2. Section 680.27(A)(2) requires an 8 AWG insulated copper bonding jumper in rigid chloride conduit (PVC) conduit. The conductor may be solid or stranded. Answer A is true. Answers B and C are false.

▶ 3. Section 680.27(A)(2) also requires the termination of the 8 AWG bonding jumper in the forming shell to be covered with, or encapsulated in, a listed potting compound to protect the connection from possible deteriorating effects of pool water. Answer D is false.

▶ 4. The correct answer is A.

QUESTION 27. A new panelboard will serve a swimming pool and is not a part of the service equipment but is supplied from an overcurrent device in the service equipment (feeder panelboard). Which one of the following statements about the equipment grounding conductor installed between the grounding terminal of the feeder panelboard and the grounding terminal of the service equipment is NOT true?

A. The equipment grounding conductor is required to be an insulated copper conductor and installed with the feeder conductors.
B. The raceway containing the equipment grounding conductor may be rigid metal conduit, intermediate metal conduit, rigid chloride conduit (PVC) conduit or electrical nonmetallic tubing where installed outside of the building.
C. The feeder conductors, including the equipment grounding conductor, may be installed in electrical metallic tubing where installed on or within the building.
D. The equipment grounding conductor shall be sized in accordance with Table 250.122 but not smaller than 12 AWG.

ANSWER _____

PROCEDURE TO ESTABLISH ANSWER
The question is about the equipment grounding conductor for new pool equipment panelboards supplied by a feeder.

▶ 1. In Index, find "Swimming pools, fountains and similar installations" under which find "Grounding 680.6, 680.7(B), 680.23(B)(4) and (F)(2), 680.24(D) and (F), 680.25(B), 680.43(F), 680.54, 680.55…"

▶ 2. Section 680.25(B)(1) requires the equipment grounding conductor to be sized in accordance with Table 250.122 but not smaller than 12 AWG and be an insulated copper conductor. Answer D is true.

▶ 3. Section 680.25(A) and its exceptions list the permitted wiring methods but do not recognize electrical nonmetallic tubing where it is installed on the outside of buildings. Answer B is false.

▶ 4. Section 680.25(A)(4) permits electrical metallic tubing to be installed on or within buildings. Answer C is true.

▶ 5. Section 680.25(B) states that an equipment grounding conductor is required to be an insulated copper conductor installed with the feeder conductors. Answer A is true.
Note: The question deals with the installation of a new panelboard so the allowances for grounding of existing panelboards are not applicable.

▶ 6. The correct answer is B.

QUESTION 28. In swimming pool installations, a feeder supplying a panelboard that is not a part of service equipment shall have a conductor installed between its grounding terminal and the grounding terminal of the service equipment. This conductor serves as which one of the following?

A. A neutral conductor
B. A grounding electrode conductor
C. An equipment grounding conductor
D. A common conductor

ANSWER _____

PROCEDURE TO ESTABLISH ANSWER
The question is about grounding of panelboards for swimming pool equipment.

▶ 1. In Index, find "Swimming pools, fountains and similar installations" under which find "Grounding 680.6, 680.7(B), 680.23(B)(4) and (F)(2), 680.24(D) and (F), 680.25(B), 680.43(F), 680.54, 680.55."

▶ 2. Section 680.25 covers *feeders* and 680.25(B) requires an equipment grounding conductor to be installed between the grounding terminal of the pool equipment panelboard and the grounding terminal of the applicable service equipment.

▶ 3. The correct answer is C.

QUESTION 29. What is the required minimum horizontal distance generally required between a switch used to control pool lighting and the inside walls of the pool where they are not separated by a permanent barrier?

A. 1.5 m (5 ft)
B. 3.0 m (10 ft)
C. 4.5 m (15 ft)
D. 6.0 m (20 ft)

ANSWER _____

PROCEDURE TO ESTABLISH ANSWER
The question is about switches near swimming pools.

▶ 1. In Index, find "Swimming pools, fountains and similar installations" under which find "Switches and switching devices, 680.22(C), 680.41."

▶ 2. Section 680.22(C) requires a minimum horizontal distance of at least 1.5 m (5 ft) unless separated by a solid fence, wall, or other permanent barrier. The question does not mention anything about switches listed as being acceptable for use within 1.5 m (5 ft).

▶ 3. The correct answer is A.

QUESTION 30. What is the minimum size equipment grounding conductor permitted for junction boxes for wet-niche luminaires on swimming pools?

A. 12 AWG
B. 14 AWG
C. 10 AWG
D. 8 AWG

ANSWER _____

PROCEDURE TO ESTABLISH ANSWER
The question is about equipment grounding conductors for boxes.

▶ 1. In Index, find "Swimming pools, fountains and similar installations" under which find "Grounding, 680.6, 680.7(B), 680.23(B)(4) and (F)(2), 680.24(D) and (F), 680.25(B), 680.43(F), 680.54, 680.55."

▶ 2. Section 680.23(F)(2) requires an insulated copper equipment grounding conductor not smaller than a 12 AWG for the purpose of grounding a wet-niche luminaire.

▶ 3. Section 680.24(F) requires the junction box in the supply circuit of the wet-niche luminaire be connected to the grounding terminal of the panelboard. Section 680.25(B)(1) reinforces the requirement for the equipment grounding conductor for the box to be a minimum size of 12 AWG insulated copper conductor.

▶ 4. The correct answer is A.

QUESTION 31. Which one of the following statements about radiant heating cables embedded in the concrete deck of a swimming pool is true?

A. They shall be located at least 1.5 m (5 ft) from the inside walls of the pool.
B. They are permitted if identified for such use and are protected by a GFCI.
C. They must be covered by at least 75 mm (3 in.) of concrete.
D. They are not permitted in or below the deck.

ANSWER _____

PROCEDURE TO ESTABLISH ANSWER
The question is about radiant heating cables in swimming pool decks.

▶ 1. In Index, find "Swimming pools, fountains and similar installations" under which find "Deck area heating, 680.27(C)."

▶ 2. Section 680.27(C)(3) prohibits radiant heating cables embedded in or below the deck.

▶ 3. The correct answer is D.

QUESTION 32. Which one of the following statements about a spa or hot tub installed outdoors is NOT true?

A. A listed packaged unit is permitted to be cord- and plug-connected with a cord no longer than 4.6 m (15 ft) providing it is GFCI-protected
B. Generally, spas or hot tubs must be installed in accordance with the requirements for permanently installed pools Part II of Article 680.
C. Metal bands or hoops used to secure wooden staves are not required to be bonded.
D. Bonding by metal-to-metal mounting on a common frame or base is permitted.

ANSWER _____

PROCEDURE TO ESTABLISH ANSWER
The question is about a spa or hot tub installed outdoors.

▶ 1. In Index, find "Spas and hot tubs" under which find "Outdoor installations, 680.42."

▶ 2. Section 680.40 requires electrical installations at spas and hot tubs to comply with the provisions of Parts I and IV of Article 680. Section 680.42 requires a spa or hot tub installed outdoors to comply with Parts I and II of Article

680 which provides requirements for permanently installed pools, including the grounding provisions. "Part I" is missing from Answer B, making the statement not true.

▶ 3. Section 680.42(A)(2) permits cord- and plug-connected listed packaged units with cords up to 4.6 m (15 ft) in length if protected by a ground-fault circuit interrupter. Answer A is true.

▶ 4. Section 680.42(B) permits bonding metal-to-metal mounting and also states in the last sentence of the paragraph that metal bands used to secure wooden staves are not required to be bonded. Answers C & D are true.

▶ 5. The correct answer is B.

Q UESTION 33. A hydromassage bathtub is installed in the master bedroom of a dwelling. Which one of the following statements regarding GFCI protection for 125-volt, single-phase receptacles in the bedroom is true?

A. None of the bedroom receptacles require GFCI protection.
B. GFCI protection is only required for receptacles serving the hydromassage bathtub.
C. GFCI protection is required for all receptacles within 1.83 m (6 ft) of the inside walls of the hydromassage bathtub.
D. All receptacles within the bedroom require GFCI protection.

ANSWER _____

PROCEDURE TO ESTABLISH ANSWER
The question is about GFCI protection for receptacles near hydromassage bathtubs. There are two key issues in the question are "Ground-fault circuit interrupter protection" and "hydromassage bathtubs."

▶ 1. In the Index find "Ground-fault circuit interrupters" under which find "Bathtubs, hydromassage, 680.71 which will end up being the most direct route to the answer.

If you find "Hydromassage bathtub" in the Index, you will find, 680–Part VII" under which find "Definition 680.2." You can scan Article 680, Part VII, and find "680.71, Protection."

▶ 2. Section 680.71 requires all 125-volt, single-phase receptacles not exceeding 30 amperes within 1.83 m (6 ft) of the inside walls of a hydromassage bathtub to be protected by a ground-fault circuit interrupter(s). Answer C is true and Answers A, B and D are not true.

▶ 3. The correct answer is C.

Q UESTION 34. Which one of the following statements about cord- and plug-connected equipment for fountains is true?

A. GFCI protection is not required for the equipment.
B. Connections with flexible cord must be permanent, except that grounding-type attachment plugs and receptacles are permitted to allow removal or disconnection for maintenance, repair, or storage, and where the connection is not located in a water-containing area of the fountain.
C. GFCI protection is required for all equipment except the power supply cord.
D. Type SPE-3 flexible cord is permitted to supply the equipment.

ANSWER _____

PROCEDURE TO ESTABLISH ANSWER
The question is about cord- and plug-connected equipment for fountains.

▶ 1. In Index, find "Fountains. *see* Swimming pools, fountains, and similar installations."

▶ 2. In Index, find "Swimming pools, fountains, and similar equipment," under which find, "Fountains, 680–Part V." You can also find "Cord-and-plug-connected equipment, 680.7, 680.21(A)(5), 680.22(B)(5), 680.31, 680.42(A)(2),

680.56." The correct reference is 680.56 but if you are not familiar the structure of Article 680 you would have to go through all the other references first. Where 680-Part V is small it may be quicker to just scan the Part and find 680.56.

▶ 3. Scan Article 680 Part V, and find "680.56, Cord- and Plug-Connected Equipment," under which subsection (A) Ground-Fault Circuit-Interrupter, requires GFCI protection for all electric equipment at fountains, including power-supply cords. Answers A and C are not true.

▶ 4. Section 680.56(D), Terminations, requires what is stated in Answer B, which is true.

▶ 5. To verify if Type SPE-3 flexible cord is permitted, 680.56(B) requires an extra-hard use cord as designated in Table 400.4. Referring to Table 400.4 under the "Use" column, Type SPE-3 cord is indicated as "Not hard usage." Answer D is not true.

▶ 6. The correct answer is B.

QUESTION 35. Which of the following statements about requirements for bonding hydromassage bathtubs is NOT true?

A. Hydromassage bathtubs are considered regular bathtubs and bonding is not required.
B. All metal piping systems, electrical equipment and pump motors are required to be bonded.
C. The bonding conductor must be not smaller than 8 AWG solid copper conductor, and can be insulated, covered or bare.
D. The 8 AWG bonding jumper is not required to be connected to a double insulated circulating pump motor.

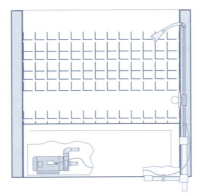

Metal piping systems, metal parts of electrical equipment, and pump motors for hydromassage bathtubs required to be bonded?

ANSWER _____

PROCEDURE TO ESTABLISH ANSWER
The question is about bonding hydromassage bathtubs.

▶ 1. In Index, find "Hydromassage bathtubs, 680– Part VII."

▶ 2. Scan Part VII of Article 680 and find "680.74, Bonding."

▶ 3. Scanning Section 680.74 reveals that statements "B" and "C" are true; All metal piping and all metal grounded parts are required to be bonded with not smaller than an 8 AWG copper conductor. Section 680.74 also specifies double insulated circulating pump motors are not required to be bonded. Answer D is true.

Also, in Index, find "Double-insulated pool pumps, 680.21(B), 680.31" which further verifies that Answer D is true.

▶ 4. The correct answer is A.

Swimming Pools | 1- and 2-Family Study Guide | 155

QUESTION 36. All of the following statements about overhead conductor clearances above and around swimming pools are true EXCEPT:

A. The minimum clearances overhead shall be taken starting from a level of 4 inches below the pool deck level.
B. The minimum clearance horizontally shall not be less than 10 feet.
C. CATV cables shall be permitted at a height of not less than 10 feet over swimming or wading pools.
D. Where a minimum clearance from the water level is given, the measurement must be taken from the maximum water level of the pool.

ANSWER _____

PROCEDURE TO ESTABLISH ANSWER
The question is about overhead conductor clearances above and around swimming pools.

▶ 1. In Index, find "Swimming pools, fountains and similar installations" under which find "Overhead conductor clearances, 680.8."

▶ 2. In 680.8, we find that answer A is not true, and that the maximum water level for the pool is the starting point for measuring the minimum distance overhead for overhead conductors. Answer D is true.

▶ 3. In Table 680.8, the stated minimum clearance horizontally is not less than 10 feet.

▶ 4. Section 680.8(B) addresses communication systems, and states that television coaxial cables shall be permitted at a height of not less than 10 feet over a swimming or wading pool.

▶ 5. The correct answer is A.

QUESTION 37. The maintenance disconnecting means for a pool pump motor and heater shall be:

A. Readily accessible
B. Within sight its equipment
C. B only
D. A and B

ANSWER _____

PROCEDURE TO ESTABLISH ANSWER
The question is about the maintenance disconnecting means for pool utilization equipment.

▶ 1. In Index, find "Swimming pools, fountains and similar installations, Art. 680." There is no reference for maintenance disconnect or disconnecting means, so you would have to scan Article 680, starting with Part 680 – Part I.

▶ 2. In the Index find "Disconnecting means" under which find "Pools, spars and hot tubs, 680.12."

▶ 3. In 680.12, we find that answers A and B are true. The disconnecting means for pool utilization equipment is required to be both readily accessible and within sight its equipment.

Note: See Chapter 1, Article 100 for the definition of *Accessible, Readily*. Readily accessible means it can be reached quickly for operation or renewal without having to climb over objects or resort to a portable means to reach the equipment. In the question, it is the maintenance disconnecting means. Equipment that is installed in front of electrical disconnects makes accessing the disconnect sometimes difficult, and may create other safety issues.

▶ 4. The correct answer is D.

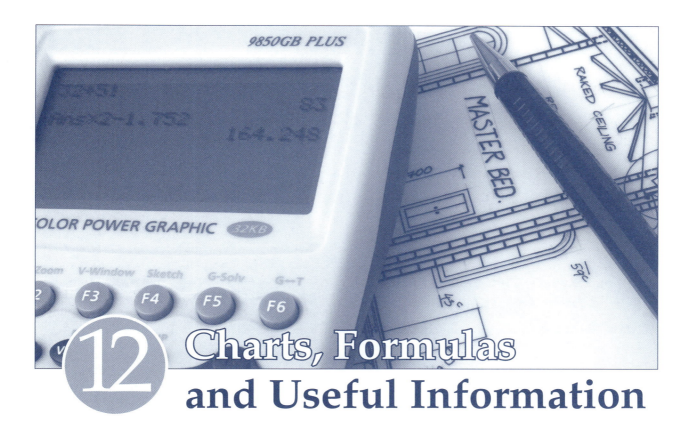

12 Charts, Formulas and Useful Information

Table 300.1(C) Metric Designator and Trade Sizes

Metric Designator	Trade Size
12	3/8
16	1/2
21	3/4
27	1
35	1 1/4
41	1 1/2
53	2
63	2 1/2
78	3
91	3 1/2
103	4
129	5
155	6

Note: The metric designators and trade sizes are for identification purposes only and are not actual dimensions. Source: *NEC*-2014, Table 300.1(C), page 146.

Adjusting Equipment Grounding Conductor Size

Calculate the minimum equipment grounding conductor size as per 250.122(B) when the ungrounded circuit conductors are increased in size (typically to compensate for voltage drop).

Example: Assume a 175-ampere circuit-breaker or fuse with a 2/0 AWG THW copper conductor to a load will exceed the acceptable voltage drop. It has been calculated that 4/0 AWG copper conductors would replace the 2/0 AWG conductors to correct the voltage drop.

Table 250.122 requires that a 6 AWG copper equipment grounding conductor is the minimum size for a 175-ampere circuit-breaker or fuse. Section 250.122(B) states: "Where ungrounded conductors are adjusted in size, equipment grounding conductors, where installed, shall be adjusted proportionately according to circular mil area."

Refer to Chapter 9, Table 8, of the *NEC* for circular mil area of conductors:

2/0 AWG = 133,100 circular mil area
6 AWG = 26,240 circular mil area
4/0 AWG = 211,600 circular mil area

Determine ratio of ungrounded conductors:

$$\frac{211,600 \; (4/0)}{133,100 \; (2/0)} = 1.59$$

Multiply area of required equipment grounding conductor by ratio determined above:
26,240 cm (6 AWG) × 1.59 = 41,721.6 minimum circular mil area

Refer to Chapter 9, Table 8, of the *NEC* for circular mil area of conductors:

4 AWG = 41,740 circular mil area; required size for EGC to counteract the effects of voltage drop

A 4 AWG copper conductors would be the minimum size equipment grounding conductor for this circuit. Follow a similar procedure for aluminum conductors.

Conductor Ampacity Basics

The insulation on conductors can withstand a certain amount of heat, but only to some specific limit! High temperatures will destroy conductor insulation completely, or will shorten the life expectancy of the insulation. This will occur during a short time exposure to extreme excessive heat, or over a long period of time to moderate excessive heat. If a conductor has an insulation rating of 140°F that means the conductor temperature under load cannot exceed 140°F. It does not mean that the conductor can be placed in a 140°F/60°C ambient temperature.

When current passes through a conductor, heat is generated. Remember: Watts = I2R. The more current-carrying conductors in a single raceway or cable, the greater the heat. The temperature of the surrounding area (ambient temperature) also has an effect on conductor insulation. See Watts Wheel (Ohm's Law, Ferm's Fast Finder).

A rule of thumb is that for every 10°C above rated temperature, the conductor's life expectancy is cut in half. The same half-life rule is applicable to electric motors and other electrical equipment.

The *National Electrical Code* contains a number of requirements that relate to potential heat problems in conductors and electrical equipment.

TERMINATIONS: Section 110.14(C) in the *National Electrical Code* tells us the temperature rating associated with the ampacity of a conductor cannot exceed the lowest temperature rating of any connected termination, conductor or device. So unless the electrical equipment used is listed and marked for use with higher temperature rated conductors, a 60°C conductor ampacity will be used for equipment rated 100 amperes or less, or marked for conductor sizes 14 AWG through 1 AWG. conductors

Without a marking for a higher temperature rating on the equipment, the 60°C, conductor ampacity must be used even though the conductors being used might be rated for higher temperatures, such as 75°C (one "H" in the insulation designation) or 90°C (two "H"s in the insulation designation) in order to maintain the designed conductor and equipment termination temperature coordinations. For equipment rated over 100 amperes or marked for conductors larger than 1 AWG, the conductor ampacity is based on a 75°C rating. This would be true even though the conductors might be rated for a higher temperature, such as 90°C. This requirement is also found in the UL White Book.

Conductors with insulation of a higher rating than specified for termination purposes are permitted for ampacity adjustment or correction (derating) purposes, such as for more than three current-carrying conductors in a raceway or cable or for ambient temperatures greater than 30°C (86°F).

Conductors with insulation of a higher rating than specified for termination purposes are permitted for ampacity adjustment or correction (derating) purposes, such as for more than three current-carrying conductors in a raceway or cable or for ambient temperatures greater than 30°C (86°F).

MORE THAN THREE CURRENT-CARRYING CONDUCTORS: Where more than three current-carrying conductors are installed in a single raceway or cable, conductor ampacity reduction is necessary according to *NEC* Table 310.15(B)(3)(a), page 164.

Question: To connect two 3-phase motors, six 1 AWG THHN copper conductors are installed in one conduit. What is the adjusted ampacity of these 1 AWG THHN conductors?

Answer: From Table 310.15(B)(16), 1 AWG THHN copper conductors have an allowable ampacity of 145 amperes. From Table 310.15(B)(3)(a), we find that an adjustment factor of 0.80 (80%) must be applied.

$$150 \times 0.8 = 120 \text{ amperes}$$

High Ambient Temperature: When conductors are subjected to ambient temperatures higher than specified in Table 310.15(B)(2)(a), their ampacity must be corrected according to the factors found in NEC Table 310.15(B)(2)(a).

Example: What is the ampacity of 1 AWG THHN copper conductors that are installed or pass through areas where the ambient temperature is expected to be 100°F?

Answer: From Table 310.15(B)(16), 1 AWG THHN copper conductors have an allowable ampacity of 150 amperes. From Table 310.15(B)(2)(a), we find that a correction factor of 0.91 (91%) for the 100°F temperature must be applied.

$$145 \times 0.91 = 131 \text{ amperes}$$

More Than Three Current-carrying Conductors and High Ambient Temperature: Where both conditions (more than three current-carrying conductors and higher than specified ambient temperatures) are encountered, the adjustment factors from Table 310.15(B)(3)(a) and the temperature correction factors from Table 310.15(B)(2)(a) must be applied.

Example: What is the final ampacity of 1 AWG THHN conductors when six are installed in one conduit? All six conductors are considered to be current-carrying. The expected ambient temperature will be 100°F.

Answer: From Table 310.15(B)(16), 1 AWG THHN copper conductors have an allowable ampacity of 145 amperes. From Table 310.15(B)(3)(a), we find than an adjustment factor of 0.80 (80%) must be applied for the number of current-carrying conductors. From Table 310.15(B)(2)(a), we find that a correction factor of 0.91 for the 100°F temperature must be applied.

$$145 \times 0.80 \times 0.91 = 105.5 \text{ amperes}$$

New Table 310.15(B)(3)(c) covers the adjustment factors to the ambient temperature of conductors installed in circular raceways on rooftops, where exposed to direct sunlight. The closer the circular raceway is to the rooftop, the more correction for higher ambient temperature must be applied resulting in less permitted ampacity for the conductors).

Conductor Fill in Conduit and Tubing

The information that follows relates to the *National Electrical Code* requirements for the maximum number of conductors permitted in a conduit or tubing. In Chapter 9 of the *NEC*, we find:

Table 1: Percent of Cross Section of Conduit and Tubing for Conductors. This table shows the allowable percentage fill based upon the number and cross-sectional area of conductors in the conduit or tubing. See *NEC* Table 1, Chapter 9.

53 percent fill
One conductor in conduit. Note that a circle inside another makes efficient use of the space.

31 percent fill
Two conductors in conduit.
Note that two circles inside another do not fit well.

40 percent fill
More than two conductors in conduit. Efficient use of the space.

Table 4: Dimensions and Percent Area of Conduit and Tubing. This table consists of twelve (12) individual tables that show the internal diameters and percent fill calculated for 100%, 31%, 40%, and 53% for twelve commonly used conduit and tubings. These tables also provide a 60% column for use with short nipples (not more than 24" in length) in accordance with Note 4 to Table 1, Chapter 9. Select the appropriate table for your installation (see *NEC* Table 4, Chapter 9).

Table 5: Dimensions of Insulated Conductors and Fixture Wires. This table provides the diameters and approximate square inch cross sectional areas for all types of conductors in use today that might be installed in a raceway or tubing.

Standard Stranding   Compact Stranding

Table 5A: Compact Aluminum Building Wire Nominal Dimensions and Areas. This table provides the dimensional data for compact stranded aluminum conductors in common use today. Compact stranded conductors have approximately 10% less diameter than regular stranded conductors and approximately 12-15% less cross-sectional area.

Table 8: Conductor Properties. This table provides conductor circular mil area, stranding data, diameters and cross-sectional area in square inches. It also provides the DC resistance values at 75°C for coated and uncoated copper conductors, and for aluminum conductors. Dimensions for bare conductors are found in this table as well.

All Conductors the Same Size and Same Insulation
Simply refer to the "Conduit and Tubing Fill Tables for Conductors and Fixture Wires of the Same Size" in Annex C of the *NEC*. Here, there are twelve tables for the most common raceways. First locate the correct table for the raceway to be used, then the conductor insulation type, then the wire size and go across the row to find the number of conductors to be installed. The column heading above the number of conductors gives the minimum raceway size.

Conductors of Different Sizes or Insulation Types
1. Find the area in square inches for the conductor size and insulation type to be installed in Chapter 9.
   Table 5 – dimensions of Insulated Conductors and Fixture Wires.
   Table 5A – Compact Copper and Aluminum Building Wire Nominal Dimensions and Areas.
   Table 8 – Conductor Properties. Use for area of bare conductors.
2. Multiply the square inch area of each conductor by the number to be installed.
3. Total the square inch areas of all conductors.
4. Refer to Chapter 9, Table 1 for the maximum fill permitted for the number of conductors to be installed.
5. Find the minimum raceway size permitted by reference to Table 4 for the type of raceway used.

Note: As indicated in Informational Note No. 1, the fill allowances permitted in Table 1 are based on reasonable conditions or proper installation of the conductors, number of bends and lengths of pulls and future expansion is not mentioned nor considered. It should be recognized that for certain conditions a larger conduit or lesser fill should be considered.

Conductors in Parallel

Section 310.10(H)(2) of the *NEC*, regarding conductor and installation characteristics, requires where run in parallel the conductors of each phase must be the same length, have the same material, etc., so each parallel conductor of the phase carries an equal amount of the current. If the conductors of each phase were allowed to be different lengths, the following procedure would demonstrate the current each conductor will carry.

Example: A 1600-ampere service consists of four conduits, each containing four 600-kcmil THW conductors. According to Table 310.15(B)(16), the allowable ampacity of a 600-kcmil THW conductor is 420 amperes. If this service is called upon to deliver the full 1600 amperes, what is the actual current flow in each of the four paralleled conductors?

Step 1: Measure the length of each set of the four conductors that are in parallel.

Step 2: Add these lengths together. Let's assume that the lengths are 20 feet, 22 feet, 24 feet, and 26 feet. 20 ft. + 22 ft. + 24 ft. + 26 ft. = 92 feet total length of all four conductors

Step 3: Set up and solve these calculations:

$$\frac{20 \times 1600}{92} = 347.8 \text{ amperes}$$

$$\frac{22 \times 1600}{92} = 382.6 \text{ amperes}$$

$$\frac{24 \times 1600}{92} = 417.4 \text{ amperes}$$

$$\frac{26 \times 1600}{92} = 452.2 \text{ amperes}$$

Step 4: *Invert* the results of the above calculations.

Ohm's Law tells us that current flow is inversely proportional to resistance. This means that the higher the resistance, the lower the current flow. In our example, the conductor with the longest length (highest resistance) will carry the least amount of current. The conductor having the shortest length (lowest resistance) will carry the most current.

Therefore, the current flow in the conductors is:

20 ft.	452.5 amperes
22 ft.	417.4 amperes
24 ft.	382.6 amperes
26 ft.	347.8 amperes

Neutral Load
Single-Phase System
The neutral conductor will carry the unbalanced current between L1 and L2.

Example:

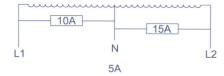

Three-Phase 4-wire Wye System

I of N = $\sqrt{I^2A + I^2B + I^2C - (IA \times IB) - (IB \times IC) - (IC \times IA)} = N$

Example:

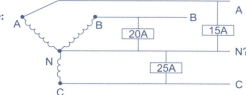

15 × 15	=	225		15 × 20	=	300
20 × 20	=	400		20 × 25	=	500
25 × 25	=	625		25 × 15	=	375
		1250				1175
	−	1175				
		75		$\sqrt{75}$ = 8.66 amps		

See 310.15(B)(5) for information on neutral conductors.

See 220.61 for load calculation methods.

---

kW or kVA to Amps
Single-phase amps = kVA × 1000 ÷ 1 phase voltage
Three-phase amps = kVA × 1000 ÷ (1.732 × phase-to-phase voltage)

Three-Phase Divisors
at 480 volts, 3φ – watts ÷ 831 = amps × 831 = watts
at 240 volts, 3φ – watts ÷ 416 = amps × 416 = watts
at 230 volts, 3φ – watts ÷ 398 = amps × 398 = watts
at 208 volts, 3φ – watts ÷ 360 = amps × 360 = watts
at 120 volts, 3φ – watts ÷ 208 = amps × 208 = watts

Short Cut

To find amps if load is given in kVA   three-phase circuits
- and voltage is 480   multiply kVA x 1.2
- and voltage is 240   multiply kVA x 2.41
- and voltage is 230   multiply kVA x 2.51
- and voltage is 208   multiply kVA x 2.78
- and voltage is 120   multiply kVA x 4.81
- and voltage is 115   multiply kVA x 5.02

To find amps if load is given in kVA   single-phase circuits
- and voltage is 480   multiply kVA x 2.08
- and voltage is 277   multiply kVA x 3.61
- and voltage is 240   multiply kVA x 4.17
- and voltage is 230   multiply kVA x 4.35
- and voltage is 208   multiply kVA x 4.81
- and voltage is 120   multiply kVA x 8.3
- and voltage is 115   multiply kVA x 8.7

kVA is same as kW without power factor
Three-phase amps to single-phase amps = multiply by 1.73
Single-phase amps to three-phase amps = multiply by .58

Power Factor

When a circuit contains only resistance, the current and voltage are in phase and you have a 100% power factor and (volt – amperes = watts).

When either inductance or capacitance is introduced, the voltage and current are no longer in phase and the power factor is then something less than 100%.

$$\text{Power factor in single-phase circuits} = \frac{\text{watts}}{\text{amps} \times \text{volts}}$$

$$\text{Power factor in three-phase circuits} = \frac{\text{watts}}{\text{amps} \times \text{volts} \times 1.732}$$

True power (in watts) is the reading obtained from a watt meter.

Apparent power (in volt amps) is obtained by multiplying volts x amps for 1φ, or volts x 1.732 x amps for 3φ.

Single-phase watts = volts x amps x power factor
   Three-phase watts = volts x 1.732 x amps x power factor
   Volt-amps = true power in watts ÷ power factor

$$\text{Power factor} = \frac{\text{true power}}{\text{apparent power}}$$

$$\text{Amps 1-phase} = \frac{\text{watts}}{\text{volts} \times \text{power factor}} \quad \text{or} \quad \frac{\text{VA}}{\text{volts}}$$

$$\text{Amps 3-phase} = \frac{\text{watts}}{\text{volts} \times 1.732 \times \text{P.F.}} \quad \text{or} \quad \frac{\text{VA}}{\text{volts} \times 1.732}$$

Power Factor (continued)

Example:
   30 amps at 240 volts single-phase = 7200 volt-amps
   watt meter reads = 6192

$$\text{Power factor} = \frac{\text{true power}}{\text{apparent power}} \quad \text{or} \quad \frac{6192}{7200} \quad \text{or } .86 \text{ or } 86\%$$

$$\text{volt-amps} = \text{watts} \div \text{power factor or } 6192 \div .86 = 7200 \text{ VA}$$

$$\text{amps} = \frac{\text{watts}}{\text{volts} \times \text{power factor}} \quad \text{or} \quad \frac{6192}{240 \times .86} \quad \text{or} \quad \frac{6192}{206.4} = 30 \text{ amps}$$

Horsepower (HP)

One watt is the power used when one ampere of current flows through a potential difference of one volt.

Mechanical power is usually measured in units of horsepower.

One watt is equal to .00134 horsepower; 746 watts is equal to one horsepower.

Formulas:

$$HP = \frac{\text{watts}}{746}$$

$$HP = \text{watts} \times .00134$$

$$\text{Watts} = HP \times 746$$

$$HP = \frac{kW}{.746}$$

$$HP = kW \times 1.34$$

$$\text{Efficiency} = \frac{\text{power output}}{\text{power input}}$$

$$HP \text{ single-phase} = \frac{\text{volts} \times \text{amps} \times \text{eff.} \times P.F.}{746}$$

$$HP \text{ three-phase} = \frac{\text{volts} \times 1.732 \times \text{amps} \times \text{eff.} \times P.F.}{746}$$

$$\text{Amps single-phase} = \frac{746 \times HP}{\text{volts} \times \text{eff.} \times P.F.}$$

$$\text{Amps three-phase} = \frac{746 \times HP}{\text{volts} \times 1.732 \times \text{eff.} \times P.F.}$$

Reciprocals

To find a reciprocal of a number, divided that number into one.

Sample: $1.732 \overline{)1.0000} = .577 \qquad \sqrt{3} = 1.732$

Square root of 3 = 1.732

To divide a number by 1.73 for a given answer, you can multiply a number by the divisors reciprocal and get the same answer.

Samples: $\quad \dfrac{208}{1.732} = 120 \qquad .58 \times 208 = 120$

$\qquad\qquad \dfrac{480}{1.732} = 277 \qquad .58 \times 480 = 277$

Ohm's Law

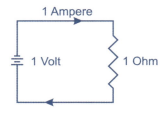

E	=	Volts
R	=	Resistance
I	=	Current
W	=	Watts (Volt-Amperes)

$$\frac{E}{I \times R}$$

Ω = Ohm

1000 Ohms = 1 Kilohm (K)
1,000,000 Ohms = 1 Megohm (Meg)
1,000 Kilohms (K) = 1 Megohm (Meg)

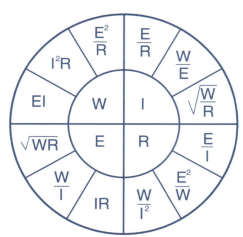

Watt's Wheel or Ohm's Law Circle

The expressions in the outer ring are equal to the expression in the inner circle.

For example, to find the resistance where the watts and current are known, divide watts by the current squared.

Residential Requirements

Service Rating

A minimum 100-ampere, three-wire service (or feeder) is required, in most cases, for any individual (dwelling unit) residence – house, cabin, apartment, etc., [see 230.42(B) and 230.79(C)]. If electric heat is installed as the heat source for an individual dwelling, a minimum 200-ampere, three-wire service should be installed, but in no case less than the minimum service required after calculations in accordance with 230.42, and 220.14. The service must be adequate for the load served calculated in accordance with the applicable requirements of Article 220. See Services Single Family Dwelling, Ferm's Fast Finder.

Service Location

Always consult the serving utility for requirements such as meter locations, mounting heights, and mast support. A list of acceptable wiring methods and raceways for service-entrance conductors is provided in 230.43. The service disconnecting means must be installed at a readily accessible location outside the building or inside the building but located nearest the point of entrance of the service-entrance conductors. The service disconnecting means can be either a single device or not more than six disconnects grouped in the same location. For service disconnecting means location and marking requirements, see 230.70, 230.71 and 230.72.

Service Grounding and Bonding Requirements

The dwelling service is required to be grounded in accordance with Parts II and III of Article 250. General grounding provisions are included in Part II and the grounding electrode provisions are found in Part III of Article 250. A metal underground water pipe is required to be supplemented by an additional electrode in accordance with 250.53(D)(2). If the supplemental electrode is a rod, pipe or plate, it must comply with 250.53(A). Metal enclosures for service equipment and conductors are required to be bonded together in a manner specified in 250.92. Metal water piping systems and other metal piping systems are required to be bonded in accordance with 250.104(A) and (B).

Service Masts and Underground Service Conductors

If a service mast is used as a support for the power service-drop or overhead service conductors, it must meet the requirements of 230.28. Refer to the service mast drawings (SM-1 and SM-2) provided in this text.

If underground service conductors are used and any part of them are exposed to earth fill, they must be listed as direct burial conductors such as Type USE. Underground service-entrance conductors must meet the depth requirements of 300.5 and must be protected from physical damage in accordance with 300.5(D).

Dwelling Lighting Requirements

A 15-ampere general purpose lighting branch circuit shall be provided for each 600 square feet of area (20-ampere circuit for 800 square feet) of a dwelling, including the basement, but not including open porches, garages, or unused or unfinished spaces not adaptable for future use [see 220.14(J), 220.12]. (15 amps x 120 volts = 1800 VA / 3 VA per sq ft = 600 sq ft)

A wall switch controlled lighting outlet must be installed at each outdoor entrance or exit as well as in each habitable room, and bathroom(s), hallway(s), stairway(s), and attached garage(s) or detached garage(s) with electric power. In habitable rooms other than bathrooms and kitchens, a switch controlling a receptacle shall be permitted in lieu of a switch controlled lighting outlet. Where switches are installed for lighting outlets for stairways, a switch control is required at each floor level (and intermediate landing areas that include an entry to the landing) where the difference in floor levels is six risers or more. An occupancy sensor for lighting control is permitted in addition to wall switches or combination units at customary wall switch locations [see 210.70(A)]. A switch controlled lighting outlet is required at each basement, also in any crawl space, attic, or utility room containing equipment that requires servicing, in addition to any space(s) used for storage. Lighting outlets are required to be located near equipment that requires servicing and the switch is to be located at the entrance to the space or room [see 210.70(A)(3)]. Surface lighting luminaries are not permitted in clothes closets unless they meet the provisions in 410.16. A flush mounted fixture with a solid lens is permitted if it meets the requirements of 410.16, 410.115 and 410.116.

Dwelling Receptacle Requirements

Receptacle outlets are required to be located in every habitable room of dwelling units so that no point measured horizontally along the floor line is more than 1.8 m (6 ft) without an outlet in that space. In other words, a receptacle outlet is needed within 1.8 m (6 ft) of every doorway or fireplace, but in the rest of the room, the receptacle outlets can be spaced 3.6 m (12 ft) apart if there is no break in the wall between them. Any wall space greater than 600 mm (2 ft) requires a receptacle outlet. A receptacle outlet installed over 1.7 m (5.5 ft) above the floor cannot be counted as the required receptacle outlet for that space. Receptacle outlets installed within 450 mm (18 in.) of the wall are permitted to be counted as the required receptacle outlet for that space. Any receptacle outlets installed in the ends of electric baseboard heaters are permitted to meet the above requirements. Such receptacles shall not be connected to the heater circuit. It should be noted that many listed electric baseboard heaters do not permit a receptacle outlet to be installed on the wall above them. See the requirements of 210.52(A).

At least one receptacle outlet is required in every hallway that is 3.0 m (10 ft) or more in length (unbroken by a door) accordance with 210.52(H). Foyers, that are not part of a hallway, with an area greater than 5.6 ms 60 ft must have a receptacle in any wall space that is 900 mm (3 ft) in width (doorways or door-side windows and similar openings that extend to the floor are not considered wall space). A receptacle outlet is required adjacent to and within 900 mm (3 ft) of bathroom basins in accordance with 210.52(D). At least one 20-ampere branch circuit is required for a dwelling unit bathroom or bathrooms to meet the provisions of 210.11(C)(3). A laundry receptacle outlet is required for dwelling units in accordance with 210.52(F) and is required to be a circuit rated at a minimum of 20-amperes as indicated in 210.11(C)(2). The circuit supplying the receptacle outlet(s) for the laundry shall supply no other load and the outlet must be located within 1.8 m (6 ft) of the laundry equipment.

For one-family dwellings and each unit of a two-family dwelling that is at grade level, at least one receptacle outlet is required in the front and back of such dwelling units. It must be accessible and located not more than 2.0 m (6.5 ft) above grade to meet the provisions of 210.52(E). Receptacles are also required at every balcony, deck, or porch.

For one-and two-family dwellings a receptacle outlet for servicing of heating and air-conditioning and refrigeration is required within 7.5 m (25 ft) of and on the same level as the equipment, whether inside or outside. This receptacle outlet is not permitted to be connected to the load side of the equipment disconnect [see 210.63].

A receptacle outlet is required for one-family dwellings at each basement, attached garage, or each detached garage or accessory building with electric power. This receptacle outlet is in addition to any receptacle(s) for specific equipment [see 210.52(G)].

In kitchens and dining areas of dwelling units, a receptacle outlet must be installed at each wall counter space 300 mm (12 in.) or wider. Receptacles are required to be located so that no point along the counter wall space is more than 600 mm (2 ft) from another receptacle. Island or peninsular countertops with a long dimension of 600 mm (2 ft) or greater and a short dimension of 300 mm (12 in.) or greater requires a receptacle outlet. Receptacles installed at the countertop spaces shall not be located more than 500 mm (20 in.) above the countertop surface. For peninsular countertops, the measurements are to be taken from the connecting edge. All countertop spaces separated by ranges, refrigerators, or sinks, etc., are considered separate countertop spaces and the provisions of 210.52(C)(1),(2), and (3) apply. An exception to 210.52(C)(1) addresses space directly behind a sink or range that exceeds the dimensions in Figure 210.52. A receptacle would then be required in such spaces [see 210.52(C)(1) Exception and 210.52(C)(5)]. Receptacle outlets located behind refrigerators, freezers, or other fixed stationary equipment are not required to be counted in the countertop wall space requirements of 210.52(C) [see 210.52(C)(4)].

Tamper-resistant receptacles are required per 406.12. Weather-resistant receptacles are required per 406.9.

Kitchen Receptacles and Circuits

The kitchen countertop area must have the receptacle outlets supplied by at least two 20-ampere small-appliance branch circuits. The receptacle outlets in the dining area must also be supplied by a 20-ampere circuit that extends from the kitchen receptacle circuits. Additional small appliance branch circuits are permitted to supply additional kitchen receptacle outlets and other rooms specified in 210.52(B)(1). The minimum required circuits provided for the kitchen receptacles in accordance with 210.52(B)(3) are required to supply only one kitchen. See 210.11(C)(1) for the minimum small appliance branch circuits required for dwellings.

Dishwashers typically require a separate properly rated circuit, and a kitchen disposal or compactor, or both, requires a separate circuit for the load that must be served in accordance with 210.23 and 220.14(A).

A circuit suitable for the load with a minimum rating of 40 amperes is required for a range of 8 3/4 kW or more, either freestanding or the drop-in type [see 220.55].

A circuit suitable for the load with a minimum rating of 30 amperes (5,000 VA) is required for each electric clothes dryer [see 220.54].

A circuit suitable for at least 125% of the nameplate of electric water heater(s) (continuous load) is required in accordance with the provisions of 422.13.

GFCI Protection for Dwelling Units

All 125-volt, single-phase, 15- and 20-ampere receptacles installed in the following dwelling unit locations require GFCI protection [see 210.8(A)].

1. All bathroom receptacles
2. All receptacles installed in garage and accessory buildings with the floor located at or below grade level not intended as habitable rooms and limited to storage areas, work areas, or areas of similar use.
3. All receptacles installed outdoors, with the exception of receptacles supplied by dedicated branch circuits for snow-melting or deicing equipment.
4. Crawl space receptacles at or below grade level
5. Receptacles in unfinished basements, with an exception for permanently installed burglar/fire alarm systems.
6. Receptacles intended to serve countertop surfaces of kitchens
7. Receptacles installed within 1.8 m (6 ft) of dwelling unit sinks
8. 125-volt, single-phase, 15- and 20-ampere receptacles installed in or at dwelling unit boathouses
9. All receptacles installed within 1.8 m (6 ft) of the outside edge of a bathtub or shower stall.
10. Laundry areas
11. All outlets not exceeding 240 volts for boat hoists at dwellings [210.8(C)].

Arc-Fault Circuit-Interrupter Protection

An arc-fault circuit interrupter (AFCI) device is designed and intended to provide protection from the effects of arcing faults for outlets of dwelling unit branch circuits. The AFCI device recognizes the characteristics that are unique to arcing faults. See the definition of arc-fault circuit interrupter provided in Article 100 of the *NEC*.

Section 210.12(A) requires all 120-volt, single-phase, 15- and 20-ampere branch circuits supplying outlets or devices of dwelling unit kitchens, family rooms, dining rooms, living rooms, parlors, libraries, dens, bedrooms, sunrooms, recreation rooms, closets, hallways, laundry areas, or similar rooms or areas to be protected by a listed arc-fault circuit interrupter, in accordance with 210.12(A)(1)-(6). This provision is applicable to branch circuits supplying outlets located in occupancies that meet the definition of dwelling in Article 100.

Note: Combination-type AFCI devices are those designed to sense parallel arcing as well as series arcing conditions. Branch circuits to burglar or fire alarm panels are not permitted to be AFCI- or GFCI-protected [see 760.41(B) and 760.121(B) and the Exception to 210.12(A)(1)-(6)].

Kilowatt Hour Monthly Consumption

For monthly kilowatt hour consumption, multiply approximate appliance wattage by the number of hours of use per month, and divide by 1000. Multiply monthly kilowatt hours by appropriate rate for monthly cost.

Example:

Food blender is 400 watts

400 w x 30 hours per month equals 12,000 watt-hours

$$\frac{12,000}{1,000} = 12 \text{ KWH}$$

If electric power costs 10¢ per KWH.

12 KWH x 10¢ = 120¢ per month.

12 x .10 = 1

Typical Wattage Rating of Residential Electrical Appliances

Appliance	Approx. Wattage
Air Conditioner (Window 120-volt)	up to 1500
Blanket (Electric)	190
Block Heater (Car)	400-800
Broiler	1500
Clothes Dryer	up to 5000
Coffee Maker (10-cup)	850
Deep Fat Fryer	1500
Dishwasher	up to 1800
Electrostatic Cleaner	60
Fan (Attic)	365
Fan (Circulating)	85
Fan (Furnace)	700
Food Blender	400
Food Freezer	335
Food Freezer (No Frost)	425
Food Mixer	125
Food Waste Disposer	1176
Frying Pan	1160
Hair Dryer	800–1250
Heat Lamp (Infrared)	250
Heater (Portable)	up to 1500
Heater, 240 v Baseboard	up to 250 w. per foot
Iron (Hand)	1250
Lawn Mower	1500
Microwave Oven	1500
Range up to 12 kW	usually 8000
Refrigerator	300
Refrigerator–Freezer	600
Refrigerator–Freezer (No Frost)	750
Rotisserie	1500
Sewing Machine	75
Shaver	15
Stereo	30–115
Sun Lamp	280
Television (Color)	100–300
Toaster	1150
Trash Compactor	600
Vacuum Cleaner	800
Waffle Iron	1080
Washing Machine (Automatic)	700
Water Heater (Quick Recovery)	4500
Water Bed	500
Water Pump	700-1920

Service Mast Installation Details SM-1

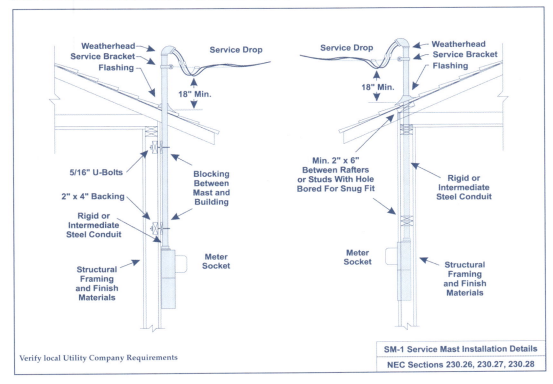

Service Mast Installation Details SM-2

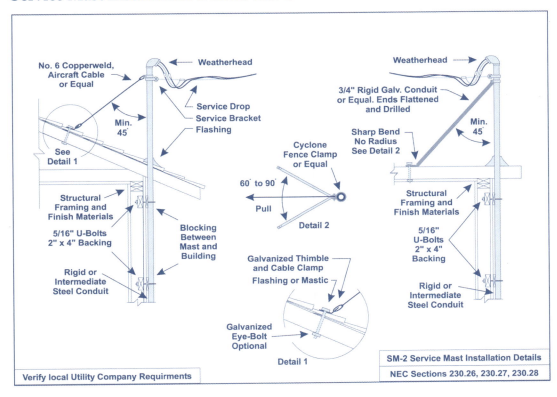

Charts, Formulas, and Useful Information | 1- and 2-Family Study Guide | 169

Resistance

Total resistance of a series circuit is the sum of all the resistance in the circuit.

R1 + R2 + R3 = RT
5 Ω + 4 Ω + 3 Ω = 12

Total resistance of parallel resistors if all the resistors are the same size.

$$\frac{\text{R of one resistor}}{\text{Number of resistors in parallel}} = RT$$

Total resistance of parallel resistors of different resistance.

5 Ω
5 Ω
$= \frac{5}{2} = 2.5\ \Omega$

5 Ω
5 Ω
5 Ω
$= \frac{5}{3} = 1.6666\ \Omega$

$$\frac{1}{\frac{1}{R1} + \frac{1}{R2} + \frac{1}{R3} + \frac{1}{R4}} = RT$$

R1 = 120 Ω
R2 = 240 Ω
R3 = 60 Ω
R4 = 120 Ω

The reciprocal of the sum of the reciprocals of the resistors in the group.

$$\frac{1}{\frac{1}{120} + \frac{1}{240} + \frac{1}{60} + \frac{1}{120}}$$

.0083333
.0041666
.0166666
.0083333
.0374998

$$RT = \frac{1}{.0374998} = 26.666\ \Omega$$

— OR —

$$\frac{R1 \times R2}{R1 + R2} = RT$$

$$\frac{120 \times 240}{120 + 240} = \frac{28,800}{360} = 80$$

$$\frac{80 \times 60}{80 + 60} = \frac{4800}{140} = 34.285714$$

$$\frac{34.285714 \times 120}{34.285714 + 120} = \frac{4114.2856}{154.28571} = 26.666\ \Omega$$

Series/Parallel Circuit

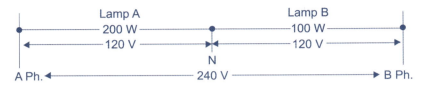

1. Solve for ohms (resistance) of lamp A.
2. Solve for ohms (resistance) of lamp B.
3. Solve for current of lamp A.
4. Solve for current of lamp B.
5. If lost neutral at panel, what is the current at lamp A?
6. If lost neutral at panel, what is the current at lamp B?
7. If lost neutral at panel, what is the voltage across lamp A?
8. If lost neutral at panel, what is the voltage across lamp B?
9. If lost neutral at panel, which lamp will burn out?

To solve, use Ohm's Law circle on page 238.

Answers:

1. Lamp A ohms $R = \dfrac{E^2}{W} = \dfrac{120 \times 120}{200} = 72$

2. Lamp B ohms $R = \dfrac{E^2}{W} = \dfrac{120 \times 120}{100} = 144$

3. Lamp A current $I = \dfrac{W}{E} = \dfrac{200}{120} = 1.6666$

4. Lamp B current $I = \dfrac{W}{E} = \dfrac{100}{120} = .8333$

5. Lamp A current $I = \dfrac{E}{R} = \dfrac{240}{72 + 144} = 1.1111$

6. Lamp B current $I = \dfrac{E}{R} = \dfrac{240}{72 + 144} = 1.1111$

7. Lamp A voltage $E = IR = 1.1111 \times 72 = 80$

8. Lamp B voltage $E = IR = 1.1111 \times 144 = 160$

9. 100 watt lamp at 160 volts   = Lamp B

Skin Effect

Alternating current flowing through a conductor will generate alternating magnetic flux linkages in and around the conductor which oppose the flow of current. The greatest number of linkages will be near the center of the conductor and will therefore cause the center of the conductor to be a higher resistance area. This condition causes more current to flow close to the surface of the conductor and is known as skin effect.

Skin effect becomes more and more a factor as the frequency of the system is increased. Skin effect is neglible at 60 Hz per second.

Ampacity of Circuit Breaker or Fuse	Sizing Equipment Grounding Conductor — Wire Type AWG – kcmil Equipment Ground Wire Size	
	Copper Conductor	Aluminum Conductor
0 through 15	14	12
16 through 20	12	10
21 through 60	10	8
61 through 100	8	6
101 through 200	6	4
201 through 300	4	2
301 through 400	3	1
401 through 500	2	1/0
501 through 600	1	2/0
601 through 800	0	3/0
801 through 1000	2/0	4/0
1001 through 1200	3/0	250 kcmil
1201 through 1600	4/0	350 kcmil
1601 through 2000	250 kcmil	400 kcmil
2001 through 2500	350 kcmil	600 kcmil
2501 through 3000	400 kcmil	600 kcmil
3001 through 4000	500 kcmil	800 kcmil
4001 through 5000	700 kcmil	1200 kcmil
5001 through 6000	800 kcmil	1200 kcmil

Note: See installation provisions for equipment grounding conductors in Section 250.120 and sizing requirements are located in 250.122. See Adjusting Equipment Grounding Conductor Size in 250.122(B)..

Volt-amp (VA)

Single-phase Circuits

Volt-amp = amps × voltage

Amp = volt-amp ÷ voltage

$$kVA = \frac{voltage \times amps}{1000}$$

Example:

180 VA at 120 V = 1.5 Amps

$$120 \overline{)180 \text{ VA}} = 1.5 \text{ amps}$$

1.5 amps × 120 V = 180 VA

Three-phase Circuits

Volt-amp = amps × voltage × 1.732

$$Amp = \frac{3\varphi \text{ kVA} \times 1000}{voltage \times 1.732}$$

$$kVA = \frac{voltage \times amps \times 1.732}{1000}$$

Example:

9000 VA at 208 V 3-Ph. = 25 amps

Amps

208 V × 1.732 = 360

$$360 \overline{)9000 \text{ VA}} = 25 \text{ amps}$$

25 amps × 360 = 9000 VA

Transformers
To find the voltage, turns and current, use the following symbols and formulas.

Symbols	Formula
E_P = Primary voltage	
E_S = Secondary voltage	
T_P = Primary turns	$\dfrac{E_P}{E_S} = \dfrac{T_P}{T_S} = \dfrac{I_S}{I_P}$
T_S = Secondary turns	
I_S = Secondary current	
I_P = Primary current	
? = Unknown	

Remove the unwanted symbols and cross multiply as in (A) or (B) below to solve for the unknown.
  (A) If the unknown is on the top, cross multiply toward the known.
  (B) If the unknown is on the bottom, cross multiply toward the unknown.

Example #1 as per (A):
A step down transformer has 120 volts on the primary and 24 volts on the secondary. With a primary current of 2 amps, what current will the secondary deliver?

$$\dfrac{E_P}{E_S} = \cancel{\dfrac{T_P}{T_S}} = \dfrac{I_S}{I_P} \quad \text{or} \quad \dfrac{E_P}{E_S} = \dfrac{I_S}{I_P} \quad \text{or} \quad \dfrac{120}{24} \diagdown \dfrac{?}{2} \quad \text{or} \quad \dfrac{240}{24} = 10 \text{ amps}$$

Example #2 as per (B):
A step down transformer has 120 volts on the primary and 24 volts on the secondary. With 1200 turns on the primary, how many turns will there be on the secondary?

$$\dfrac{E_P}{I_S} = \dfrac{T_P}{T_S} = \cancel{\dfrac{I_S}{I_P}} \quad \text{or} \quad \dfrac{E_P}{E_S} = \dfrac{T_P}{T_S} \quad \text{or} \quad \dfrac{120}{24} \diagup \dfrac{1200}{?} \quad \text{or} \quad \dfrac{28{,}800}{120} = 240$$

Additional formulas on next page.

Transformer Formulas

To find the **primary voltage** when the turns and the secondary voltage are known.	$E_P =$	$\dfrac{E_S \times T_P}{T_S}$
To find the **primary voltage** when the current and secondary voltage are known.	$E_P =$	$\dfrac{E_S \times I_S}{I_P}$
To find the **secondary voltage** when the turns and primary voltage are known.	$E_S =$	$\dfrac{E_P \times T_S}{T_P}$
To find the **secondary voltage** when the current and the primary voltage are known.	$E_S =$	$\dfrac{E_P \times I_P}{I_S}$
To find the **primary turns** when the secondary turns and both voltages are known.	$T_P =$	$\dfrac{E_P \times T_S}{E_S}$
To find the **primary turns** when the current and the secondary turns are known.	$T_P =$	$\dfrac{I_S \times T_S}{I_P}$
To find the **secondary turns** when the currents and the primary turns are known.	$T_S =$	$\dfrac{T_P \times I_P}{I_S}$
To find the **secondary turns** when the voltages and primary turns are known.	$T_S =$	$\dfrac{E_S \times T_P}{E_P}$
To find the **secondary current** when the voltages and the primary current are known.	$I_S =$	$\dfrac{E_P \times I_P}{E_S}$
To find the **secondary current** when the turns and the primary current are known.	$I_S =$	$\dfrac{T_P \times I_P}{T_S}$
To find the **primary current** when the voltages and the secondary current are known.	$I_P =$	$\dfrac{E_S \times I_S}{E_P}$
To find the **primary current** when the turns and the secondary current are known.	$I_P =$	$\dfrac{I_S \times T_S}{T_P}$

Note: Open delta transformer connection will produce 57.7% of the power of the closed delta connection.

Voltage Drop

Voltage drop is only mentioned in some sections of the *NEC* as informational notes, and is required to be calculated in other sections of the *Code*. These sections are 210.19(A) informational note 4, 215.2(A)(4) Informational Note 2, 310.15(A)(1) informational note 1, 647.4(D), and 695.7. Permitted or required amounts of voltage drop may range from 1.5 to 15 percent of the feeder or branch-circuit voltage. Five percent maximum is generally suggested on a circuit.

Informational notes are not mandatory *Code* requirements, but are explanatory material intended for informational purposes only [see 90.5(C)]. However, manufacturer's installation instructions, which are required to be followed in 110.3(B), often require a minimum voltage rating to be maintained in order for a particular type of utilization equipment to function in the manner intended by the manufacturer, and to be listed by an electrical equipment nationally recognized testing laboratory. To perform voltage drop calculations, it is essential to have the following information: 1) the k-factor, 2) the length of the feeder and/or branch circuit to the load, 3) the amperage load of the circuit, and, of course, 4) the circuit voltage. The k-factor is a multiplier representing the DC resistance for a given size conductor 1,000 feet long and operating at 75°C. From this information, the code user can find either the minimum size conductor needed to carry the load (measured in circular mils or kcmils), and/or the percentage of voltage drop.

The formulas included here are based on conductor dc resistance values provided in Chapter 9 Table 8 of the *NEC*, and are viewed as generally acceptable for voltage drop calculations. Table 8 is based on 75 °C/167°F, and provides a k-factor constant of 12.9 for copper, and 21.2 for aluminum conductors. — See note below.

For example, to find the k-factor, you multiply the resistance of the conductor per foot by the circular mil of the conductor. Remember that Table 8 states resistance in ohms per 1,000 feet. For voltage drop calculations when copper wire is used, be sure to select the value from the "uncoated copper" column, as most copper conductors are uncoated. To be "coated" means that there is a tin or other type of coating on the copper conductor, which changes its resistance value. If a conductor is "coated," then use the "coated" column resistance value. Remember that "coated" does not refer to the conductor installation. Note the examples below.

For Copper Wire, use the dc resistance measured in ohms from Chapter 9, Table 8:

The dc resistance of a 1,000 kcmil copper conductor is 0.0129 ohms per 1,000 feet.

(0.0129 ohms per 1,000 feet divided by 1,000 = .0000129 ohms per foot)

0.0000129 ohms per foot x 1,000,000 circular mils = 12.9 k-factor — for copper wire

For Aluminum Wire, the dc resistance measured in ohms per 1,000 feet of conductor from Chapter 9, Table 8:

(0.0212 ohms per 1,000 feet divided by 1,000 = .0000212 ohms per foot)

0.0000212 ohms per foot x 1,000,000 circular mils = 21.2 k-factor — for aluminum wire

Note: It is important to note that to find the k-factor, *you multiply the resistance of the conductor per foot by the circular mil sizes of the conductor.* For any copper or aluminum conductor found in Chapter 9, Table 8, the k-factor will roughly be 12.9 or very close to it for copper, and 21.2 or very close to it for aluminum. Therefore, these two amounts are chosen as k-factor constant values for uncoated copper or aluminum conductors operating at 75°C/167 °F ambient temperatures and rated amperage.

75°C/167°F temperature rating is often used in today's electrical circuits, as most new lugs in electrical distribution equipment and utilization equipment are rated 75°C/167°F; and 90°C/194°F rated conductors are used at the 75°C ampacity because of the termination requirements found in 110.14(C). The formula used is also generally acceptable for 60°C/140 °F conductor installations. Voltage drop is calculated for single-phase installations with the understanding that the current will be returning from the load either from a line-to-line or line-to-neutral load; therefore, the multiplier 2 is added into the formula for the resistance of the conductor to the load and back. This is necessary to complete the circuit and to clear a fault, (keeping 250.122(B) in mind, which will be discussed later). The formula for three-phase installations uses 1.732 instead of 2 as the multiplier. Current flows out to the load and back on the phase conductors.

Once the *volts dropped* have been determined, use the formula below to determine the percent of voltage drop for the circuit or system.

Example 1: $\dfrac{7.2 \text{ volts dropped}}{240 \text{ volts (1 phase)}} = 3\%$ voltage drop

Example 2: $\dfrac{24 \text{ volts dropped}}{480 \text{ volts L-L}} = 5\%$ voltage drop

Choose a formula based on the conductor size used, or the maximum amount of voltage drop acceptable to the AHJ. (3%, 5%, etc.)

Voltage Drop Formulas for 1-phase Installations:

Volts dropped = $\dfrac{2 \times \text{Length of conductors to load} \times \text{k-factor (copper or aluminum)} \times \text{I (amperage)}}{\text{The circular mils or kcmils of the conductor used}}$

Voltage Drop Formulas for 3-phase Installations:

Volts dropped = $\dfrac{1.732 \times \text{Length of conductors to load} \times \text{k-factor (copper or aluminum)} \times \text{I (amperage)}}{\text{The circular mils or kcmils of the conductor used}}$

To determine size in circular mils required (single-phase) = $\dfrac{2 \times L \times K \times I}{\%\text{ Voltage Drop}}$

To determine size in circular mils required (three-phase) = $\dfrac{1.732 \times L \times K \times I}{\%\text{ Voltage Drop}}$

These formulas may be used to determine the maximum length of a conductor, the circular mil size needed for a conductor, or the voltage drop in a system or circuit.

Voltage-Drop Formula

Where

$\dfrac{2 \times K \times I \times L}{CM} = VD$

$\dfrac{2 \times K \times I \times L}{VD} = CM$

$\dfrac{CM \times VD}{2 \times K \times I} = \text{maximum length}$

$\dfrac{CM \times VD}{2 \times K \times L} = \text{maximum I (amps)}$

VD = actual volts dropped (*not* percentage)

K = assumed specific resistance

L = length of run to load

I = load in amps

CM = area of wire, circular mils

Note: For 3-phase formulas, replace the multiplier 2 with 1.732.

Note: To find k-factor, multiply resistance per foot of conductor by circular mils.

Example: K for 1 AWG copper at 75°C = .000154 × 83690 = 12.9

Note: Chapter 9 Table 8 dc resistance values for k-factor and voltage drop on ac circuits are used for simplicity and consistency. Resistance values for a given size wire in Chapter 9 Table 8 are very close to the values given in Chapter 9 Table 9, regardless of which wiring method is used.

Hazardous Classified Locations (Defined)

Hazardous area are divided into three classes:

CLASS I, CLASS II, and CLASS III.

Class I Locations, Article 501 and Article 505

Hazardous due to the presence of flammable gases & flammable liquid-produced vapors.

Group A, B, C or D is determined by ignition temperature and explosion pressure of gases and vapors. [Section 500.6(A)]

Groups IIC, IIB and IIA are used for Class I, Zone 0, 1 and 2 locations. [Section 505.6]

- DIVISION 1, Section 500.5(B)(1)

    Hazardous under normal operating conditions.

- DIVISION 2, Section 500.5(B)(2)

    Hazardous under abnormal operating conditions.

- ZONE(s) 0, 1 and 2. Article 505
- ZONE(s) 20, 21, and 22. Article 506

Class II Locations, Article 502, Article 506

Hazardous due to the presence of combustible dust.

Group E, F or G is determined by ignition temperature and conductivity of the dust.

- DIVISION 1, Section 500.5(C)(1)

    Hazardous under normal operating conditions.

- DIVISON 2, Section 500.5(C)(2)

    Hazardous under abnormal operating conditions.

- ZONE(s) 20, 21, and 22.

    Article 506 (note Article 506 provides the requirements for both locations containing combustible dust as well as fibers/flyings.)

Class III Locations, Article 503

Hazardous due to the presence of ignitible fibers (or combustible flyings).

- DIVISION 1, Section 500.5(D)(1)

    Where easily ignitible fibers are handled, manufactured or used.

- DIVISION 2, Section 500.5(D)(2)

    Where easily ignitible fibers are stored or handled, but not in the process of manufacture.

    • See "Recommended Practice for the Classification of Flammable Liquids, Gas, or Vapors and of Hazardous (Classified) Locations for Electrical Installations in Chemical Process Areas," NFPA 497.

    • See "Recommended Practice for the Classification of Combustible Dusts and of Hazardous (Classified) Locations for Electrical Installations in Chemical Process Areas," NFPA 499.

    • See "Classification of Flammable Liquids, gases, or Vapors and of Hazardous (Classified) Locations for Electrical Installations," NFPA 497.

    • Each room, section, or area shall be considered individually in determining its classification. See 500.5(A) in the *NEC*.

    • Documentation of hazardous (classified) locations required. Section 500.4(A) in the *NEC*

Unclassified Locations

Locations determined to be neither Class I, Division 1; Class 1, Division 2; Class I, Zone 0; Class I, Zone 1; Class I, Zone 2; Class II, Division 1; Class II, Division 2; Class III, Division 1; Class III, Division 2; or any combination thereof. [Section 500.2]

NEMA SIZE	NEMA SIZE MOTOR STARTERS FULL VOLTAGE STARTING				
	MAXIMUM HORSEPOWER SINGLE PHASE MOTORS		MAXIMUM HORSEPOWER POLYPHASE MOTORS		
	115V	230V	200V	230V	460V/575V
00	–	1	1½	1½	2
0	1	2	3	3	5
1	2	3	7½	7½	10
1½	3	5	–	–	–
2	3	7½	10	15	25
3	7½	15	25	30	50
4	–	–	40	50	100
5	–	–	75	100	200
6	–	–	150	200	400
7	–	–	–	300	600
8	–	–	–	450	900
9	–	–	–	800	1600

How to Determine the Circular Mil Area of a Busbar

Circular mils = $\dfrac{\text{square mils}}{0.7854}$ or square mils × 1.2732365 or

Circular mils = $\dfrac{\text{square inches}}{0.0000007854}$

Square mils = $\dfrac{\text{square inch}}{0.000001}$

Example: A busbar sized at 1" x 1/4" is equal to 318,309.14 circular mils

Multiply 1" x ¼" (0.25) and divide by 0.000001 which equals 250,000.

Square Mils = $\dfrac{1.00" \times .25"}{.000001}$ = 250,000 square mils

250,000 square mils × 1.2732365 = 318,309.12 circular mils

Therefore, a 1" x ¼" busbar = 318,309 cm wire size (next size up is 350 kcmil)

Divide by 0.7854 = total of 318,309.14 cm or we could take the square mils of 250,000 × 1.2732365, which equals 318,309.12 cm.

Additional calculations for sizing a busbar can be performed using the above example and changing the size of the busbar.

Short-Circuit Current Available Summary

The fault currents in an electrical system can be calculated if sufficient information about the electrical system is known. The point-to-point method for short-circuit calculations follows this summary.

Section 110.9 covers interrupting rating. Equipment that is intended to break current at fault levels must have an interrupting rating sufficient for the nominal circuit voltage and the current that is available at the line terminals of the equipment. Equipment intended to break current at other than fault levels, must have an interrupting rating at nominal circuit voltage sufficient for the current that must be interrupted (see also 110.10 of the *NEC*).

The degree of current limitation of a circuit breaker or fuse depends on the type of breaker or fuse and the available short-circuit current. A breaker or fuse is current-limiting only for short-circuit currents in its current-limiting range. The larger a breaker or fuse, the lesser the degree of current limitation.

Where a large electrical distribution system (typically 800 ampere and larger) has short-circuit currents exceeding circuit-breaker interrupting ratings or component short-circuit current (withstand) ratings, it is not generally sufficient to just put a current-limiting fuse in only the service main.

The large main service fuse may be capable of protecting the larger or higher interrupting rated circuit breakers, but it cannot be assumed that the smaller circuit breakers in the system would have protection. It is recommended that the entire system should be analyzed for proper interrupting rating and current limitation by a qualified person with specialized knowledge.

Point-to-Point Method for Short-Circuit Calculations

(Reprinted by permission Cooper industries, Bussmann Division, P.O. Box 14460, St. Louis, Missouri 63178, revised version 2008.) Bussmann Technical Services

Adequate interrupting capacity and protection of electrical components are two essential aspects required by the *National Electrical Code* in 110.9, 110.10 and 240.1.

The first step to assure that a system has proper interrupting capacity and component protection is to determine the available short-circuit currents.

With this method, the available short-circuit currents can be determined with a reasonable degree of accuracy at various points for either 3-phase or 1-phase electrical distribution systems. This method assumes unlimited primary short-circuit current (infinite bus). Obtain transformer percent impedance from electric utility or from nameplate. The steps are as follows:

1. Determine transformer full-load amperes from nameplate, tables, or the following formula:

    for three-phase transformers

    $$I_{F.L.A.} = \frac{Kva \times 1000}{E_{L-L} \times 1.73}$$

    for single-phase transformers

    $$I_{F.L.A.} = \frac{Kva \times 1000}{E_{L-L}}$$

2. Find transformer multiplier:

    $$\frac{100}{\text{transformer percent impedance } Z} = \text{multiplier}$$

3. Determine transformer let-thru short-circuit current (I_{SCA}) from tables or use the following formula: transformer I_{FLA} × multiplier

4. Determine "f" factor for three-phase faults:

    $$f = \frac{1.73 \times L \times I}{N \times C \times E_{L-L}}$$

    for single-phase, line-to-line (L-L) faults on single-phase, center-tapped transformers:

    $$f = \frac{2 \times L \times I}{N \times C \times E_{L-L}}$$

    for single-phase, line-to-neutral (L-N) faults on single-phase, center-tapped transformers:

    $$f = \frac{2 \times L \times I^*}{N \times C \times E_{L-N}}$$

Where L = the length of circuit to the fault in feet (one way).

I = the available short-circuit in amperes at the beginning of the circuit.

C = the constant from Table C for the type of conductors and circuit arrangement.

E = line-to-line or line-to-neutral voltage.

N = the number of conductors in parallel.

5. After solving for "f", locate in Chart M the proper multiplier "M" or calculate using formula.

6. Multiply the available short-circuit current at the beginning of the circuit by multiplier "M" to determine the available symmetrical short-circuit current at the fault.

$$I_{SCA} \text{ at fault} = I_{SCA} \text{ at beginning of circuit} \times M$$

*See Note 2

NOTE 1. Motor short-circuit contribution, if significant, may be added to the transformer secondary short-circuit current value as determined in Step 3. Proceed with this adjusted figure through Steps 4, 5, and 6. A practical estimate of motor short-circuit contribution is to multiply the total motor load current in amperes by 4.

NOTE 2. The L-N fault current is higher than the L-L fault current at the secondary terminals of a single-phase center-tapped transformer. The short-circuit current available (I) for this case in Step 4 should be adjusted at the transformer terminals as follows:

At L-N Center-tapped Transformer Terminals

I = 1.5 x L-L Short-circuit Amperes at

Transformer Terminals

At some distance from the terminals, depending upon wire size, the L-N fault current is lower than the L-L fault current. The 1.5 multiplier is an approximation and will theoretically vary from 1.33 to 1.67. These figures are based on change in turns ration between primary and secondary, infinite source available, zero feet from terminals of transformer, and 1.2 x %X and 1.5 x %R for L-N vs. L-L resistance and reactance values. Begin L-N calculations at transformer secondary terminals, then proceed point-to-point.

Fault No. 1

Step 1. $I_{FLA} = \dfrac{KVA \times 1000}{E_{L-L} \times 1.73} = \dfrac{3000 \times 1000}{208 \times 1.73} = 833 \text{ A}$

Step 2. Multiplier $= \dfrac{100}{.9^* \times \text{Trans. } \% Z} = \dfrac{100}{1.8} = 55.55$

Step 3. $I_{SCA} = 833 \times 55.55 = 46{,}273$ A at transformer secondary

Step 4. $f = \dfrac{1.73 \times L \times I}{C \times E_{L-L}} = \dfrac{1.73 \times 20 \times 46{,}273}{22{,}185 \times 208} = 0.347$

Step 5. $M = \dfrac{1}{1 + f} = \dfrac{1}{1 + .0347} = 0.742$ (See Table M)

Step 6. $I_{SCA} = 46{,}273 \times 0.742 = 34{,}343$ A at Fault No. 1

Fault No. 2

Step 4. $f = \dfrac{1.73 \times 20 \times 34{,}343}{5906 \times 208} = 0.968$

Step 5. $M = \dfrac{1}{1 + f} = \dfrac{1}{1 + 0.968} = 0.508$ (See Table M)

Step 6. ISCA = $34{,}343 \times 0.508 = 17{,}447$ A at Fault No. 2

Notes: For simplicity, the motor contribution was not included.

*Transformer % Z is multiplied by .9 to establish a worst-case condition.

Example:

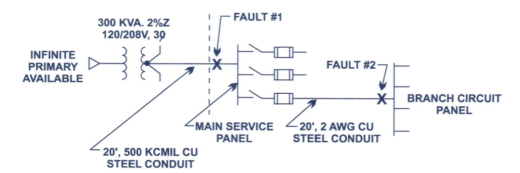

Table of "C" Values (Cable)

AWG or kcmil	Copper Three Single Conductors In Magnetic Duct 600V	Copper Three Single Conductors In Magnetic Duct 5kv	Copper Three Single Conductors In Nonmagnetic Duct 600V	Copper Three Single Conductors In Nonmagnetic Duct 5kv	Copper Three-Conductor Cable In Magnetic Duct 600V	Copper Three-Conductor Cable In Nonmagnetic Duct 600V	Aluminum Three Single Conductors In Magnetic Duct 600V	Aluminum Three Single Conductors In Nonmagnetic Duct 600V	AWG or kcmil
12	617	617	617	617	617	617	375	375	12
10	981	981	981	981	981	981	598	598	10
8	1557	1551	1558	1555	1559	1559	951	951	8
6	2425	2406	2430	2417	2431	2433	1480	1481	6
4	3806	3750	3825	3789	3830	3837	2345	2350	4
3	4760	4760	4802	4802	4760	4802	2948	2958	3
2	5906	5736	6044	5926	5989	6087	3713	3729	2
1	7292	7029	7493	7306	7454	7579	4645	4678	1
1/0	8924	8543	9317	9033	9209	9472	5777	5838	1/0
2/0	10755	10061	11423	10877	11244	11703	7186	7301	2/0
3/0	12843	11804	13923	13048	13656	14410	8826	9110	3/0
4/0	15082	13605	16673	15351	16391	17482	10740	11174	4/0
250	16483	14924	18593	17120	18310	19779	12122	12862	250
300	18176	16292	20867	18975	20617	22524	13909	14922	300
350	19703	17385	22736	20526	22646	24904	15484	16812	350
400	20565	18235	24296	21786	24253	26915	16670	18505	400
500	22185	19172	26706	23277	26980	30028	18755	21390	500
600	22965	20567	28033	25203	28752	32236	20093	23451	600
750	24136	21386	28303	25430	31050	32404	21766	25976	750
1000	25278	22539	31490	28083	33864	37197	23477	28778	1000

Table of "C" Values (Cable)

Ampacity	Plug-In Busway Copper	Plug-In Busway Aluminum	Feeder Busway Copper	Feeder Busway Aluminum	High Imped. Busway Copper
225	28700	23000	18700	12000	---
400	38900	34700	23900	21300	---
600	41000	38300	36500	31300	---
800	46100	57500	49300	44100	---
1000	69400	89300	62900	56200	15600
1200	94300	97100	76900	69900	16100
1350	119000	104200	90100	84000	17500
1600	129900	120500	101000	90900	19200
2000	142900	135100	134200	125000	20400
2500	143800	156300	180500	166700	21700
3000	144900	175400	204100	188700	23800
4000	---	---	277800	256400	---

Table M (multiplier) $M = \dfrac{1}{1+f}$

f	M	f	M
0.01	0.99	1.50	0.40
0.02	0.98	1.75	0.36
0.03	0.97	2.00	0.33
0.04	0.96	2.50	0.29
0.05	0.95	3.00	0.25
0.06	0.94	3.50	0.22
0.07	0.93	4.00	0.20
0.08	0.93	5.00	0.17
0.09	0.92	6.00	0.14
0.10	0.91	7.00	0.13
0.15	0.87	8.00	0.11
0.20	0.83	9.00	0.10
0.25	0.80	10.00	0.09
0.30	0.77	15.00	0.06
0.35	0.74	20.00	0.05
0.40	0.71	30.00	0.03
0.50	0.67	40.00	0.02
0.60	0.63	50.00	0.02
0.70	0.59	60.00	0.02
0.80	0.55	70.00	0.01
0.90	0.53	80.00	0.01
1.00	0.50	90.00	0.01
1.20	0.45	100.00	0.01

THREE-PHASE TRANSFORMER FULL LOAD CURRENT RATING IN AMPERES

VOLTAGE line-to-line	150 KVA	167 KVA	225 KVA	300 KVA	500 KVA	750 KVA	1000 KVA	1500 KVA	2000 KVA
208 volts	417	464	625	834	1388	2080	2776	4164	5552
220 volts	394	439	592	788	1315	1970	2630	3940	5260
240 volts	362	402	542	722	1203	1804	2406	3609	4812
440 volts	197	219	296	394	657	985	1315	1970	2630
460 volts	189	209	284	378	630	945	1260	1890	2520
480 volts	181	201	271	361	601	902	1203	1804	2406
600 volts	144	161	216	289	481	722	962	1444	1924

SINGLE-PHASE TRANSFORMER FULL LOAD CURRENT RATING IN AMPERES

VOLTAGE	25 KVA	50 KVA	75 KVA	100 KVA	150 KVA	167 KVA	200 KVA	250 KVA	333 KVA	500 KVA
115/230	109	217	326	435	652	726	870	1087	1448	2174
120/240	104	208	313	416	625	696	833	1042	1388	2083
230/460	54	109	163	217	326	363	435	544	724	1087
240/480	52	104	156	208	313	348	416	521	694	1042

Charts, Formulas, and Useful Information | 1- and 2-Family Study Guide | 181

Information Concerning Available Short-Circuit Current Tables

The Bussmann Manufacturing Division point-to-point method for short-circuit calculations, as presented in *Ferm's Fast Finder*, was used to calculate all the tables.

Tables give maximum fault-current values for various distribution transformer connections and sizes as a function of secondary conductor size and length. The table values have been calculated using the assumptions as outlined below and are applicable for both underground and overhead construction. Due to the assumptions made, the tabulated values will normally be somewhat greater than actual maximum fault currents. Hence the use of the tabulated values for determining the minimum rating of service-entrance equipment will usually yield conservative results. If there is any question, check with the local authority enforcing the code in your area.

The tables have been calculated using aluminum conductors as taken from the table of "C" values for three single conductors in nonmagnetic duct 600 volts. See extreme right side column in table of "C values. As a rule of thumb, the tables may be used for copper conductors by using the table value for the aluminum conductor two sizes greater than the actual copper conductor size.

Assumed percent impedance on all transformers in the following tables is 1.6 percent. This value is typical of newer transformers. The larger the percent impedance of the transformer, the smaller the available short-circuit current.

The 120/240-volt single-phase transformers were calculated both line-to-line and line-to-neutral. The larger of the two figures appears in the tables. See Note 2 in Bussmann formula. All other transformers were calculated line-to-line.

Maximum short-circuit current at the secondary terminals of an open wye/open delta bank made up of equal kVA transformers, is the same as for a closed delta bank. If unequal sized transformers are used, maximum short-circuit current will fall between the single-phase short-circuit current for the largest transformer and the three-phase short-circuit current for a closed delta bank made up of three transformers the same size as the largest transformer.

If the effect of secondary conductors is to be included in the calculation, it is much simpler to assume a closed bank of the three transformers of the size of the largest in the open bank and utilize the tables or equations as presented here. This will yield answers on the safe high side for available short-circuit current.

For a more detailed explanation, you should consult a qualified electrical engineer.

Where more than one overcurrent device is in series as shown as the "main service panel" and "branch-circuit panel" in the example, each equipment must be rated for the fault current available at its supply terminals unless it is part of a series rated system. In a series rated system, the downstream devices may have a rating lower than the available fault current when installed as part of a tested and listed series rated system. The equipment suitable for installation to achieve the series rating is marked on the equipment by the manufacturer.

For additional charts and formulas, see Ferm's Fast Finder, 2014.

13 Answers

Raceways
1. B *NEC* 310.106(C)
2. B *NEC* 230.6(5)
3. D *NEC* Chapter 9, Table 1, Note 2, 358.22
4. B *NEC* Chapter 9, Tables 4 and 5
5. D *NEC* 362.30(A)
6. B *NEC* 352.22; Chapter 9, Table 1, Note 1; Annex C, Table C10
7. B *NEC* 348.30(A)
8. C *NEC* 348.30(A)
9. B *NEC* 352.10(G), 300.5(A), Table 300.5
10. C *NEC* 352.10(G), 300.5(A), Table 300.5
11. A *NEC* 300.11(B), 300.11(B)(2)
12. A *NEC* 230.43
13. A *NEC* 250.64(B) and 250.64(E)
14. B *NEC* 358.30(A)
15. D *NEC* 344.22; Chapter 9, Table 1; Annex C, Table C8
16. B *NEC* 230.28(A) & (B)
17. A *NEC* 230.54(A)
18. D *NEC* 310.15(B)(3)(a)
19. C *NEC* 358.22, Chapter 9, Table 1, Note 4
20. D *NEC* 250.92(B)(1), (2), (3), & (4)
21. A *NEC* 386.10(1), 386.12(1) and (5)
22. B *NEC* 352.30(A) & (B)
23. C *NEC* 358.20(B)
24. C *NEC* 342.20(A) & (B), 342.30(A) & (B)
25. B *NEC* 358.26
26. B *NEC* 348.10, 348.12, 230.43(15), 348.12(1), 348.12(6)
27. A *NEC* 352.10(A), (C), (G), (H) and 352.12(B)
28. D *NEC* Article 100, Definitions, 310.10(C) & Table 310.104(A)
29. B *NEC* 300.4(G), 312.6(C)
30. C *NEC* 312.5(C), Ex
31. D *NEC* 344.24, Table 2, Chapter 9
32. D *NEC* 348.30(A) & Ex. No.2 (1)

Cables
1. B *NEC* 300.5(A), Table 300.5
2. C *NEC* Article 334
3. C *NEC* 340.10, 300.5(A), Table 300.5

4. A   *NEC* 334.10(A)(1), 334.12(B)(4), 334.12(A)(3), 334.12(A)(9)
5. B   *NEC* 334.80, 310.15(B), Table 310.15(B)(16)
6. A   *NEC* 314.17(C), 334.30
7. C   *NEC* 334.24
8. D   *NEC* 300.4(F) Ex. No. 1
9. A   *NEC* 230.51(A)
10. A   *NEC* 314.17(C)
11. C   *NEC* 334.30
12. B   *NEC* 334.15(C)
13. C   *NEC* 334.112
14. A   *NEC* 340.10(1), (4), (5), 340.12(8)
15. A   *NEC* 340.10(1), 300.5(D) (1)
16. D   *NEC* 300.5(A), Table 300.5, Column 1
17. C   *NEC* 310.120(A)
18. A   *NEC* 334.10(1), 334.12(B)(4), (A)(3), (A)(9), (B)(2)
19. C   *NEC* 338.10
20. D   *NEC* 338.10(B), (B)(2) Exception, 338.10(A), 250.140 Exception
21. A   *NEC* 300.14
22. D   *NEC* 340.116
23. C   *NEC* 334.80
24. A   *NEC* 334.10(1), (A)(1), and (A)(2), 334.12(B)(4)
25. B   *NEC* 334.23, 320.23(A)
26. A   *NEC* 334.17, 300.4(B)(1)
27. A   *NEC* 314.17(B) & (C), 334.30
28. C   *NEC* 340.104
29. A   *NEC* 314.17(C)
30. C   *NEC* 300.4(D)
31. D   *NEC* 312.5(C), 312.5(C) Ex. (a) (c) & (e)
32. B   *NEC* 334 Part III, 334.30, and 334.80
33. C   *NEC* 340.112
34. C   *NEC* 352.44, 352.10(H), 352.6, 352.22

Conductors

1. B   *NEC* 314.16(A) & (B)(1) through (5)
2. A   *NEC* 250.140 Ex., (2), (3)
3. D   *NEC* 250.64(A)
4. C   *NEC* 310.15, 310.15(B)(7)(2) Table 310.15(B)(16)
5. D   *NEC* 310.15(B)(4), 310.15(B)(7)(1), Table 310.15(B)(16)
6. B   *NEC* Article 100
7. A   *NEC* 210.11(C)(1), 210.52(B)(1) & (2)
8. C   *NEC* 110.14(B)
9. A   *NEC* 250.66, Table 250.66
10. D   *NEC* 250.148(E), and (C), 250.8(B)
11. A   *NEC* 334.80
12. C   *NEC* 250.122, Table 250.122
13. C   *NEC* 422.10(A), Table 310.15(B)(16), 240.4(D)(7), 334.80, Ohm's Law
14. D   *NEC* 348.12(1)
15. B   *NEC* 210.11(C)(3), 210.23(A)
16. C   *NEC* 310.15, 310.15(B)(3)(a), Table 310.15(B)(3)(a)
17. C   *NEC* 110.5
18. B   *NEC* 210.11(C)(1), Table 310.15(B)(16), 220.4(D)
19. B   *NEC* 310.15(B), 310.15(B)(7)(1)
20. C   *NEC* Chapter 9, Table 5
21. A   *NEC* 310.15(B), Table 310.15(B)(16), 240.4(D)
22. D   *NEC* 250.122, Table 250.122
23. C   *NEC* 310.15(B), 310.15(B)(7), 110.14(C)(1), Table 310.15(B)(16)
24. A   *NEC* 225.19(C)
25. C   *NEC* 310.104(A), 225.4, 310.10(C)
26. D   *NEC* 402.6
27. D   *NEC* 250.134(A), 250.118(1), (14), 250.118(5)(c)
28. B   *NEC* 334.80, 310.15(B), Table 310.15(B)(16)
29. B   *NEC* 310.10(D), 310.104(A), 310.10(C), 225.4, Footnote 4 to 310.104(A)
30. A   *NEC* 310.15(A)(1), 310.15(B), 310.15(B)(2)(a), Table 310.15(B)(3)(a), 334.80
31. D   *NEC* 300.4(B)(1), 300.4(A)(2), 300.4(A)(1) Exception 1 and 2
32. B   *NEC* 314.16(B), 300.14
33. C   *NEC* in 314.16(B)(2)
34. D   210.8, 210.8(A)(6), 210.8(A)(10)

Service Equipment

1. B   *NEC* 230.24(B)(1)
2. C   *NEC* 110.26(A)(1), Table 110.26(A)(1)
3. A   *NEC* 230.43

4.	D	*NEC* 250.64(B) & (E)		5.	D	*NEC* 404.2(A), 402.2(A) Ex.
5.	B	*NEC* 250.24(A)(5), Informational Note; 250.142(A) & (B)		6.	D	*NEC* 404.14(A)(3)
6.	D	*NEC* 230.42(B), 230.79(C)		7.	B	*NEC* 210.8(A)(8)
7.	C	*NEC* 550.32(C)		8.	C	*NEC* 725.135, 725.136(A), (D)(1), and (I)(1), 300.11(B)(2)
8.	B	*NEC* 250.53(A)(2) Exception		9	A	*NEC* Article 100
9.	A	*NEC* 110.26(D)		10.	D	*NEC* 210.8(A)(1), (2), & (6)
10.	C	*NEC* 110.26(A)(1) & (2)		11.	C	*NEC* 210.50(C)
11.	B	*NEC* 250.53(D)(2)		12.	D	*NEC* 240.50(C)
12.	D	*NEC* 230.71(A)		13.	A	*NEC* 210.52(C)(2) & (3)
13.	B	*NEC* 230.79(D)		14.	C	*NEC* 314.24
14.	A	*NEC* 230.26, 230.24		15.	B	*NEC* 404.2(B)
15.	B	*NEC* 230.24(B)(2)		16.	A	*NEC* 210.4(B)
16.	C	*NEC* 230.42(A), 310.15, Table 310.15(B)(16)		17.	A	*NEC* 422.31(C), 422.33
17.	C	*NEC* 230.42(B), 230.79(B), Table 310.15(B)(16)		18.	C	*NEC* 210.8, 210.8(A)(2)
				19.	B	*NEC* 430.81(B)
18.	C	*NEC* 110.26(E)(1)(a)		20.	D	*NEC* 210.12(A), 210.12(A)(1), (4), and (6)
19.	B	*NEC* 230.2(A), (B), (C), & (D), Article 100, Definitions		21.	C	*NEC* 210.4(C) Ex. 1 & 2, 240.15(B)(2)
				22.	A	*NEC* 210.70(A)(2)(c)
20.	B	*NEC* 230.72(A) Ex.		23.	D	*NEC* 210.52(E)
21.	C	*NEC* 230.79(C)		24.	A	*NEC* 110.9
22.	D	*NEC* 230.46, 110.14(B), 300.5(E)		25.	C	*NEC* 110.14(C)(1)
23.	C	*NEC* 230.54(A), (C), & (F)		26.	D	*NEC* 404.14(E)
24.	A	*NEC* 250.53(A)(3)		27.	A	*NEC* 404.9(B), 404.14(A)(3), 404.11
25.	C	*NEC* 110.26(A)(3)		28.	A	*NEC* 210.12(A), 210.12(B)(1) and (2), 210.12(A)(5)
26.	B	*NEC* 250.24(A)(1) & (5)				
27.	C	*NEC* 230.50(B)(1)		29.	D	*NEC* 210.12(A)(1)-(6)
28.	D	*NEC* 408.36, 230.71				
29.	D	*NEC* 230.24(A)				
30.	B	*NEC* 250.66, Table 250.66, Chapter 9, Table 8, 250.66(B)		**Utilization Equipment**		
				1.	A	*NEC* 422.16(B)(1), (2), and (4)
31.	D	*NEC* 230.70(B), 230.66, 408.30		2.	B	*NEC* 424.3(B), Article 100, 210.19(A), 210.20(A)
32.	C	*NEC* 230.82				
33.	C	*NEC* 250.102(A) & (C)(1) & (2), Table 250.102(C)(1)		3.	C	*NEC* 422.13, Article 100, 210.20(A)
				4.	D	*NEC* 314.27(C), 422.18
34.	D	*NEC* 250.24, (C)(1) & (2), 250.102(C)(1), 310.15(B)(7), 220.61(A) and (B), 310.10(H)		5.	D	*NEC* 220.54
				6.	A	*NEC* 210.11(C)(1), 210.52(B)(2), 210.23(A)(2)
				7.	B	*NEC* 410.16(C)(2)
				8.	C	*NEC* 424.3(B), 210.20(A)
Control Devices				9.	C	*NEC* 110.13(A)
1.	C	*NEC* 424.19, 424.20(A)		10.	B	*NEC* 220.18(A)
2.	C	*NEC* 404.8(A)		11.	C	*NEC* 404.8(A)
3.	B	*NEC* 424.65, 424, 19(A)		12.	B	*NEC* 210.21(B)(2), Table 210.21(B)(2)
4.	A	*NEC* 422.31(C)		13.	A	*NEC* 250.140, 250.134, 250.138

14. B *NEC* 215.2(A), 220.53
15. B *NEC* 410.16(B)
16. C *NEC* 410.116(A) & (B)
17. A *NEC* 422.16(B)(l)(2)
18. D *NEC* 422.32, 422.34, 422.33, 422.16(B)(2)(2)
19. B *NEC* 410.10(D)
20. D *NEC* 422.16(B)(3), 422.33(A)
21. C *NEC* 422.11(E)(3)
22. C *NEC* 424.22(B)
23. D *NEC* 400.6
24. A *NEC* 410.10(A)
25. C *NEC* 410.16(C)(1)
26. D *NEC* 410.16, 314.23, 314.27(A)(2)
27. A *NEC* 410.116(B)
28. D *NEC* 424.3(A)
29. B *NEC* 210.70(A)(2)(b)
30. D *NEC* 424.19(A)(1), 424.20(A)(4)
31. A *NEC* Article 100
32. B *NEC* 424.41(B)
33. C *NEC* 410.42, 410.44, and 250.110
34. D *NEC* 424.3(B), 424.13, 424.11, 422.12
35. D *NEC* 422.16(B)(1)-(5)

Cabinets

1. C *NEC* 300.4(G)
2. B *NEC* 110.28, Table 110.28
3. C *NEC* 312.3
4. D *NEC* 312.2, Article 100
5. D *NEC* 408.55, 408.55 Ex. 1, Table 312.6(A), Table 312.6(B)
6. A *NEC* 312.2
7. A *NEC* Article 100 Definitions
8. C *NEC* 408.4, 110.22
9. C *NEC* 312.5(A) & (C), and 312.5(C) Exception
10. C *NEC* 312.6(B)(2), 310.15, 310.15(B)(7), Table 312.6(B)
11. A *NEC* 300.4(G)
12. B *NEC* Article 100, Definitions
13. D *NEC* 312.7, 312.8, 312.9, 312.11
14. D *NEC* 376.56 (A)
15. C *NEC* 110.26(A)(1), Table 110.26(A)(1)
16. B *NEC* 366.22(A)
17. D *NEC* 312.11, 312.11(A) & (B)
18. C *NEC* 312.8, 312.8(1) – (3)
19. A *NEC* 408.55, 312.6(A), Table 312.6(A)
20. D *NEC* 408.36(A)
21. A *NEC* 312.5(C) Exception Conditions (b), (d), and (f)
22. C *NEC* 408.55 Table 312.6(A)
23. D *NEC* 312.2(A)
24. B *NEC* 230.82(3), 230.94 Ex. 5.

Calculations

1. D Ohm's Law
2. B *NEC* 220.12 Table 220.12, 210.11(A) and (B)
3. B *NEC* Table 220.55
4. B *NEC* Table 220.55
5. D *NEC* Table Ohm's Law, 110.14(C)(1)(0)(1), Table 310.15(B)(16)
6. C *NEC* 220.54
7. B *NEC* 424.3(B), Article 100 – Definitions, 210.20(A)
8. A *NEC* 430.22, Table 430.248, Table 310.15(B)(16)
9. B Ohm's Law
10. A *NEC* 310.15(B), Table 310.15(B)(16), 310.15(B)(5), 310.15(B)(2)
11. C *NEC* 422.13, 422.11(E), Article 100 – Part 1, 210.20(A), 422.11(E)(3), 240.6
12. C *NEC* Table 220.55
13. A *NEC* Table 210.11(C), 220.12, 220.52, 220.42, 220.55, Table 220.55
14. B *NEC* Table 220.12, 220.52(A) and (B), and 220.42
15. D *NEC* 220.14(J), 220.82, 220.82(A), (B), and (C)
16. C *NEC* 230.42, 220.80, 220.82
17. A *NEC* 230.42, Table 220.12, 210.11(C)(1) and (C)(2), 220.52(A) and (B), Table 220.42, 220.55 Note (4), 220.60, 220.51
18. B *NEC* 230.42, 220.80, 220.82 (A), (B) and (C)
19. D *NEC* Table 220.12, 220.14(J), Informative Annex D
20. C *NEC* 314.16(B)
21. A *NEC* 550.31, Table 550.31
22. B *NEC* 220.52(B), 220.42

23. C *NEC* 314.16(B)(1) and (B)(5), Table 314.16(B)
24. A *NEC* 314.16(B), Table 314.16(B)
25. B *NEC* 440.33, Table 310.15(B)(16), 110.14(C)(1)(A)
26. A *NEC* 210.19(A)(3), Ex 2
27. C *NEC* 310.15(B), Table 310.15(B)(16), 230.90(A) Ex. 5, 310.15(B)(7)
28. C *NEC* 424.98(A)
29. B *NEC* 358.22, Chapter 9, Table 1, Table 4, Table 5
30. B *NEC* 312.5(C), Chapter 9, Table 1
31. A *NEC* 220.83
32. C *NEC* 220.54
33. A *NEC* 310.15(B), Table 310.15(B)(16), 310.15(B)(5)(a), 310.15(B)(3)(a)

25. A *NEC* 680.71, 680.72, 410.10(D)
26. A *NEC* 680.27(A)(2)
27. B *NEC* 680.25(B)(1), Table 250.122, 680.25(A)(1) & (4)
28. C *NEC* 680.25(B)
29. A *NEC* 680.22(C)
30. A *NEC* 680.23(F)(2), 680.25(B)(1), 680.24(F)
31. D *NEC* 680.27(C)(3)
32. B *NEC* 680.42(A)(2) & (B), 680.40
33. C *NEC* 680.71
34. B *NEC* 680.56(A), (B), and (D), Table 400.4
35. A *NEC* 680.74, 680.21(B), 680.31
36. A *NEC* 680.8, Table 680.8, 680.8(B)
37. D *NEC* 680.12

Swimming Pools
1. C *NEC* 680.22(A)(2) & (3), 680.8(A), Table 680.8, 680.10
2. B *NEC* 680.22(A)(2)
3. D *NEC* 680.26(B)(1)-(7)
4. C *NEC* 680.22(B)
5. B *NEC* 680.22(B)
6. A *NEC* 680.8(B)
7. C *NEC* 680.8(A), Table 680.8
8. D *NEC* 680.7(A) & (B)
9. D *NEC* 680.21(A)(1), (3) & (4)
10. A *NEC* 680.23(B)(2)
11. D *NEC* 680.24(D)
12. C *NEC* 680.22(A)(1), (2),(3) & (4)
13. B *NEC* 680.33(A) & (B)
14. C *NEC* 680.23(A)(3), (4), and (5)
15. B *NEC* 680.22(A)(1), (2), & (3)
16. D *NEC* 680.2
17. A *NEC* 680.22(B)
18. C *NEC* 680.20, 680.10
19. A *NEC* 680.22(C), 680.12
20. B *NEC* 680.9
21. D *NEC* 680.23(A)(4)
22. B *NEC* 680.23(A)(7), 680.23(A)(4), 680.23(A)(3)
23. A *NEC* 680.24(A)(2)(c)
24. C *NEC* 680.26(C), 250.8(1)

Notes

Notes

Going mobile?
We've got an app for you.

Download Your FREE Preview Issue Today

Whatever platform you choose, IAEI has got you covered.
Keeping up with the electrical industry is now only a tap away.

Receive 6 digital issues of *IAEI* magazine for only $47.94
(savings of 25% off digital newsstand price)

Get started at **www.iaei.org/digital**
FREE to current IAEI members. No need to apply.

Explore new ideas on IAEI's new website.

Explore IAEI's fully redesigned and updated website. Created with a fresh new look and user-friendly navigation, our new site has exciting features such as a social networking community, multimedia, RSS feeds, forums, and photo galleries all within your section, chapter or division. As a member, you can actively connect and collaborate with colleagues as well as continue your professional growth and development.

Even with all the new features, our site continues to provide you with the latest up-to-date industry news and events as well as information on our products and services. So go ahead, look around, and discover what's inside at **www.iaei.org**.

IAEI MEMBERS save LIVES every DAY...
YOU CAN TOO.

IAEI members can become your strongest allies when support, expertise, and resources are needed to get the job done right. With 137 chapters nationwide, your membership allows you access to a wealth of knowledge in the electrical field.

IAEI membership provides:
- Vital safety requirements in all electrical safety codes
- Continued education and training seminars
- Career growth and development opportunities

Join IAEI today and become a vital part in promoting electrical safety throughout the industry.

Member Type	1-Year Membership	3-Year Membership
Associate Members	$102.00	$286.00
Inspector Members*	$102.00	$286.00
Section Members	$105.00	$295.00
Inspection Agency Members	$204.00	$572.00
National Members	$525.00	$1,475.00
International Members	$525.00	$1,475.00
Student Members**	$78.00	N/A

New members, other than students, may choose the multiyear plan when they complete the application form.

Return the application to:
International Association of Electrical Inspectors
P. O. Box 830848 ■ Richardson, TX 75083-0848

MEMBERSHIP APPLICATION *PLEASE PRINT*

Name - Last _____ First _____ M.I. _____

Title _____

Employer _____

Address of Applicant _____

City _____ State or Province _____ ZIP or Postal Code _____

(Area Code) Telephone Number _____

Email _____ Date of Birth _____

Student applicants give school attending** _____ Graduation date _____

Applicant's Signature _____

Chapter, where you live or work, if known _____ (Division, where appropriate) _____

If previous member, give last membership number and last year of membership. _____

Endorsed by _____ Endorser's Membership Number _____

☐ MasterCard ☐ Visa ☐ AMEX ☐ Money Order
☐ Discover ☐ Diners Club ☐ Check

Name on Card _____

Charge Card Number _____ Expiration Date _____

☐ Inspector ☐ Associate ☐ Student ☐ Other _____
Amount Paid $ _____ Specify member type _____

Inspector Member MUST sign below:

I, _____ meet the qualification for inspector member as described below.

*Inspector members must regularly make electrical inspections for preventing injury to persons or damage to property on behalf of a governmental agency, insurance agency, rating bureau, recognized testing laboratory or electric light and power company.
** Student member must be currently enrolled in an approved college, university, vocational technical school or trade school specializing in electrical training or approved electrical apprenticeship school.

Contact IAEI customer service department for information on our other membership categories – Section, National and International Member; Sustaining Member (Bronze, Silver, Gold, or Platinum); and Inspection Agency Member.

Mail to: IAEI, P.O. Box 830848, Richardson, TX 75083-0848
For information call: (972) 235-1455 (8–5 CST) 12SG14

For Office Use | Section _____ Chapter No. _____ Division No. _____

1- and 2-Family Dwellings Study Guide
Electrical Inspector Certification Program

Editor-in-Chief
David Clements

Director of Education
L. Keith Lofland

Education, Codes and Standards Coordinator
Joseph Wages, Jr.

Director of Marketing
Melody Schmidt

Director of Publishing
Kathryn Ingley

Designer
Laura L. Hildreth

Creative Director / Cover Design
John Watson

Technical Review
Mark R. Hilbert
David Clements
L. Keith Lofland
Joseph Wages, Jr.

Illustrations & Photographs
Brady Davis
Thinkstock

Composed at:
International Association of Electrical Inspectors
in Palatino Lt Std by OpenType©
Printed by Walsworth Print Group on 60# Book. Bound in 12 pt. Cover.